PRUSSIA: MYTH AND REALITY

PRUSSIA:
MYTH AND REALITY

THE ROLE OF PRUSSIA
in GERMAN HISTORY

by

E. J. FEUCHTWANGER

HENRY REGNERY COMPANY
CHICAGO

Contents

Maps (drawn by Mr. A. S. Burn, G.Inst.T., Chief Cartographer in the Department of Geography, University of Southampton)

Prussia: Myth and Reality

Preface

Few general histories of Prussia have been written in German, let alone in English. The term itself creates difficulties; for in a strict sense, a history of Prussia might cover only the period between 1701, when the Elector of Brandenburg assumed the title of King in Prussia, and 1870, after which date the story of Prussia becomes almost completely merged with that of Germany. The present book does not attempt to give a fully comprehensive summary of the rise and fall of Prussia, but tries to discuss Prussia as a problem of German history. The stress is on the factors which made a heterogeneous collection of territories into a political entity, with its own ethos and dynamism, capable of imposing an unmistakable imprint on its citizens. Cultural and ideological influences which shaped Prussia have been given considerable attention; diplomatic history and foreign affairs are only briefly sketched—here the non-German reader is well supplied with many excellent books. Chronologically the main emphasis is on the period between the death of Frederick the Great in 1786 and the Franco-Prussian War of 1870. It was during this time that the impact of Prussia on the development of Germany was crucial.

The author found that the massive work done on Prussian history in the heyday of German historiography has stood the test of time well. The structure of fact established by historians from Ranke onwards is not likely to be radically revised. With the disappearance of Prussia and even of a unified Germany our perspective has, however, changed fundamentally. There are many questions to which we would like an answer, which were not asked in the past. Unfortunately much of the documentary evidence is in the eastern part of Germany and not easily accessible to scholars.

My special thanks are due to Professor John Bromley, of the University of Southampton, for many valuable suggestions, and for reading the completed manuscript and improving it on many points of detail.

E. J. Feuchtwanger

Introduction

THE PROBLEM OF PRUSSIA

Prussianism is a life style, an instinct, a compulsion.... The officer corps, the bureaucracy, the workers of August Bebel, "the" people of 1813, 1870, 1914, feel, desire, act as a super-personal whole. This is *not* herd instinct; it is something immensely strong and free, which *noone* who does not belong can understand. Prussianism is exclusive. (Oswald Spengler in *Prussianism and Socialism,* written in 1919.)

Abolition of the State of Prussia

The Prussian State which from early days has been a bearer of militarism and reaction in Germany has *de facto* ceased to exist.

Guided by the interests of preservation of peace and security of peoples and with the desire to assure further reconstruction of the political life of Germany on a democratic basis, the Control Council enacts as follows :

Article I

The Prussian State together with its central government and all its agencies is abolished.

(Law No. 46 of the Allied Control Council,
25th February 1947.)

Prussia has been cast both as the hero and the villain of German history. To generations of Germans the creation of the new Reich in 1870 seemed the culmination of German history and it was to Prussia that they owed this saving grace. "How do we deserve God's grace that lets us witness such great and mighty events? And how shall we live after this? What for twenty years has been the goal of our work and wishes has now been fulfilled in this infinitely wonderful way : Where can I, at my age, find a new goal for my future life?"[1] Thus wrote Heinrich von Sybel when Bismarck was completing the edifice of the new Germany. Sybel was one of that group of historians who had taught the Germans that the path to a modern German nation state lay through Prussia. The Hohenzollern monarchy would combine with the German liberal national movement to create the unified country which would enable the Germans to face the other great nations of Europe on terms of equality. The failure of 1848 had produced disillusionment but not final disappointment. The spectacle of the Italians achieving their national unity revived German hopes. And they were not disappointed. With dramatic speed and prodigious skill Bismarck brought about what had proved elusive for so long. But how different was the path of unification as trodden by Bismarck from what most had imagined! The articulate classes of Germany were, however, not entirely unprepared for what happened. The failure of 1848 had taught many of them the importance of power in political action. Nevertheless the wars of 1864, 1866 and 1870 were a stunning and unexpected demonstration of the use of force for the achievement of great ends. The path to unity was very different from what German liberals had expected, but when they saw the blessed land they found it good.

The majority of Germans were completely overwhelmed by the demonstration of Prussian might and deeply grateful to the Prussian state, its leaders and its armies, for what they had done. Historians like Sybel or Treitschke and many lesser writers and publicists celebrated the consummation of what they had so long and so ardently desired. They now had no difficulty in persuading their countrymen that Prussia had always been destined to create the new German state and end centuries of disunion. The Prussian state had arisen mysteriously out of dynastic accident and had been set on the path to greatness by a unique succession of brilliant and ambitious rulers. In retrospect nothing was easier than to link Bismarck with Frederick the Great, and even the Great Elector was portrayed as a ruler aiming for German recovery after a period of great humiliation. Writers like Heinrich von Kleist and philosophers like Hegel, so it now seemed, had foreseen the destiny of Prussia. Over generations the qualities and instruments had been fashioned to fit Prussia for the great task : a powerful army, a military caste to provide it with officers, an efficient bureaucracy to muster the resources of the state, an educational system to train the people. Prussia seemed unique in her ability to create a spirit of mutual confidence between the state and its citizens. And thus it was that Prussia was finally able to lead Germany, in spite of all the handicaps of history, towards a greater and more glorious future.

There was at least enough truth in this picture of Prussia to make it acceptable to the generation of Germans who lived through the creation of the second Reich and for those who grew up in it. Prussia was a military-dynastic state like many others; it was distinguished by the size, and sometimes by the efficiency of its army, and by the effectiveness of its administrative system. Before the 19th century, however, it was completely divorced from any sense of German nationhood; and even in the 19th century the Prussian state was frequently hostile to German nationalism. Although the social structure of Prussia was so heavily impregnated with the military spirit, the country was, after Frederick the Great and until Bismarck, timid and cautious in her external policy. But all this was overlooked in the euphoric atmosphere of the new Reich and dissenting voices were few. That the great and powerful modern Germany was the culmination of Prussia remained the conviction of many Germans.

It is not surprising therefore that those who had no reason to love the new Germany or had crossed swords with her accepted the same picture. Much of mankind in the first World War thought the bad Prussians were leading the good Germans astray. Few of those who accepted this popular image knew that the Prussians were not an ethnic group; that they were merely citizens of a state; and that since this state had become a part of a greater and more important one it was at least an open question to what extent Prussia and the Prussians still existed. The question could be put more meaningfully by asking what qualities in the new Germany were derived from Prussia, but even to this question there could be no simple answer. During the first World War the German historian Friedrich Meinecke wrote an essay taking issue with writers like Cecil Chesterton and Ramsay Muir who had presented the case against Germany in terms of militarist Prussia as the corrupter of German culture. Meinecke, the author of a classical study on the subtle interactions of nationalism and cosmopolitanism and of Prussia and Germany in the 19th century, had no difficulty in showing that such simple explanations were false.[2] There was never any straight antithesis between the Germany of the poets and thinkers and the Prussia of soldiers and barrack-rooms.

Yet the Prussian myth went on agitating friend and foe. As the old Prussian military-dynastic state receded into the remote past it became possible to propagate ideas about it with greater freedom. Among many disorientated Germans of the 1920s Prussia stood for the tough, lean qualities of the warrior, for the true sense of community to pit against the disintegrating individualism of the age, for a native form of strong government to overcome the debilitating regime of parties imported from the West. Prussia was, however, also one of the bulwarks of the Weimar Republic and men of the Left saw the black-red coalition government of Prussia as continuing an old tradition of social responsibility and progressive administration. To others again both inside and outside Germany Prussia was still the centre of militarism and of political reaction. Finally Hitler, most adept of propagandists, took up the Prussian myth. He used it to convince the German middle class that his revolution only meant the restoration of German greatness in the tradition of Frederick the Great and Bismarck. When the propaganda machine of Goebbels went to such lengths to convey this picture of continuity, at least at some moments in the career of the Nazi regime, it was hardly surprising that those who realized the menace of Hitler were sometimes led to think that the Austrian Corporal fitted into a long Prussian tradition.

Thus Prussia and the role of Prussia in Germany history has been for a century or more the property of myth makers. Even earlier Prussia had a very definite image in the rest of Germany. It was, after all, an "artificial" state, whose essence lay not in certain ethnic characteristics but in the qualities which it impressed upon its citizens. Some time early in the 18th century, probably in the reign of Frederick William I, the administrative machine created by the Hohenzollern rulers acquired an ethos of its own. This Prussian ethos carried many connotations which were sometimes the reverse of those conveyed by the Prussian idea in more recent times. Prussia in the 18th and early 19th centuries meant sobriety, lack of ostentation, perhaps a poverty of spirit, and parsimonious but enlightened administration. It meant a concentration of resources on things military, but it did not mean aggression. "Travailler pour le roi de Prusse" meant working hard for little material reward; Prussian public servants and even ordinary citizens were thought to have a well-developed sense of duty. The Prussian state might be a barrack square, but it was well run; and it was sufficiently free and tolerant to attract its share of the great flowering of German civilization at the end of the 18th century. The reform era did not radically alter the Prussian image. Until the age of Bismarck the South Germans continued to regard Prussia with a mixture of condescension, aversion and respect. Prussia was considered culturally backward, tightly disciplined and joyless, but efficient and incorruptible. The notion of Prussia leading Germany towards unity made only gradual headway and received a major setback in 1848.

Now that Prussia has disappeared, probably beyond recall, it has become easier to look at her history and her role in German affairs without emotion. Prussia appears now neither as a villain nor as a hero. The rise of the Hohenzollern state remains a remarkable story which has much to tell us about some of the essential factors of European history : the nature of the state, the basis of nationality, the interplay of liberty and authority. It is a story which needs to be told in its own right and not from the point of view of having reached its culmination in 1870. The formation of modern Germany now seems more like the end rather than the apotheosis of the old Prussia, for by the 1860s the Prussian state had itself become out of date in some of its most characteristic features. If Bismarck had not come to the rescue, Prussia could only have survived in the modern world at the price of a radical transformation. Prussianism became synonymous with militarism, aggression and ruthless efficiency; the real weakness of the traditional Prussia lay in the failure of her institutions and her ruling classes to adapt themselves to the industrial age.

CHAPTER I

Origins

THREE elements had to come together to produce the Prussian state: the March of Brandenburg, the dynasty of the Hohenzollerns, and the states on the Baltic founded by the Order of Teutonic Knights, from which the name Prussia is derived. The fusion of these elements was finally accomplished at the beginning of the 17th century.

The establishment of the March Brandenburg is part of the process of German eastward penetration which went on for most of the Middle Ages. The colonization of the lands east of the Elbe was the most positive German achievement of the medieval period and without it the Germans could never have become the great Central European nation of more recent times. Nationalist historians have seen it as compensating for medieval Germany's failure to lay the foundation for a modern nation state, a failure which stands in such marked contrast to the development of her western neighbours. The area which later became known as Brandenburg stretched on both sides of the Middle Elbe. In this region there existed, as early as the 10th century, the Northern March of the Empire on the west bank of the river; while on the east bank Otto the Great founded the bishoprics of Brandenburg and Havelberg as an assertion of imperial rights. At this stage German colonization made little progress. The Slav tribes east of the Elbe, known to the Germans as Wends, reacted against their colonizers and the religion they brought with them and in a great uprising in 983 destroyed what advances had been made.

The German progress eastward was resumed in the 12th century when Albrecht the Bear, of the Ascanian dynasty, became margrave of the North March. He and his successors extended the region under their control, which became generally known as Brandenburg, east to the Oder and beyond, north into Pomerania and south into the archbishopric of Magdeburg, which had also been founded by Otto the Great. Under the aegis of the Ascanian margraves German settlers flooded in, lured by the prospect of a freer life than they could enjoy further west. They were of all classes—noblemen, knights, peasants, monks and burghers—and

pressure of population as well as natural disasters drove them east-
wards. The Slavs were absorbed rather than conquered, and the
German and Slav nobilities became largely amalgamated. Ethni-
cally the population became a mixture of Teuton and Slav, but in
an area such as Brandenburg east of the Elbe, where the indigenous Slavs had been sparsely settled, the German element was
probably predominant. There was a distinct Flemish influence, for
many of the settlers came from the Low Countries. In the early
stages of colonization, the pressures of the feudal system east of the
Elbe were probably much lighter than farther west and the landowner was the peasant's neighbour rather than his lord. Monastic
orders, particularly the Cistercians and Premonstratensians, played
an important role in the colonization and the conversion of the
Slavs. Is it possible to see in the strenuous way of life of these
monks, inspired by the Benedictine injunction *Ora et Labora*,
prayer and work, an early incarnation of the Prussian spirit?
Moeller van den Bruck, a nationalist writer of the 1920s who has
the dubious distinction of being the originator of the concept of
"The Third Reich", draws this parallel and it is true that the
colours of the later Prussian state, black and white, hark back to
the Cistercians and to the Teutonic Order. "Prussia was black and
white even in her beginnings. The ascetic feeling of Cistercians
and Teutonic Knights had subconsciously chosen these serious,
abstract, northerly colours which because of their lack of hue are
not really colours—and the zeal with which they pursued their
voluntary labours of love and their life's work, proclaims the earliest
and most genuinely Prussian traits."[1]

   The Ascanian House died out in 1319 and there followed a
century of external decline and internal disintegration for Brandenburg. The March became successively an appendage of the
Houses of Wittelsbach and Luxemburg. These princes, without
roots in the March, were unable to impose their rule effectively
and were often concerned only to extract what resources they could
from this distant and inhospitable territory. An event worthy of
note in this confused period was the conferment, in 1351, of the
electoral dignity on the rulers of the March, an act confirmed by
the Golden Bull of 1356. The importance of the March was hardly
sufficient to warrant the elevation of its rulers to the ranks of the
seven Electors. The Emperor Charles IV, who promulgated the
Golden Bull, may have acted in anticipation of the time when he
and his House would take over Brandenburg from the Wittels-
bachs. He in fact became the only prince in this turbulent century
who really tried to improve the condition of the country. To him
we owe a land register, compiled in 1375, from which comes much

of our information about the state of society in medieval Brandenburg. Fate might have drawn Brandenburg in any of a number of
different directions in the 15th century. The territory might have
become a means of giving the House of Wittelsbach a foothold in
north Germany as well as in the south, thus making it into a
dynasty more powerful than the Habsburgs were about to become.
Under the Luxemburgers the March might have become aligned
with Bohemia in an entirely different axis of power. An amalgama-
tion with Poland was another possibility and complete disintegration of the lands amassed by the Ascanians was not to be ruled out.
It was entirely fortuitous that Brandenburg became a new base of
the House of Hohenzollern and, in the long run, the most significant
one.

The Hohenzollerns were a Suabian family, who, at the end of
the 12th century, partly through marriage, partly through the
favour they enjoyed with the Emperor Frederick Barbarossa, became
Burgraves of Nuremberg. This position, originally an imperial
office, was like so many others gradually transformed into a territorial principality. The powers of the Hohenzollern at Nuremberg
were, however, always challenged and restricted by the burghers
of the city as well as by the Emperor; the importance of Nuremberg to the Hohenzollerns lay mainly in giving them a foothold in
Franconia from where they were able to acquire territory in the
region. These acquisitions formed the basis of the Franconian possessions of the dynasty which centred round Bayreuth and Ansbach
and which they retained until the 19th century. The Burgraves of
Nuremberg were elevated to the rank of imperial princes in the
14th century and often played important roles in the affairs of the
Empire. A first fleeting contact with Brandenburg occurred in
1345, when one of the Burgraves acted as governor in the March,
on behalf of the Wittelsbach ruler. In 1411 the Burgrave Frederick
VI, who ruled in Ansbach as well as Bayreuth, was made Vicar-
General in the March Brandenburg by the Emperor Sigismund, to
whom he had rendered conspicuous service in the acquisition of the
imperial crown. The Emperor conferred the full electoral dignity
on Frederick in 1415 and he was formally invested as Margrave
and Elector Frederick I of Brandenburg in 1417. The most important single step in the formation of the Prussian state had been
taken.

Like his predecessors, Frederick had to fight hard to make his
rule effective in his new dominion. He had to battle with the over-
mighty nobles, among them the legendary Quitzows. He had some
successes: the new cannon, fired with gunpowder, helped him to
reduce the castles of recalcitrant subjects. But his plans to extend

his dominions in the March and North East Germany foundered amid the complex cross-currents of the time. After 1426 Frederick never saw Brandenburg again; he concentrated his attention on his Franconian lands and on imperial affairs. The first Hohenzollern ruler of Brandenburg was essentially a medieval figure, an imperial prince and functionary rather than a territorial ruler.

The task of the Hohenzollerns in Brandenburg was more difficult than that which had faced the Ascanians two hundred years earlier. The territory was surrounded by powerful neighbours both to the north and to the east. Moreover, some time passed before Brandenburg took pride of place among Hohenzollern possessions. Constant subdivision to provide for a number of sons was still the practice. Two of Frederick I's sons divided Brandenburg between them and only the death of one of them reunited the March in the hands of the other, Frederick II. The next elector, the knightly Albrecht Achilles, laid it down, in the so-called *Dispositio Achillea,* that not more than three Hohenzollerns were to rule simultaneously. This meant that Brandenburg was not to be divided and that normally the Franconian lands would be separated from it, which indeed they were till the end of the 18th century. Thus Brandenburg became the centre of Hohenzollern power. At the end of the 16th century the family treaty of Gera confirmed that Brandenburg, the electoral title, and any claims attaching to it, should pass as a unit in the main male line of the House of Hohenzollern. The claim of the House of Brandenburg to the Duchy of Prussia was thought worthy of specific mention.

The century of the Reformation brought stability and prosperity to Brandenburg. The Hohenzollerns were converted to Lutheranism, following rather than leading their subjects, and a new though by no means radically changed order of service in the churches was introduced in 1540. Monasteries were dissolved and the Elector assumed the Headship of the Church, exercising it through superintendents and a consistory. Along with Saxony, Brandenburg became one of the leading Protestant principalities in Germany; but the Hohenzollerns, then and for a long time to come, were also anxious to maintain their links with the Catholic Emperor and retained a loyalty to the Empire. They attempted to play a balancing role and were reluctant to commit themselves fully to a league of Protestant princes.

Internally, the most notable development was the growing strength and privileges of the landowning aristocracy and the decline in status of the peasantry. No longer were the nobles the lawless robber barons of a century earlier; they were becoming economically powerful estate-owners, taking more and more land under cultivation and farming it with peasants who were being degraded to the position of serfs. The German word for serfdom was "leibeigen", which meant that the serf was owned by the master to the extent of life and limb, and it describes a state of affairs increasingly common in the whole of eastern Europe. It stands in marked contrast to developments in western Europe at this time, where the feudal system was being gradually dissolved into relationships based on cash, wages and rent. The drift towards serfdom in eastern Europe was due to economic causes: rising prices made the export of corn more profitable; this in turn produced the incentive to bring more land under cultivation and a way had to be found to tie labour to the land. The social structure of many countries, particularly Poland, was profoundly affected by this transformation. In Brandenburg the 16th century marks the real beginning of the Junkers, that powerful noble class destined to be one of the main pillars of the later Prussian state. The Junkers also exercised much influence in the direction of affairs through the periodic meetings of the Estates. The Electors had to treat with the representatives of the Junkers at these meetings, mainly over finance. The rulers themselves were gradually developing instruments of centralized control and jurisdiction, culminating in the formation of a Privy Council in 1604, but Brandenburg was still a long way from having an absolute monarchy equipped with an effective bureaucracy. Towns had never been highly developed in the March and by the 16th century their heyday was passed. With their experience of battling with the burghers of Nuremberg the Hohenzollerns were anti-urban. By the end of the 16th century Brandenburg was still overwhelmingly agricultural and the great trade-routes were passing it by. The territory seemed likely to remain a backwater.

In the meantime the third main element in the future Prussian state had come within the orbit of the Hohenzollerns, the former state of the Teutonic Order of Knights on the Baltic. In 1511 Albrecht, a grandson of the Elector Albrecht Achilles and son of Frederick, Margrave of Ansbach and later also of Bayreuth, was elected the last High Master of the Order. The Order had been founded in 1198 in Palestine to help with the conquest of the Holy Land. It later moved its activities to Transylvania, but owing to political friction had to leave again in 1225. Then the opportunity occurred for the Order to transfer its missionary work to the country east of the mouth of the Vistula. This area was inhabited by the Baltic tribes known as Prussians, who were fiercely resisting conversion to Christianity. In the Golden Bull of Rimini of 1226 the Emperor Frederick II empowered his friend Herman of Salza,

High Master of the Teutonic Order, to govern the territories to be conquered as part of the Empire. The enfeoffment also received papal sanction. Within a short time an area similar in extent to the Province of East Prussia after 1918 was conquered. German settlers were brought in to colonize the land according to a systematic plan; the Prussians, in so far as they were prepared to accept Christianity, were absorbed. When in 1308 the Knights won Danzig and Pomerelia (roughly the area covered in our century by the controversial Polish corridor) from the Poles, the seat of the High Master was transferred to the Marienburg, a formidable palace at Danzig.

The 14th century was the peak period of the Order; at one time the territories under its control stretched from the Newmark, the part of Brandenburg east of the Oder, up to Estonia, although its writ never ran very effectively beyond the Memel. The Order was one of the most important powers on the Baltic, its trade stretched from England to Russia, it controlled many important towns and co-operated closely with the Hanseatic League. This country, ruled by a monastic order, was one of the best-governed states of the Middle Ages. It maintained full archives, which to this day afford an excellent insight into its colonization procedures and social and economic policies. Its bureaucracy was guided by effective and uniform rules. One cannot therefore help wondering whether something of this spirit survived to the later Prussian state, which had similar characteristics. A modern German historian has said that the officials and administrators of the Order, with their self-discipline, sobriety and responsibility, and their achievements in colonization and administration, anticipated the spirit of later Prussia; he thinks that the corporate and ascetic spirit of the Knights experienced a transformation and reincarnation in the Prussian officer corps.[2] This may be an idealization both of the medieval Knights and the later Prussian officers, but we may grant that the parallel is too obvious to be ignored. Some authorities take the view that part of the administrative structure of the Order did, indeed, survive the chaos of the 15th century and the secularization of the 16th century to influence the later state of Brandenburg-Prussia.[3]

The state of the Teutonic Order also had its weaknesses. The most obvious was that members of the Order were celibate monks with no roots in the country. Under them there grew up a native German nobility and peasantry, although the presence of the Order, as long as it remained fully effective, always limited the power of the nobility. When external pressure against the state and territories of the Order grew, it was not surprising that the nobility sometimes attacked their masters from the rear and made common cause with the external enemy. The Polish-Lithuanian Union at the end of the 14th century presented the Order with a major challenge. The Knights attempted a pre-emptive strike, but were severely beaten at the battle of Tannenberg in 1410 and many of them were killed. Later attempts by the Order to gain more support from the populations they ruled through their Estates failed. At the second Peace of Thorn in 1466 the Knights lost important territories to the Poles and had to swear allegiance to the Crown of Poland. The remaining rump of their state had therefore ceased to be part of the Empire. In a last desperate attempt to save themselves the Knights began to elect various members of German ruling houses as High Masters. It was in those circumstances that Albrecht of Brandenburg-Ansbach was chosen High Master in 1511. One of his qualifications was that his mother was a Polish princess and that he might be able to save the territory of the Order from being finally swallowed by the Poles. In this he succeeded, but he failed to save the Order.

Albrecht was a cultivated man, a humanist and a friend of Erasmus, and with the agreement of the Estates of Prussia he early on became a convert to Lutheranism. The Reformation spread with miraculous rapidity in the territory of the Order. Luther himself advised Albrecht to secularize the territory and to acknowledge the suzerainty of the Polish Crown, a step which he had long been reluctant to take. Thus the Duchy of Prussia, held in fief from the Kings of Poland, began its existence in 1525. It was a territory of minor importance, not comparable to the state of the Teutonic Order at the height of its power. It was, however, an outpost of Protestantism in that part of the world, with the University of Königsberg, founded in 1544, already the centre of Protestant learning. As in the rest of eastern Europe, the nobility became very much the dominant force in the Duchy, while the peasantry gradually declined into serfdom.

The fact that Prussia was a Lutheran island in a sea of Catholicism, and that it was ruled by Hohenzollern princes, made an eventual union with Brandenburg more than probable. In 1569, on the death of Duke Albrecht, the Elector Joachim II of Brandenburg secured the co-enfeoffment of the Duchy for himself and his heirs from the Kings of Poland. A further step to strengthen the Brandenburg claims on Prussia was taken in 1594 when Johann Sigismund, son and heir of the Elector Johann Georg, married a daughter of Albrecht's son, the feeble-minded and increasingly incapacitated Duke of Prussia. When this pathetic potentate finally expired in 1618 without leaving any male heirs, Johann Sigismund, now Elector of Brandenburg, became Duke of Prussia and swore allegiance as such to the King of Poland. The Prussian Estates rendered homage to the new Duke, though with little enthusiasm and intending to preserve their independence to the full. Despite these limitations, the third major element in the emergence of the future Prussian state had slipped into place, "truly a great step for the country and the dynasty", as Ranke put it.[4]

Two further developments at the turn of the 16th and 17th centuries were necessary to create the full framework and the tension from which the Prussia of the future was to arise : the Cleves-Jülich succession, that terror of school history books, and the conversion of the Hohenzollern rulers to Calvinism. A number of rich and strategically important territories on the Lower Rhine— Cleves, Jülich, Mark, Berg, Ravensberg and Ravenstein—became the object of rival claims at the end of the 16th century. The Brandenburg stake derived from the same marriage of Johann Sigismund in 1594 which had strengthened his claim on Prussia : the Duchess Marie Eleanor of Prussia, who became his mother-in-law, was a sister of the last Duke of Cleves who died insane in 1609. There were at least four other parties in the ring : the Emperor, the Elector of Saxony, and the Counts Palatine of Neuburg and Zweibrücken. The problem of the succession was inextricably interwoven with the balance between Catholics and Protestants on the Lower Rhine, in Germany and in Europe, the struggle between Spain and the Netherlands, and the ambitions of the House of Habsburg to gain a foothold in the Low Countries. Where so many great issues were at stake and powerful contestants stood embattled, the voice of Brandenburg was feeble and her military effort in the warface which ensued derisory.

Nevertheless the Peace of Xanten of 1614, which for the time being resolved the problem, acknowledged the right of the Electors of Brandenburg to rule in Cleves, Mark, Ravensberg and Ravenstein but not in Jülich and Berg, predominantly Catholic areas. The Estates of the territories swore allegiance to the Elector Johann Sigismund, while intending, like their counterparts in Prussia, to take little heed of him in practice. The important fact was that the rule of the Hohenzollerns was brought to the Rhine, from whence it would not depart, except for a brief interlude in the Napoleonic period, until 1918, and this at the very moment when it was also reaching the Baltic a thousand or more miles away. The feeble Electorate of Brandenburg was now deeply involved in Western, Central and Eastern Europe. Could such a chance agglomeration of lands have any meaning or any permanence? Only if a great effort of will was forthcoming to knit these disparate territories together and imbue them with a common spirit. It was inevitable that so extended a position could be held together only by armed force.

In creating the will to make a state out of this inauspicious inheritance the conversion of the Hohenzollerns of Brandenburg to Calvinism was of critical significance. The Calvinist form of Protestantism produced a strenuous breed of humanity. Its adherents escaped from the terrors of Predestination by finding in worldly success the assurance of belonging to the elect. In the Low Countries, the British Isles, among the French Huguenots, Calvinism stimulated the rise of modern capitalism and entrepreneurial activity. In Brandenburg the Reformed religion implanted in the Hohenzollern dynasty a strong belief that the rising fortunes of their House were the clearest token of divine grace. Only by the most devoted attention to the administration of their territories, careful financial husbandry, unceasing improvement of their armies and intrepid maintenance of their European position could they assure themselves of remaining in a state of grace. As important as instilling a will to greatness in the rulers was the effect of Calvinism in promoting religious toleration. Ever since the Elector Joachim II had embraced Lutheranism in 1539 the Hohenzollerns had shied away from religious extremism. At first many Catholic rites and practices were maintained and, later, sectarian violence within the Protestant camp was discouraged. When the electors became Calvinists they continued to preside over the Lutheran Church, and in Brandenburg and Prussia over a predominantly Lutheran population. A good deal of live-and-let-live in matters of religion became inevitable.

The Elector Johann Sigismund, in whose reign many of the strands of the Prussian story seemed to come together, became a member of the Reformed Church in 1613. It was partly a calculated act of state, partly a matter of personal conviction. The Estates of Cleves and Mark had made their allegiance conditional on the recognition of the three religious denominations of the territories. The establishment of the Elector's position in the western territories depended much on the Netherlands, predominantly Calvinist. By turning to the Reformed Church the Elector could also hope to gain greater independence from the Estates of Brandenburg and Prussia. Having taken the step, Johann Sigismund recognized that a policy of religious toleration had become a necessity. His conversion unleashed a flood of polemical literature, but in 1614 he issued a so-called Toleration Edict, which made it an offence to preach hatred of other Christian faiths from the pulpit. The principle of *cuius regio eius religio*, which had prevailed in Germany since the Peace of Augsburg sixty years earlier, had perforce to be abandoned in Brandenburg now that a Calvinist prince stood at the head of a mainly Lutheran people. The Elector had to admit freedom of conscience and to declare that he would not dictate to his subjects in matters of faith. All these attitudes were well ahead of the times.

All the elements which were to go into the making of the Prussian state were now present : the acquisition of Prussia, the Cleves-Jülich succession, the conversion to the Reformed Church of the Hohenzollerns; but it still needed a ruler of genius to start the process of fusion. For the moment he did not appear. During most of the terrible Thirty Years War the Brandenburg lands were ruled by the ailing and vacillating Elector Georg Wilhelm, who hovered uneasily between the Protestant and the Imperial camp. Religion and opposition to the selfish policy of the Habsburgs in Germany should have inclined Brandenburg towards the Swedes, and indeed the Elector was married to a sister of Gustavus Adolphus. But one of the aims of Sweden was to retain a foothold on the southern shores of the Baltic, in Pomerania; and Brandenburg had a claim to Pomerania which became effective with the death of the last Pomeranian Duke of the Greifen dynasty in 1637.

For most of his reign Georg Wilhelm's Chief Minister and most powerful adviser was Schwartzenberg, a Catholic nobleman from the Rhineland, who had been a counsellor to the prince when he was Governor of Cleves before his accession. After 1626 Schwartzenberg became increasingly convinced that Brandenburg should form an alliance with the Emperor. He was in eclipse while Sweden was at the height of her power, but returned to favour later, especially after Saxony had made it up with the Emperor in the Peace of Prague in 1635. For the last three years of the reign, from 1637 to 1640, Brandenburg fought actively against the Swedes, with the acquisition of Pomerania as one of her main aims. The Elector's resources were totally inadequate for this fight and the small forces he could raise largely ineffective. The March was almost entirely overrun, not for the first time in this war, and suffered severely. The Electoral Court took refuge in Königsberg, where Georg Wilhelm died in December 1640, to be succeeded by his son, Frederick William, better known as the Great Elector. Here at last was the ruler who was to prove capable of developing the potentialities of the Brandenburg inheritance. Disastrous as was the situation of his House at the moment of his accession, these potentialities were even now not irretrievably lost.

The Great Elector can be regarded as the real founder of the Brandenburg-Prussian state. He turned to advantage what to his predecessors had been a source of weakness, Brandenburg's simul-

taneous involvement in Western, Central and Eastern Europe and
the pressure upon her of the great rival powers—Austria, France,
Sweden and Poland. Throughout his reign he was forever changing
alliances and was often regarded as unreliable. What actuated him
was the relentless determination to safeguard the interests of his
House and his territories. This was his real aim, even if he occasionally tried to mobilize German imperial sentiment behind his
policy. Frequently he miscalculated and overestimated the help the
Dutch or later the French would bring him. The territorial gains
he made were not impressive and mostly came to him as a result
of the power balance at the time of the Peace of Westphalia. The
acquisition of the whole of Pomerania and particularly of the
mouth of the Oder eluded him all his life. Yet his endless ma-
noeuvres and the complex diplomatic web he spun brought him
growing prestige : Brandenburg became a power with which every
chancellery in Europe had to reckon. In Germany the Hohenzollerns became second only to the Habsburgs.

The linchpin of this position of strength built up by the Great
Elector was the army, which by the end of his reign numbered
30,000 well-trained troops, where at the beginning there had been
a rabble of a few thousand. The creation of this force provided
more than anything else the motivation for the revolution in government which the Great Elector carried out and which was much the
most important of his achievements. He gave the three parts of his
dominions, which at first hung together only because they were
theoretically subject to him and over two of which his control was
shadowy, a reasonably uniform and centralized administration. He
battled with the most powerful force of regionalism, the Estates,
in all three parts and won. He thereby brought Brandenburg-
Prussia in line with the practice of absolute monarchy as applied
elsewhere in Europe. The nobility, particularly the Junkers in
Brandenburg and Prussia, deprived of their collective influence on
affairs of state, were taught to find satisfaction in individual service
to their sovereign, especially in the army. Impressed as he was by
the advantage of having strong military forces, even to a degree
out of proportion to the resources of his lands, the Great Elector
was also keenly aware of the need to develop these resources. In
his youth he had admired the commercial and trading prosperity
of the Dutch and he pursued a policy of "peuplierung" in true
mercantilist fashion throughout his reign. The main spiritual driving force behind the Great Elector's ceaseless labours to make his
state "formidabel" and "konsiderabel" was his Calvinist religion,
which made him personally work at the business of ruling to an
extent unusual in princes of his time.

Frederick William detested the anti-Swedish policy of Schwartz-enberg, his father's favourite, but he was at first not strong enough to overthrow it. The death of Schwartzenberg within a few weeks of the new Elector's accession was providential and eased Frederick William's task in making peace with the Swedes. This change was greatly welcomed in the March, where the population had been halved since 1618 and on which the exactions of Schwartzenberg had lain heavily. The Elector, however, soon found that the disbandment of his small forces made him more than ever the plaything of stronger powers and in 1644 he reversed this policy by raising new troops. From that time he was never without a standing army and this became the central point of all his endeavours. The new troops were sworn to him and no longer to the Emperor. A memorandum of one of his councillors, dating from these years, recommended a standing army based on compulsorily recruited peasants, officered by the Brandenburg nobility, which served in so many armies of the period, and supported by permanent revenues and taxes. These ideas could not be immediately implemented, but pointed to the shape of things to come.

Frederick William maintained a large delegation at the negotiations at Münster and Osnabrück which finally produced the Peace of Westphalia. With the help of his new forces he was able to recover from foreign occupation some fortresses and territory in the March and in Cleves. He tried to strengthen his position further by a proposal to marry Christina of Sweden and by his actual marriage, in 1646, to a princess of the House of Orange. Yet in spite of his strong legal claim to Pomerania the settlement of 1648 gave him only Eastern Pomerania, called Hinterpommern in German, while Western Pomerania, Vorpommern, including the all-important mouth of the Oder with the port of Stettin, remained in Swedish hands. Sweden was in actual occupation of the whole of Pomerania and it took Frederick William another five years to get possession of the part allotted to him. In compensation for having given up the lion's share of Pomerania, Brandenburg obtained the secularized bishoprics of Minden and Halberstadt and the reversion of the archbishopric of Magdeburg.

Disappointed in one direction, Frederick William tried, in 1651, to improve his standing in the still unresolved Cleves-Jülich question by an armed intervention in Jülich, which was then under the control of his hated Catholic rival, the Count Palatine of Neuburg. This operation was completely unsuccessful and made the Elector highly unpopular as a breaker of the peace so recently established. Even this fiasco, however, indicated that the Elector had become completely disenchanted with the policy of neutrality which his

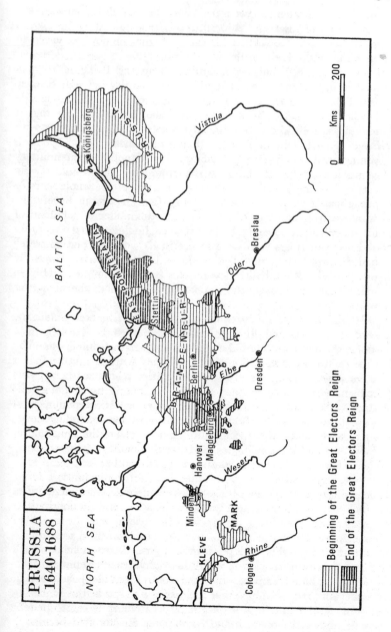

PRUSSIA
1640-1688

NORTH SEA

BALTIC SEA

Königsberg

P·R·U·S·S·I·A

Vistula

Kms 200

0

Oder

Breslau

P·O·M·E·R·A·N·I·A

Stettin

B·R·A·N·D·E·N·B·U·R·G

Berlin

Elbe

Dresden

Magdeburg

Hanover

Weser

Minden

KLEVE

MARK

Rhine

Cologne

Beginning of the Great Electors Reign

End of the Great Electors Reign

father had so often followed and which he had also adopted in the early years of his reign. A posture of strength, and determination to use it actively to further his cause, is what he now conceived to be in the best interests of Brandenburg.

When another major war broke out in the Baltic in 1655, a further instalment in the long-drawn-out rivalry between Sweden and Poland, the Elector was determined to intervene on one side or the other. Before it was over, in 1660, he had in fact fought for and against the two main adversaries. While in alliance with Sweden, he fought in 1656 the battle of Warsaw, which gave his young army its first major victory and established the military reputation of Brandenburg. Apart from this, the results of the battle were meagre as indeed were the fruits of the whole war for Frederick William. There was only one important benefit he obtained from it: the recognition by both Sweden and Poland of his independent sovereignty in Prussia. He thus joined the ranks of European rulers who were sovereign *de jure*; a situation which had already been established *de facto* for all German princes by the Peace of Westphalia. Beyond this he gained immeasurably in self-confidence through the important role he had played in this war.

In the meantime Frederick William's assertive policy and the central role allotted to the Army had pushed him a long way along the path of internal transformation in his dominions. The changes involved him in decisive clashes with the Diets in his three main territories and in administrative reorganization of permanent significance in the evolution of the Prussian state. The struggle with the Estates was least bitter in Brandenburg, most violent in Prussia. In Brandenburg the situation became increasingly tense when the Elector refused to disband the troops after the Peace of Westphalia, as had been customary in peace-time. The Estates, in a long rearguard action, refused to grant the Elector the revenues necessary for the maintenance of the forces and repeatedly presented him with long lists of grievances. In 1653, after much wrangling, they gave way by voting him money for six years ahead. Effectively this meant that the Diet's and the nobility's role in the making of policy was at an end. In return the Junkers had all their rights and privileges confirmed, in particular their "police" powers, a wide term in those days, their exemption from general taxes and imports, and their control over the peasants. The master-serf relationship which had become so marked over the last century in the March, was once more legally endorsed and thereby made even more onerous and inescapable for the peasants.

In Cleves the struggle with the Estates was more difficult. The

general situation was inimical to an increase of princely power and
there was also the neighbouring example of Jülich where a much
more liberal regime prevailed. Up to the time of the Swedish war
the prince made little headway in increasing his control over his
western provinces; in practice, however, he extracted quite a lot
of money for the upkeep of his forces from these rich territories.
Although on paper there was little change after 1660, the Elector's
growing self-confidence and enhanced military reputation created
a more favourable situation for him. He was now able to recruit
and quarter troops in Cleves and the other Rhenish territories, and
the Estates became accustomed to granting him revenues. It was
of major importance to the Elector's position in the West that the
partition of the Cleves-Jülich inheritance with Neuburg was acknowledged as permanent after 1666. Even so the Great Elector was
only partially successful in integrating his western provinces with
the rest of his dominions : the social structure was very different
here, the relationship between landlord and tenant more commercial than in the feudal East and the towns more important.

The fiercest struggle between ruler and Diet ensued in Prussia.
Frederick William had personally experienced, in the last years of
his father's reign and the early years of his own, how little the
Electors of Brandenburg counted for in their eastern province.
The main element in the weakness of the Hohenzollerns in Prussia
was the Polish suzerainty to which they had to submit. The Prussian nobility and important towns like Königsberg could always
play off the Crown of Poland against the Elector. If Poland
seemed to be weakening the Swedes could be appealed to. These
props of Prussian independence were knocked away when the
Peace of Oliva, at the end of the Swedish-Polish War in 1660,
recognized the sovereignty of the Electors of Brandenburg in their
capacity as Dukes of Prussia.

The conflict between the Elector and the Estates of Prussia now
entered its crucial stage, when the changed legal circumstances
required the Diet to render homage anew to the sovereign Duke
of Prussia. Although the conditions which the Elector attached to
the document of allegiance were quite moderate, the resistance to
his demands took its stand on ancient constitutional rights. Particularly the urban opposition in Königsberg found a resolute and
popular champion in Hieronymus Roth, the chairman of the city
court of law. It required the appearance of Frederick William
with an armed force outside the city and the arrest of Roth to
calm the opposition. The Estates and Königsberg agreed to grants
of money and also to the holding of office by members of the
Reformed Church. Even then resistance to the Elector's demands

was not finally quelled. When he needed more money for military purposes in 1669, the Estates again prevaricated and this time a member of the nobility, Colonel von Kalckstein, became the chief leader of the recalcitrants. He was typical of those Junkers, who, modelling themselves on the Polish aristocracy, would not admit any diminution of their independence. The Elector determined to make an example of Kalckstein and finally had him executed.

Thus the princely power advanced inexorably throughout the Hohenzollern dominions. The Estates were not fighting a battle for freedom and were only partially motivated by the desire to maintain regional independence. For the most part they were spurred on by the determination to maintain their vested interests and the established privileges of their rank. The Elector, on the other hand, was not fighting for the lower orders. Such overtones were perceptible only to a minor degree in his actions and the effect of his policy was to strengthen the rights of the nobility. He was merely following the fashion of the times in building up an absolute monarchy with a strong military establishment. He was moving pragmatically towards the situation which thinkers like Hobbes, Bossuet and Pufendorf were elaborating theoretically. On the debit side, the Great Elector's defeat of the Estates meant the disappearance in Brandenburg-Prussia of almost all vestiges of the representative principle except at the very local level. This undoubtedly contributed to the weakness of parliamentary government in Germany right down to our own day.

The struggle with the Estates was accompanied by major administrative and financial reforms. The main motive power was again the need to sustain the army. By the end of the Swedish-Polish war one can definitely speak of a standing army, for this war had brought about a unified force for all three parts of the Hohenzollern state, and although it was reduced when peace came in 1660, it was never again completely disbanded. This army was still in the main mercenary in character, in that, for example, the colonels of regiments were engaged on contract and then provided the officers and men to make up a regiment. The Elector tried to move away from this system by gaining more control over the appointment of subordinate officers, by choosing more native-born officers and by setting up a small military academy. He maintained close personal contact with a small staff of senior officers, the beginnings of a General Staff, of whom the two successive Field Marshals, Sparr and Derfflinger, were the most prominent. Frederick William aimed at acquiring a state army instead of a *condottieri* force. The Junkers, who had opposed him so bitterly over the taxes required to feed the troops, soon began to take service in the army, and also in the civil administration, and thus was born a tradition vital to the Prussian state. It would be premature however to think of the Great Elector as the founder of the Prussian officer corps—this task remained for his grandson to accomplish.

The maintenance of the army entailed far-reaching changes in the system of taxation. It was the Elector's aim to introduce as his main instrument of raising revenue a tax on consumption, called "Akzise" in German, or excise. He had seen this in operation in Holland where it proved very productive. One of its advantages was that it would by-pass the tax immunity of the nobility, which would compensate for its rather heavier incidence on the poorer classes. It would make unnecessary the periodic wrangle with the Diets. For this reason and in order to preserve their immunity, the nobility fiercely resisted the excise tax and the Great Elector was never able to overcome this resistance. The towns, however, did adopt this tax after 1667 and thus a dual system of taxation, one for town and another for country, came into being. This was itself a major factor in weakening the Estates as an important political element. The collection of the tax in towns was in the hands of the Elector's own officials who got an increasing grip on the whole of urban administration. The strength and power of the central-ized state bureaucracy increased immeasurably thereby, at the expense of local initiative, the ancient right of self-government and middle-class independence. The Elector's tax collectors and officials were in their turn responsible to the "General-Kriegskommissariat", a powerful new agency in the unification of the Hohenzollern lands. A hierarchy of officials, spread through all provinces down to the Kreis level, worked under the head of this department whose main function was to supply the army. The Privy Council was also used methodically as an instrument of unification. Origin-ally effective only for Brandenburg, it became after 1651 a body on which all the various territories of the ruler were represented and they became accustomed to having much of their business trans-acted there.

In the choice of men to staff his bureaucratic instruments the Great Elector was less hidebound than many rulers of the period; men of sometimes quite humble origins were given their oppor-tunity. It would again be anticipating the future to think of Frederick William as the founder of that efficient civil service which became, along with the army, one of the pillars of Prussia; but at any rate the beginnings of this system and its uniform functioning throughout all provinces may be placed in this reign. For all his innovations in the field of taxation and administration,

the Great Elector was never able to raise enough money to maintain his army in time of war and was dependent on foreign subsidies.
This severely limited his room for manoeuvre in foreign affairs.

The Great Elector knew enough about the prevailing mercantilist
theories of his time to be aware that better machinery of taxation
was not enough. One had to develop the economic life of the
country to produce rising revenues. Frederick William attempted
throughout his reign to raise the level of activity in agriculture and
industry in his relatively backward territories, further impoverished
by war; he was particularly interested in counteracting the depopulation brought about by the Thirty Years War. His successes
were limited, for Brandenburg-Prussia had not the geographical
advantages of Holland or England; but among his achievements
were the building of an Oder-Spree Canal, the improvement of
postal communications, and even the beginnings of naval and
colonial enterprise. Early in his reign he encouraged the immigra-
tion of Dutch settlers, particularly for their skill in drainage. One
of his boldest strokes came towards the end of his reign in the Edict
of Potsdam of 1685. It offered asylum to French Huguenots displaced by the revocation of the Edict of Nantes. It brought a
considerable French colony into Brandenburg and thenceforth
names like La Motte-Fouqué, Fontane and Le Coq Devrient
occupy an honourable place in the annals of Prussia. Not the least
important effect of the Huguenot influx was the role which French
educators now began to play in the training of generations of
Hohenzollern rulers and princes.

This was part and parcel of the policy of religious toleration
traditional in the House of Brandenburg particularly since their
conversion to Calvinism. The Great Elector was remarkably undogmatic in his view of Christianity and felt that the two main
branches of Protestantism should be regarded as indistinguishable
in practice. This outlook involved him in some bitter battles with
rigid Lutheran orthodoxy among the clergy of Brandenburg and
Prussia. The Great Lutheran divine Paul Gerhardt, author of many
famous hymns, went into exile in neighbouring Saxony and
Frederick William was unable to induce him to return. The policy
of toleration was most fruitful in the Cleves territories where
Catholics, Lutherans and Calvinists lived in close proximity. A
mixture of motives of mercantilist advantage and religious toleration also led to the readmission, in 1671, of Jews into Brandenburg,
from whence they had been driven almost exactly a century earlier
in the full flush of Reformation fanaticism.

After the Swedish-Polish war, Brandenburg experienced more
than a decade of relative peace, but from 1672 until the end of

the Great Elector's reign in 1688 there was again almost incessant warfare. Brandenburg once more switched from one alliance to another, won many a famous victory but gained little thereby because she was still at the mercy of the Great Powers. The most legendary of the victories was the Battle of Fehrbellin of 1675, where, led by Frederick William himself and by the old Field Marshal Derfflinger, the armies of Brandenburg, unaided by any allies, chased the Swedes out of the March. At a moment of humiliation at the hands of Napoleon, in 1810, Heinrich von Kleist, one of Prussia's foremost dramatists and a scion of one of her most famous families, recalled this battle to his countrymen in the play *The Prince of Homburg*. After Fehrbellin followed the conquest of Pomerania including the great port of Stettin, an acquisition which the Elector had long desired. Unfortunately, the French forced him, in 1679, to disgorge all these gains again and give them back to their friends, the Swedes. Frederick William was deeply embittered and felt deserted by his allies, the Emperor and the Dutch. This led him to switch alliances yet again and to become for some years virtually a pensioner of the French. Their huge subsidies enabled him to maintain his large army, but he had to condone Louis XIV's "reunions", the acquisition of much German territory in Alsace, including the city of Strassburg. It has always been a grief for German nationalist historians that a hero-figure like the Great Elector had so little German patriotism in him. The French in time brought the Elector as much disappointment as his other allies had done, especially over Pomerania, and towards the end of his life we find him again in league with the Emperor and the Dutch. Throughout all these years the Elector's court and even his family were often bitterly rent into French or Imperial and Dutch factions.

The Great Elector was the first Hohenzollern of European importance and reputation, though he could not compare with contemporaries like Mazarin or Richelieu, Gustavus Adolphus or Cromwell, for he lacked the power base they enjoyed. He instilled into the rag-bag collection of territories he inherited the beginnings of a common sense of statehood. Likewise the army and the civil service, two institutions of capital importance in the Prussia of the future, had their origins in his reign. In his testament the Great Elector came close to destroying what he had created : in his anxiety to provide for the numerous and vigorous offspring of his second marriage he ordered a degree of splitting up, the very danger his predecessors had laboured so hard to exorcise. These provisions were never carried out and the eldest son of his first marriage succeeded him as Frederick III in all his territories.

CHAPTER II

Prussia becomes a State 1688–1740

HALF a century elapsed between the death of the Great Elector and the opening of Frederick the Great's reign. These fifty years saw an intensification of the tendencies and characteristics of which we traced the beginnings in the reign of the Great Elector. The transformation of a chain of territories, within each of which the ruler exercised limited powers, into a unified state subject to an absolute monarch was completed. The centralizing administrative structure was further strengthened and a while class of officials devoted to the service of the monarch and the state was created. The army remained a vital feature of the state, giving Prussia a weight on the international scene much greater than her real resources warranted. The effort required to maintain the army was so all-embracing that all Prussian institutions and policies became imbued with the military spirit and style. Shorn of its corporate power but retaining its privileged status, the nobility was the main recruiting ground both for the civil administration and the officer corps—it was tamed in the service of monarch and state. The inferior status of the peasantry was in no way altered, but the mass of the population benefited a good deal from efficient administration and from the deliberate policy of raising the potential of the country. The towns and the middle classes remained weak and the spirit of self-government non-existent. The ethos of the Prussian state became a reality both to its citizens and the outside world. Its positive and negative qualities could be clearly perceived : on the one side a devotion to duty, an addiction to efficiency and sobriety, a certain regard for the common weal; on the other side an excessive reliance on authority, the pervasive atmosphere of the parade ground, a certain poverty of spirit.

The decisive factor in the consolidation of the Prussian state and in Prussia's propulsion towards Great Power status remained the determination of her rulers to achieve these ends. The general situation in Europe was also favourable. A limit was set to the hegemony of France by the maritime powers, England and Holland. At the same time Austria remained sufficiently weakened not to impede the progress of Prussia, while on the Baltic Sweden declined without, as yet, producing too marked a preponderance of Russia. Of the two reigns which cover this period, the first, that of Frederick III (King Frederick I after 1701), was the less significant in moulding the enduring features of the country. However, when Frederick made himself a king it was more than a symbolic act : in an entity as artificial as Prussia aspiration and achievement were closely related and much depended on an effort of will. Prussia's second king, Frederick William I, has been called her greatest domestic ruler. The "sergeant king" was certainly more responsible than any other single man for the peculiar Prussian qualities, the Calvinist striving, the Puritan parsimony and rectitude, the addiction to things military, the authoritarianism. Good and bad aspects of Prussia became more clearly distilled than before under his rule. All this enabled his son to wield to the full the instrument created by his predecessors and to establish Prussia as the fifth Great Power of Europe and as the rival of Austria for the leadership of Germany.

Frederick III was the exception among the four generations of Hohenzollern rulers which began with his father. A typical baroque prince, fond of luxury and ostentation, he spent much of his resources on his elaborate and expensive court. A poor physical specimen, he was not prepared to labour at the daily tasks of government. His favourites came to occupy almost the position of a modern prime minister. The first of these was Danckelmann, one of seven remarkable sons of a middle-class family which had been raised to higher status by the Great Elector. Danckelmann had been a tutor to Frederick and had gained the favour of his pupil. From the beginning of the reign until 1697 the policy of the state was made by him. Brandenburg was fully aligned with the Grand Alliance which fought Louis XIV between 1689 and 1697. As in the days of the Great Elector, the considerable army which she was able to put into the field had to be supported by subsidies from her allies, thus making an independent policy impossible. Brandenburg, in spite of her considerable military contribution to the alliance, was treated with scant respect and obtained virtually nothing at the Peace of Ryswick in 1697. This was one of the causes of Danckelmann's fall. That stern Calvinist statesman had continued the tradition of parsimonious administration started under the Great Elector. The financial organization of the electoral domain was greatly improved through the foundation of a collegiate central control office (*Geheime Hofkammer*) in 1689. This was mainly the work of Dodo von Knyphausen, one of the Great Elector's most able officials, which now reached its full fruition in the centralization of financial control throughout the Hohenzollern

lands. It was one of the unfortunate consequences of Danckelmann's eclipse that Knyphausen and much of his work was swept
away with him.

In other ways, too, the fall of the favourite in 1697 represents
a major interruption in the development of an efficient central
bureaucracy for Brandenburg-Prussia. The Privy Council, for
example, ceased to be a central policy-making organ, as it had
been under Danckelmann; but it was not replaced by effective
government from the royal cabinet, because Frederick was not able
to provide it. Instead he acquired another, much less worthy,
favourite in Kolbe von Wartenberg. As it turned out, the interruption in Prussia's administrative development was only temporary, for Frederick William I more than made good what had been
allowed to slide under his father.

Danckelmann's fall was due to a variety of factors besides the
relative lack of success in the Nine Years War. His severe Calvin-
istic outlook and his constant regard for *raison d'État* in matters
of finance, administration and policy were well in tune with the
Prussian tradition as it was to develop in the future; but these
qualities accorded ill with the pleasure-seeking and pomp in vogue
at Frederick III's court. They went against the grain with the
Electress Sophia Charlotte, a Hanoverian princess, the first blue-
stocking to sit on Prussia's throne. She and many courtiers were
jealous of Danckelmann and his six brothers, and a regular cabal
went on against him. In the end the Elector himself found his
magisterial favourite irksome. He seems to have blamed him for
the lack of progress in his pet scheme, the acquisition of the royal
title. Danckelmann was shamefully treated; for years he was kept
imprisoned while proceedings were pending against him. These
eventually collapsed for lack of evidence, but even after he was
freed his property remained confiscated and he had to live on a
state pension.

The acquisition of the royal title now became the central concern of the Elector. The matter was made more urgent by the
election of Augustus of Saxony as King of Poland in 1697; and by
the conferment of the electoral dignity on the Duke of Hanover in
1692 and the prospect of the English inheritance for Hanover.
When his neighbours were thus going up in the world Frederick
of Brandenburg could not afford to hang back without real loss
of status and power. Frederick the Great thought his grandfather
was moved by vanity, but his judgement was hardly just. Brandenburg was not strong enough to take such a step independently; the
royal title could be meaningful only if it was internationally recognized. The consent of the Emperor was particularly important, in

spite of the fact that the title was to be derived from the Duchy of Prussia, which lay outside the Empire and was the only fully sovereign territory ruled by the Hohenzollerns. This shows that the Holy Roman Empire, however shadowy, had not yet lost all significance. There were many ups and downs in the negotiations with Vienna, which went on for at least a decade. There were even unofficial efforts to bring about a conversion of the House of Brandenburg to Catholicism and hints that a more friendly attitude to the Roman religion might facilitate the matter in the eyes of both Emperor and Pope. The decisive factor in the end was the need for Brandenburg's military support in the War of the Spanish Succession. In return for this the Emperor gave his consent to the assumption of the royal title by the Elector of Brandenburg in respect of the Duchy of Prussia, but any suggestion that the Emperor had conferred the title was carefully avoided by the Prussian negotiators. In order not to offend the Poles the title had to be "King in Prussia", for West Prussia remained part of Poland. Only after the first partition of Poland in 1772 was the title changed to King of Prussia. It had been a strange chain of events which thus gave the name of a long extinct Baltic tribe to the heterogeneous collection of territories which the Hohenzollerns were in process of moulding into one of the Great Powers of Europe.

The coronation of the Elector of Brandenburg as Frederick I, King in Prussia, took place in Königsberg on 18th January 1701. On the same day, 170 years later, his descendant William I was proclaimed German Emperor at Versailles. In a strict sense the entire history of Prussia proper is embraced in this time span. The pomp and circumstance surrounding the ceremony at Königsberg severely taxed the limited resources of the Hohenzollern territories. Frederick placed the crown on his own head and then crowned his Queen; only then did the royal couple proceed to ecclesiastical anointment, performed by a Calvinist and a Lutheran bishop, both of them especially created for the occasion. Although the royal title was held only in respect of the former Duchy of Prussia, officials, institutions, armies throughout the Hohenzollern lands, except those ruled by the secondary branches, were now called royal. The name Prussia began to be used for the whole conglomeration, even though it remained usual for many decades yet to speak of the Prussian states rather than one Prussian state. All this was a unifying factor of some considerable importance. On the day before the coronation, the Order of the Black Eagle, with the imperial eagle and the device *suum cuique* in its coat of arms, had been instituted, harking back to the traditions of the Teutonic Order of Knights, the founders of the Prussian state.

The acquisition of the royal title remained the most important achievement of a reign which otherwise was an interlude in Prussia's progress towards greater power and higher organization. The epoch was fruitful, however, in culture and the arts and significant in religion. Frederick I and his consort Sophia Charlotte made a contribution by their artistic and philosophical interests and by continuing the Hohenzollern tradition of religious toleration. An Academy of Arts was founded in 1696 and a Society of Sciences, of which Leibniz became the first president, in 1700. Neither institution was as yet able to evoke enough response to give the new kingdom a broad cultural basis; even in this respect the reign was an interlude between arid stretches. Frederick himself, however, employed the gifted Danzig architect and sculptor Andreas Schlüter to design a number of important buildings in his capital, including a new palace, which embodied a specifically Prussian variant of the baroque style. At the gates of Berlin Schlüter built a palace for Sophia Charlotte, later named Charlottenburg. Here the Queen created her own court. A lover of music, she had operas, an art form only recently arrived from Italy, performed on a small stage; the King, in general tolerant and certainly eager for spectacle, could not master his Calvinist prejudices sufficiently to attend these performances. The Queen conversed with Leibniz about his wide-ranging philosophical and religious ideas. The English theist writer Toland, author of *Christianity Not Mysterious*, visited her, explained his views to her and addressed to her his "Letters to Serena". On her death bed she is reported to have said "Do not grieve for me. I shall soon satisfy my curiosity about the causes of things, and give the King an opportunity for a wonderful funeral pageant."[1]

Of more permanent significance than the artistic and philosophical ventures of the court was the rise of Pietism and its influence on the spirit of Prussia. Revivalist trends can be observed in many Protestant countries in the 17th and 18th centuries. On the other hand, Lutheranism had by the second half of the 17th century, perhaps even earlier, lost its spiritual freshness and Lutheran theology had degenerated into dogmatic hair-splitting. This situation gave rise to Pietism, a movement which in its broadest sense put the emphasis not on dogma, but on personal rebirth manifesting itself in a pure, humble, pious, charitable and loving mode of life. The peculiar importance of the movement for Prussia lies in the fact that here it was given official encouragement from the rulers and the nobility downward, while in many other parts of Protestant Germany it met with resistance from Lutheran orthodoxy. This had the further result that Pietism, which from its very essence was often predominantly inward-looking or quietist in character, was able to play a more active social role here. It encouraged concern for the welfare of the poorer and weaker members of society and thus became one of the motivating forces in that "state socialism", which can be regarded as an enduring feature of Prussia. In the conventicles all men were equal. Pietism became an important ingredient in the professional ethics of Prussian officialdom, while among ordinary citizens it fostered social responsibility. Combining with the tradition of religious toleration it created a climate of opinion favourable to the Enlightenment, although there were elements inherent in its attitudes which later clashed with the Enlightenment. The major Prussian centre of Pietism was the University of Halle. It was opened in 1692, under Frederick III, and solemnly inaugurated two years later. It was intended as an institution which would give the Hohenzollern lands, as they evolved from princely territories into full statehood, a secular and ecclesiastical *élite,* dedicated to the public good and to an undogmatic, tolerant Christianity.

Among the professors at the new University was August Hermann Francke, from the Prussian point of view perhaps the most important representative of Pietism, a man of manifold activities stretching far beyond his adopted country. His view of revived Christianity was anything but quietist, for he was deeply committed to an all-embracing reform of society. By strict devotion to the basic and original Christian principles not only the individual but society was to become reborn. In pursuit of his aims Francke became the founder of many schools and orphanages and attempted to spread education among all social classes. His work was regarded with official favour both under Frederick I and especially under Frederick William I; it made an important impact on Prussian education and more generally on the paternalistic care of the Prussian state for its subjects. It added an optimistic reformist element to inward-looking Lutheranism and is a notable example of what the German sociologist Max Weber later termed secular asceticism (*innerweltliche Askese*).

Another important figure at Halle was the jurist Christian Thomasius. He is often bracketed with the better-known Samuel Pufendorf as a founder of the German natural law school. Thomasius was one of those who freed jurisprudence and the theory of the state from the remnants of medieval scholasticism and from the predominance of religious dogma, and who secularized the view of the state, law and morality. He attacked the use of Latin in higher education and pioneered the use of German in his lectures. Thomasius and Pufendorf laid the theoretical basis in Germany for enlightened absolute monarchy : the ruler, freed from the trammels of religious dogma and divine right, has the duty to govern for the welfare of his subjects. It was part of this duty to order ecclesiastical affairs on the lines of peaceful coexistence of the different Christian churches. All this fitted in admirably with developments in Prussia in the first few decades of the 18th century. Thomasius came to Brandenburg as a refugee from Saxony, where Lutheran orthodoxy still reigned supreme, and was received with honour by Frederick III. His work at Halle raised a generation of Prussian officials trained in the new secular jurisprudence. Two other distinguished refugees, to whom Frederick's tolerant policy allowed a new sphere of activity in Brandenburg, were Philipp Jakob Spener, regarded as the head of the Pietist movement, and Gottfried Arnold, whose famous book on the Church and Heresy advocated the view that heretics were often truer apostles of real Christianity than the Church.[2]

The years at the turn of the 17th and 18th century were the first period when a distinctive culture came into being in the arid environment of Brandenburg and when some of the ideas and movements arose which went to form the peculiar ethos of Prussia. Their full impact was not felt until Frederick William I was on the throne. For the time being Prussia played a secondary and somewhat inglorious role in the War of the Spanish Succession. Prussian troops fought throughout and in many places and took part in some of Marlborough's famous battles, for examples Ramillies and Malplaquet. Yet Prussia was only an auxiliary power, Frederick a *roi mercenaire*.[3] Like his predecessor he was dependent on the subsidies of his allies, but unlike the Great Elector, Frederick and his advisers were unable to extract any real advantage from their situation. To some extent they were paying the price for the Emperor's consent to the acquisition of the royal title; in addition the hope of inheriting, after William III's death, the scattered territories of the House of Orange kept Prussia in the allied camp. It might have been more in her long-term interests to have used her resources in the Great Northern War, which was being fought simultaneously with the War of the Spanish Succession, rather than in the West. In the northern conflict Sweden, Russia, Denmark and Saxony-Poland were the principal combatants and the chief stake for Prussia would have been the Swedish territories in Germany, the acquisition of which had so often eluded the Great Elector. A more purposeful Prussian intervention on the Baltic had to await the accession of Frederick William I. Prussia's contribution to the Western war brought only minor gains, some of which were so distant and isolated as to be no more than a liability.

Prussian occupation of Mörs, Lingen and Neufchâtel, all part of the Orange inheritance, was confirmed at Utrecht and she also received the district of Geldern on the Lower Rhine. Frederick's foreign policy was thus no more successful in the War of the Spanish Succession than it had been in the Nine Years War, while domestic policy and administration drifted into greater disarray.

Kolbe von Wartenberg was formally recognized as Prime Minister in 1702 and ruled entirely through the personal ascendancy he enjoyed over the King. The Privy Council was set aside as a policy-making body. Wittgenstein, another royal favourite, was in charge of the domain administration, and what had been a showpiece of effective financial control under Knyphausen became corrupt. The very loss of taut supervision from the top and the atmosphere of instability and intrigue round the King made it necessary to rely more than ever on some of the professional, often non-noble, administrators who had been raised up under the Great Elector. Having to meet the financial demands of an ever-voracious court the system finally underwent a crisis in 1710, when the plague devastated East Prussia and adjoining territories and decimated the revenues from these areas. Wartenberg and Wittgenstein fell and for the first time the influence of the Crown Prince, the future soldier-king, made itself felt in the counsels of the state and in the administration. His strange personality was to dominate the affairs of Prussia for the next thirty years.

Frederick William's image has suffered in comparison with that of his more brilliant son.[4] The world knows him as a martinet who turned his country into a barrack yard. Even to those more familiar with the period he appears as a deeply flawed, tortured personality, severaly psychoneurotic, subject to uncontrollable moods and outbursts, driven by an unbalanced sense of mission and duty to make impossible demands even on his own family. We now know that some of the King's grosser aberrations were due to the disease from which he most probably suffered, porphyria, the royal malady, which also afflicted George III, Mary Stuart, James I and Frederick the Great.[5] Even apart from his personal defects Frederick William's historical achievement is as ambivalent as Prussia herself, to the making of which he contributed so much. His regime was a marriage of Pietism and the drill square : it was militaristic, philistine, lacking in freedom, caste-ridden, but it was also relatively efficient, administratively progressive, imbued with a sense of duty from the top downwards, and it paid some regard to social justice.

Frederick William was completely unlike the typical ruler of his age. His style of life was thoroughly unaristocratic and he felt most comfortable in the philistine atmosphere of his "tobacco college"; he ate off wooden tables, washed in the open, walked in the streets, personally checked up on his officials and even spied on his subjects. There is the story of him beating a terrified man whom he had encountered on one of his walks and who had not the presence of mind to give a quick affirmative reply when asked whether he loved his King. Perhaps from some sense of eschatological doom, he tried with the utmost violence to force his subjects and all those round him into a mould of living and thinking which he thought would lead them to salvation. A vital early influence in his life was his Huguenot tutor Philippe Rebeur, who transmitted to his pupil the full rigour of Calvinist teaching on predestination. Frederick William believed profoundly from an early age that the hour of destiny had struck for the House of Brandenburg when it embraced the Reformed religion in 1613. The doctrine of predestination stirred up great inner conflicts in him and it was not until about the age of twenty that he arrived at a conviction of being saved. With fanatical determination, born of deep anxiety, he kept to the path of salvation for himself and his family; but he forbade the teaching of predestination to his children, so shaken was he by his own upheaval. His personal make-up, combined with an element of mental illness, often led Frederick William into excess. Nonetheless as a public figure he is one of the most formidable examples of the Protestant-bourgeois ethic of work, sober utility, rational organization and calculated economy. In 1712 Frederick William was brought into contact with Francke and the Pietist movement. Having previously only seen the emotionalism of the Pietists and found it repugnant, his eyes were now opened to the practical reformist side of Francke's work and the careful husbandry practised in his educational establishments. This fitted in exactly with his own inclinations and guided him in his career as a ruler.

From the age of fourteen, in 1703, Frederick William had taken part in the work of the Privy Council, which was then mainly concerned with domestic administration. He heard about plans to commute the remaining feudal obligations of the nobility, steps which he himself carried out later. He proposed the formation of a cadet company, a move to accustom the aristocracy to service in the army and this was again to become one of the more notable achievements of his reign. When he appeared at court, then dominated by Wartenberg, he was ill at ease and withdrawn. His mother, with her leanings towards the West and the Enlightenment, tried to broaden his outlook by sending him on journeys to France and the Low Countries, but he came away impressed only by the

Dutch concern for social welfare. He met Marlborough when the great General visited Berlin in 1705 and put to him his view that Prussia should intervene in the Northern War. Later he was present at the battle of Malplaquet and vowed to himself that Prussia should have an army independent of foreign subsidies. The court of Frederick and Sophia Charlotte and her successor Sophia Louise was repugnant to him and he spent most of his time at his own establishment at Wusterhausen. There he raised and drilled a model battalion of tall grenadiers, "lange Kerls"—a life-long obsession for which he has become notorious. The collapse of the Wartenberg-Wittgenstein regime increased his influence. The administrative disorganization, the weakness of the country demonstrated by Russian and Swedish incursions in defiance of Prussian neutrality, all this gave Frederick William the chance to carry out a revolution from above as soon as he was in possession of the full royal powers in 1713. His accession virtually coincided with the Peace of Utrecht and normally, with the cessation of foreign subsidies, this would have entailed a sharp cut-back in the size of the Prussian army. These were the circumstances, necessities and opportunities which propelled Frederick William into a drastic break with the previous regime. He paused only long enough to give his father a funeral such as the pomp-loving first King of Prussia would have expected. He then immediately proceeded to dismantle the extravagant court of his predecessor, ruthlessly axing officials and courtiers and cutting the salaries of those who remained. He sold his father's coronation robes, melted down his table silver. These acts, symbolic of so much that was to follow, spread alarm and despondency among his subjects, who began to realize that they were entering upon an age of joyless severity.

Unpopular and frightening though the new ruler was, he had great administrative gifts. The first decade of his reign is the most important period of reorganization of the Old Regime in Prussia; much of the spirit and some of the institutions survived even the great upheavals of the early 19th century. An edict issued within a few months of Frederick William's accession forms the backcloth to his reforms : it declared all territories of the Hohenzollern state an indivisible and inalienable trust. It was thus once more solemnly emphasized that all the heterogeneous collection of territories ruled by Frederick William now constituted one state. By combining this declaration with a statement about the royal domains the King showed that he still had a patrimonial concept of the state, regarding it almost as his family property.

Administratively Frederick William inherited two major authorities, the domain administration and the war commissariat. The former, the Hofkammer or control office had, as we have seen, reached its full fruition under Knyphausen and had been temporarily eclipsed through the fall of Danckelmann. It revived in 1711 when the maladministration of Wartenberg and Wittgenstein came to an end and when Frederick William first acquired influence. It was now on his accession renamed General Finance Directory and given control over all the domains and other regalia. The war commissariat, the Generalkriegscommissariat of the Great Elector, dealt with taxation to maintain the army; its officials at a lower level played, as we have seen, predominant roles in the government of towns. The war commissariat was no longer only concerned with the army, which was now in any case an integral part of the state and had, in addition to its military functions, many civilian tasks. It was put on a collegiate basis in 1712. The two main administrative organs were frequently at loggerheads. The General Finance Directory was linked to an older concept, the personal property of the prince, and was concerned mainly with the agrarian sector of the economy. The war commissariat had arisen from a more modern concept of the state and tried to develop the commercial and industrial potential of the country through a mercantilist policy.

To unify his administration and cut out interdepartmental squabbles the King personally drew up the plans for a single new authority, the General Directory, which began to operate in 1723. It was composed of five vice-presidents or ministers, the presidency remaining vacant for the King himself. It was sub-divided into four provincial departments, staffed by fourteen councillors, each dealing with a group of territories as well as with functions for the country as a whole. Frederick the Great later added further departments. Attached to the General Directory was a Supreme Auditing Office, but the war and the domain budgets remained separate. Every penny had to be accounted for. The new body was again collegiate : decisions were taken by all ministers and councillors deliberating together. In each province of Prussia a war and domains board was instituted as a counterpart to the General Directory at the centre, containing the previously separate domains and war administrations.

A logical administrative system, adequate to a centralized state, was thus created. The supreme direction of policy was entirely in the King's hands. From his Cabinet he issued written instructions to his principal ministers and administrators through confidential secretaries. This was the meaning of cabinet government in Prussia and the real core of absolute monarchy. All this left the Privy Council a shadow of its former self. A constant off-loading of functions and diminution of status seems to be the history of all such bodies. After 1728 the day-to-day conduct of foreign affairs was also vested in a separate bureau, but this was merely the final formal recognition of a development which had gone on for a long time. Since the beginning of his reign Frederick William had handled his diplomatic business principally in consultation with Ilgen, an official very experienced in this field.

Alongside the institutions of the centralized state there still existed in the provinces the authorities which in the heyday of the provincial diets had exercised the plenitude of governmental powers. However high-sounding their titles remained, real power had progressively been stripped away from them. By the time Frederick William had carried out his reforms there were left to them, as to the Privy Council at the centre, only certain judicial functions. Only in one institution did the old regional system and the new central order meet: in the *Landrat*—an approximate translation might be county councillor. He was, and his predecessors had been, the agents of the local nobility within each Kreis or district; he also became, from the beginning of the 18th century, the agent of the ruler and the authorities acting under him. In the reigns of Frederick William and his son more and more functions —taxation, public order, execution of royal orders—were heaped upon him. Yet he was normally a prominent local Junker who assumed the office, which carried only meagre pay, for the sake of influence and status. The office of Landrat, which existed originally only in Brandenburg, was established, chiefly under Frederick William, in all the other Prussian provinces; it bore a marked resemblance to the office of Justice of the Peace in England. The King was, in spite of his ruthless policy of centralization, eager to conciliate the Junkers.

The relationship of the nobility and other social classes to Frederick William's system of government and the spirit engendered by his work are of even greater importance than the details of the institutional changes he initiated. The Junker aristocracy of Brandenburg, Pomerania and Prussia was neither rich nor culturally distinguished. Unlike the nobility in some other parts of Germany, for example in Vienna, it could not begin to compare in splendour with the French and English aristocracies of the 18th century. The Junkers lived close to the soil; they were usually efficient farmers and retained a tight hold over their peasant serfs. Yet many of them were relatively poor and had to eke out their income by seeking official employment. This they found relatively easy to obtain in what remained of the old territorial governments, but in the new centralized bureaucracy they faced much

competition from commoners, middle-class professionals, and even
from the Huguenots, who had come in towards the end of the
17th century.

Frederick William I pursued a mixed policy in the recruitment
of his civil servants. Some of the most eminent officials, for instance
the presidents of the provincial war and domains boards, were
usually drawn from the nobility. It was clearly important that men
in such positions should be able to gain the confidence of the landowners in their areas. On the other hand the soldier-king also had
many non-nobles in high office—for example, Ilgen, who founded
a dynasty of leading Prussian civil servants, and Krautt, the merchant banker who became head of one of the four departments of
the General Directory. Although Frederick William was suspicious
of book-learning, he founded a number of chairs for "cameral
science" at Prussian universities and gradually this had the effect
of making expertise rather than rank a qualification for the public
service. A commoner of ability might well be promoted over the
head of a noble. The King compensated his aristocracy for the
injuries he inflicted upon them by calling them to service in the
army; in the creation of the Prussian officer corps the marriage
between the Hohenzollern monarchy and the Junkers was fully
consummated. It was a marriage which the soldier-king initiated
in the interests of his dynasty and state; but as time went on, and
certainly by the 19th century, the often reactionary class interests
of the Junkers had imperceptibly become the predominant factor
and this contributed to the ultimate disaster of both monarchy
and aristocracy.

For the officer corps Frederick William insisted that only men
of noble origin should be recruited and he made sure, if necessary
by force, that the sons of the nobility should serve their King and
country in this way. Service abroad, which had been customary,
was prohibited. In place of the existing small military academies
he started the cadet corps in Berlin. He ordered lists to be prepared of all young noblemen between the ages of twelve and
eighteen and he personally chose those to be admitted to the cadet
corps. Officers could consider themselves personal vassals of the
King, who wore their uniform, the first European sovereign habitually to do so. To an aristocracy which was proud but not affluent
the officer corps offered many advantages : the chance of achieving high authority, great social prestige, close association with the
King, the security and companionship of a strictly regulated life.
By the end of Frederick William's reign association with the army
had become completely accepted by the nobility, and Frederick
the Great was to put even greater emphasis on the aristocratic

character of the officer corps. No doubt a nobleman was not necessarily the best officer : for example Derfflinger, the Great Elector's leading general, had risen from humble birth. Yet for the time being Prussia and the Hohenzollerns benefited greatly from having the Junkers thus tied to the state and to themselves with hoops of steel, and from having at the head of their army a caste of officers imbued with a strong *esprit de corps*.

In the less homogeneous civil service the situation was not so clear-cut. To some extent Frederick William succeeded here too in creating a new type of civil servant who no longer regarded his office as conferring the right to line his own pockets. By his own fanatical devotion to work the King set an example and he saw to it that it was followed in his service codes for the various branches of the administration. He laid down detailed orders about the working day for his officials, even the time they were allowed for meals. Outside Prussia the proverbial "travailler pour le roi de Prusse" meant working hard for little pay. The Calvinist tradition, the Pietist movement, neo-stoic ideas coming in from the West, all this combined with relentless pressure from the top, did produce in the Prussian administration perhaps the first example of the modern vocational man : the person who does not work in order to live, but who lives for his work, who finds his whole *raison d'être* in meeting the demands of the bureaucratic machine of which he is part.[6] It was of great significance for the future of Prussia and of Germany that the administrators employed by the soldier-king and his successors gained the confidence of the population and that there never arose that mistrust of officialdom common in Anglo-Saxon countries. The positive side of this was that the Prussian state could take on many constructive tasks in the social and economic field; the reverse side of the coin was that the authoritarian and paternalistic elements, which were already so strong and pervasive in Prussia, were further reinforced.

It is easy to idealize the administrative system of Prussia under the Old Regime and many German historians have succumbed to this temptation. The moralistic, puritanical, strenuous code of Prussian officialdom was sometimes more honoured in the breach than the observance. Even if the grosser forms of corruption were eliminated nepotism was still rife and many offices were virtually hereditary. The collegiate system itself led to much mutual spying. The King personally, and through so-called fiscals, kept a watchful eye on all that was going on. All initiative within the administration was thus stifled. Probably much of its regulative activity in the economic field was deadening rather than stimulating. The proverb "travailler pour le roi de Prusse" was by no means always apposite : being a Prussian bureaucrat could produce considerable affluence, partly because the deep involvement of the state in economic affairs afforded numerous opportunities for collecting fees and other emoluments. The whole system was shot through with rivalries, jealousies and petty bickerings, arising from the competition between different departments, from the continuing fight between the remnants of the old territorial administrations and the new state bureaucracy, and from the juxtaposition of nobles and non-nobles. Frederick William I's fusion of the war and domains administration in 1723 removed only one major source of conflict. The custom initiated by the Great Elector of ennobling commoners who had risen high in the royal service could only in the very long run eliminate friction arising from social prejudices and exclusiveness. The recently ennobled judicial reformer Cocceji could find himself frustrated by the obstruction of colleagues with long pedigrees.

The development of a state bureaucracy in Prussia, for which the reign of Frederick William I was the crucial period, has its parallels all over Europe. What was distinctively Prussian was that nobility was not entirely dependent on service, as it was in Russia under Peter the Great; nor was there, as in France, a strong enough corporate aristocratic power to resist royal absolutism on the one hand, the pretensions of a wealthy middle class on the other. Under Frederick William the Junkers were absorbed into state service, mainly but not entirely through the army; it was not until the end of the 18th century that the Prussian military and civil *élite* had become so strong that it forced royal absolutism into decline.

The skill with which the soldier-king tamed the Junkers was made necessary by the economic burdens he inflicted on them. In 1717 he turned all land held on the ancient feudal tenure of knight service into free hereditary property; in return for this he levied a tax calculated on the number of horses which had been part of the knight service. This imposition was fiercely resisted by the nobility in Brandenburg, because their feudal obligations had long fallen into disuse and they regarded themselves as absolute owners of their lands. In East Prussia the Junkers had not, since the days of the Teutonic Order, been entirely exempt from taxes, but they had got off increasingly lightly. A more equitable distribution of the burden between the different social classes was now initiated. It was in this connection that the King made the often quoted remark, "I will ruin the authority of the Junkers and establish the sovereignty like a rocher de bronce".

Even so, and in spite of other measures to spread taxation more justly and levy it more efficiently, the burden on the peasantry remained heavy. Some 40 per cent of the net income of peasant holdings went to the state, and possibly as much again to the land-owners. This was, however, not dramatically greater than in other European countries, for example France and the Habsburg lands, while the outcome in terms of national solvency was vastly more favourable. Frederick William was as aware as his grandfather that people were his most valuable resource and that the lives of the peasants must therefore not be made intolerable. He tried to ameliorate the conditions of serfdom, particularly for the crown peasants. Serfdom remained, however, the central fact of life for the vast majority of the population. A strikingly successful instance of Frederick William's policy of conservation was the rehabilita-tion of East Prussia, particularly its Lithuanian borderlands, which had been badly depopulated in the plague epidemic of 1709. New villages and even towns were founded; in 1732 there were brought into the province nearly 20,000 men, women and children, Pro-testants who because of their faith had been expelled by the Arch-bishop of Salzburg. Prussia thus again reaped great benefit from the practice of religious toleration. Frederick the Great, who was hardly an admirer of his father, gave him full credit for restoring East Prussia to economic health.

One of the chief aims of Frederick William's administrative reforms was the effective economic development of his country. Prussia's mercantilist policy, initiated by the Great Elector, was not essentially different from that of other contemporary European governments; but Prussia's resources were unusually meagre, while on the other hand her success in making the most of them was quite exceptional. The reform of the domain administration proved financially very productive. At the end of Frederick William's reign about a third of the agriculturally useful area of the country was in the domain and the income from it had nearly doubled since 1713. Nearly half the total income of the state came from the domain. Many of the measures to produce these results were repugnant to the Junkers. Frederick William adopted the policy of leasing out estates of the domain on six-yearly leases, instead of on hereditary leases as in the previous reign. These temporary leases were normally not given to members of the nobility, but to middle class farmers and merchants with a certain amount of capital. Pressure could be put on such men to treat the domain peasants reasonably and to farm efficiently. Land which had been alienated from the royal domain was recovered. Junker estates which had become encumbered with debt were sometimes bought up by the King. All this was not popular with the nobility but beneficial for the public revenue.

The towns were another major target for Frederick William's mercantilist policy. The commissars who under the Great Elector had largely taken over town government had their authority further enhanced and all vestiges of urban self-government were snuffed out. Thus armed with full powers the royal administration put the budgets of towns on a sound basis and treated them as virtually part of the royal domain. The excise tax became the main instrument for regulating trade in a mercantilist sense. Prussia's territory was so split up that no customs barriers could be put around it, and so the gates of cities within which the excise was levied became the effective point for imposing tolls on imported foods.

It would be idle to pretend that Frederick William's cleansing of the administration, "conservation" of the peasants or his mercantilism sprang ultimately from a concern for the welfare of his people. The real motive, felt with Calvinist intensity, was dynastic ambition and the centre of that ambition was the army. Without a large army Prussia was nothing and could quickly be degraded again below the rank of other German states. Under Frederick I the Prussian army had numbered some 40,000 men in peacetime; by the end of Frederick William's reign it was over 80,000 strong in peacetime, in a country with a population of less than $2\frac{1}{2}$ million. Eighty per cent of all revenue went to the army, compared with 60 per cent in France and 50 per cent in Austria; on the other hand only 2 per cent went to maintain the court under Frederick William and his son, as against perhaps 6 per cent in Austria under Maria Theresa and possibly 20 per cent in Bavaria.[7]

The army, its requirements and the military style penetrated the state at all levels. There were as yet hardly any barracks; soldiers were quartered out and had to provide their own food and even uniforms. If they were married their wives often engaged in small trading, and during periods of leave the soldiers themselves would work for wages. The economic life of garrison towns was thus closely bound up with the army and the King himself said that when his army was on the march the proceeds of the excise tax dropped by a third. The local garrison commander had as much say as the *Steuerrat,* the royal commissar. The encouragement of manufacture and industry, for example gunpowder, iron mines and textiles, was in the main geared to military needs. and even agricultural production was stimulated by the requirements of the army. Men who had served in the army were to be found in the civil service of the state at all levels; both Frederick William and his son liked to use the lower positions in the war and domains boards for ex-quartermasters and sergeants; while officers went on to serve in the higher civil posts, though not necessarily in the highest where training and expertise was needed. It is not surprising that a military tone predominated even in the civil service : Frederick William's codes and instructions for his administrators read very much like those for his officers. This complete intermarriage of army and state constitutes the real meaning of militarism. It is not enough to say, as some German historians have done, that Frederick William I never used his army to make aggressive war.[8] It is only fair to point out, however, that a good many other European states of the 17th and 18th centuries, for example Sweden and Russia, were closely geared to military needs. In Prussia this marriage was perhaps more successful and had greater long-term results.

Besides his reform of the officer corps Frederick William brought in another major organizational change in the army : the cantonal system of recruiting. Prussian press-gang methods caused grave disquiet and disturbance in the country. It was not uncommon for village churches to be surrounded by recruiting officers during Sunday service and for all suitable young men to be carted off. From time to time the King was forced publicly to renounce such methods, in order to avoid open resistance or the danger of depopulation, but such gestures made little difference in practice. The activities of Prussian press gangs in neighbouring territories, and particularly the King's passion for "tall fellows", caused considerable international tension from time to time.

In order to improve the situation and to regularize existing practices Frederick William instituted, by an edict of 1733, a system by which each infantry regiment was given a district or "canton" of 5,000 hearths to recruit from and each cavalry regiment one of 1,500 hearths. It was not a system of universal military service, for all the higher or more skilled social classes had exemption, so that the obligation to serve was in practice confirmed to peasants and journeymen. The peasant "cantonist" in the army found himself obeying the same officer to whom he had to do obeisance at home as his lord. In many ways this feudal bond constituted a firm basis for the discipline of the Prussian army and at least some effort was made to look after the welfare of the soldier. In Potsdam, for example, a great military orphanage was founded, on the model of the schools of the Pietist leader Francke, where soldiers' children could be given an education. Even at the end of Frederick William's reign there were still two foreigners to one Prussian in the army : it was sometimes said of Frederick the

Great's army that the Prussian element was chiefly used to stop the foreign soldiers from deserting. Any army so constituted, however large, had its limitations in the field. This made it the more necessary to have an absolutely reliable officer corps and explains the determination with which the soldier-king and his son created and maintained a homogeneous officer caste recruited from the Junker aristocracy.

In everything concerning the army Frederick William took a close interest. Together with his friend Prince Leopold of Anhalt, the Old Dessauer, he personally drilled his regiments, particularly the tall grenadiers. This was not entirely a game. Battles were conducted on the basis of so-called linear tactics, rows of men advancing with complete precision, and for this drill was essential. It was a further advantage, when it came to fighting with bayonets, to have tall men, particularly in the first row. To speed up the rate of firing an iron instead of a wooden ramrod was introduced. The King was happiest with his soldiers, attending to military detail, or in the "tobacco college", surrounded by his cronies, smoking long Dutch pipes and indulging in coarse humour.

Frederick William was convinced that the power of his state and its place in Europe rested on his army. In view of his immense effort it is surprising that he was so timid in his foreign policy and achieved so little. Perhaps he was afraid to hazard what he had built up so painfully; but there is no doubt that he was genuinely inhibited by moral and religious scruples. His essential simple-mindedness left him singularly ill-equipped for diplomatic finesse. His participation in the Northern War in the early part of his reign was slow and unsure, but it did finally result in concrete gain, the acquisition of Stettin and the mouth of the Oder. Brandenburg had coveted this important port ever since the days of the Great Elector, who saw in it the key to sea-power and world-wide commerce for his country; but the acquisition in 1720 came too late to enable Prussia to develop as a maritime and commercial power on the Dutch model. It remained, however, the one external success of Frederick William. Thereafter the soldier-king became involved in clumsy manoeuvrings between the great powers, Austria, France, England-Hanover and Russia, which brought in little gain. Frederick William was at heart still an old-type territorial prince who wanted to be loyal to the Emperor, provided he was recognized as the most powerful ruler in Northern Germany. Instead, the Austrians treated him like a "Prince of Zipfel-Zerbst" and failed to advance what he considered his just claim to Jülich-Berg. This part of the old Cleves-Jülich inheritance was likely to become vacant again with the prospective end of the Palatinate-Neuburg line, with whom Brandenburg had hitherto had to share these Rhenish territories.

Frederick William's famous and horrific quarrel with his son arose out of the twists and turns of his diplomacy. In 1730 the King was set on a pro-Habsburg course; the Queen and Crown Prince were in favour of an English alliance to be sealed by the double marriage of Frederick and his sister into the House of Hanover. The King saw plots everywhere, felt himself unequal to the diplomatic intrigue being spun around him and had for long been deeply unhappy about his son's attitude and mode of life. When the plans of the Crown Prince to escape from his father's tyranny were betrayed Frederick William was beside himself. He treated his son like an officer who had deserted and heaped every indignity upon him. In a supreme effort to make him see the error of his ways, a kind of attempt at religious conversion, he made the Crown Prince witness the execution of his closest friend and associate. The unbalanced side of the King's mind and religion is here clearly seen. Later relations between father and son improved, largely because the latter learnt how to humour the King. When Frederick William lay on his death bed he is said to have pointed to his son with the words: "There stands he who will revenge me". He was expressing his sense of betrayal and ill-treatment at the hands of the Emperor. If the statesmen of Vienna had perceived more clearly the rising power of Prussia they might well have found a way of retaining the loyalty and co-operation of Berlin and the great challenge flung down by Frederick as soon as he came to the throne might never have come.

However repugnant many sides of Frederick William's character were, his domestic achievement was remarkable. In spite of the meagre resources of Prussia and in addition to building up the fourth largest army in Europe, he cleared all state and domain debts and left his son a war chest of 10 million Thaler, packed away in boxes in the cellars of his Berlin palace. Perhaps more than any other man he was the maker of Prussianism and the Prussian state. His positive and negative qualities left their mark on the people and on generations to come.

CHAPTER III

Prussia becomes a Great Power 1740–1786

FREDERICK WILLIAM I and Frederick the Great were both essential to the rise of Prussia, but their personalities and style of government could hardly have been more different. The father was bourgeois, the son aristocratic, the father a devout Calvinist, the son a sceptical deist. Frederick William was a timid and incompetent player on the diplomatic chessboard where his son was bold and resourceful. The father's choleric, involuted character has always remained repellent whereas the fascination of the son's glittering, many-sided personality has survived to the present day. The catalogue of contrasts could be long. Yet Frederick the Great's character was in large measure formed by his ambivalent love-hate relationship with his father. The sharp antagonism between the two, beginning at a tender age and leading to cruel treatment and atrocious suffering, would have stunted and warped all but the strongest nature.

In spite of it all Frederick retained a regard and even veneration for his father and came to admire increasingly what his predecessor had achieved for the Prussian state. Thus he felt the need to prove himself against his father's accomplishments and this may have been one of the deeper motives behind the attack on Silesia with which he began his reign. When he came to the throne the world expected him to shine in the arts of peace and the ink was hardly dry on his *Anti-Machiavel*[1] in which he had proclaimed the duty of the ruler to adhere to the same ethical code in his public as in his private actions. By seizing Silesia from Maria Theresa, Frederick committed the one clearly unprovoked act of aggression in Prussian history and plunged his country into many years of warfare. Was he not trying to prove to the ghost of his father that he, the *littérateur* and flute player, was greater than any previous Hohenzollern as a builder of the state and hero of the battlefield?

Frederick's love of things beautiful, interest in literature, the arts and music, had first started the breach between him and his father. Such tastes were highly suspect to the neurotic martinet who sat on Prussia's throne and made him fear for the future of Prussia when it should pass into the hands of his son. The King did not realize that Duhan de Jandun, the Huguenot tutor he had appointed for the Crown Prince, was in fact stimulating the literary and artistic leanings of his pupil. The first report of the King expressing public displeasure at his son's mode of life dates from 1724, when Frederick was only twelve. There followed the years of growing estrangement and suspicion, culminating in Frederick's attempt to escape in 1730 and subsequent imprisonment at Küstrin. It required much persuasion from many quarters, including the Imperial Court at Vienna, to restrain the King from executing his son and heir. From this low point relations gradually improved : Frederick learnt to conform, at least outwardly, with the plans his father made for him. He worked his passage by labouring hard in the provincial administration at Küstrin. He married against his inclinations the wife Frederick William chose for him, Elizabeth-Christine of Bevern-Brunswick. It was a marriage in name only; if the rumours about Frederick's sexual incapacity were true, it may never have been consummated. The King was perhaps never quite taken in by his son's new-found orthodoxy, but he was sufficiently appeased to let Frederick live his private life without interference.

In 1736 the Crown Prince set up his own court at Rheinsberg and the next four years were the happiest of his life. He collected around him a circle of friends, among them Dietrich von Keyserlingk, a Courland noble, affectionately nicknamed Caesarion by Frederick, Charles Étienne Jordan of Huguenot origin, who acted as secretary to the Crown Prince and Algarotti, a young Venetian. Frederick liked to think that Rheinsberg was a corruption of Remusberg and that his country place had had associations with the brother of Romulus. In language and culture his court was French and this was the language in which he himself spoke, thought and wrote ever since his earliest youth. His German, so he said, was no better than a coachman's. At Rheinsberg Frederick was a voracious reader, sometimes grudging himself sleep to carry on a relentless process of self-education. All was grist to his mill—philosophy, literature, history, even science and mathematics. He carefully annotated his texts and he wrote a great deal himself.

This was the beginning of a large literary output which continued right through his life. Frederick wrote historical and philosophical treatises, he dabbled in political thought, as in his *Anti-Machiavel*, he poured out quantities of verse and conducted a huge correspondence. He worked out for himself a political doctrine which guided him when he was King : the doctrine of benevolent despotism of which he became probably the most nearly perfect example in history. In contrast again with his father, who had never been able to rid himself of patrimonial and feudal notions of kingship, Frederick developed a strong sense of the majesty of the state and thought of the ruler as the first servant of the state. But in this position the monarch had to be absolute, all-seeing, omnipotent, ever-active in all phases of the national life. It was on this conception of kingship that he modelled himself. What is striking about Frederick is his extreme liveliness of mind rather than his originality or profundity. As his later career was to show, he was really a man of action, with great powers of decision, but he combined this with insatiable intellectual curiosity and a remarkably wide range of interests. Frederick's correspondence with Voltaire started at Rheinsberg, but it was some years before the two men met; then the occasion was tinged with a slight sense of disappointment.

Frederick's relations with his father continued to fluctuate, but on the whole physical distance between the two courts minimized friction. The Crown Prince had for long been critical of Frederick William's foreign policy and, for all his youthful cosmopolitan idealism, felt deeply the humiliations which Prussia was suffering, particularly at the hands of the Habsburgs. No doubt there was building up within himself the determination to prove himself better than his father and to knit the Prussian lands together by an active policy of acquisition. When the old King died after much illness in 1740, Frederick, in spite of all past unhappiness, felt the loss acutely, but the new King's subjects were looking forward to great changes after years of austerity and drudgery.

These expectations were not entirely disappointed. The new monarch made some liberal gestures. Torture was abolished as part of the judicial process. This regulation had to be kept secret for a time and there were still some exceptions to it. Barbarous punishments were abolished, for example the drowning in leather sacks, sewn by themselves, of unmarried mothers found guilty of infanticide. New punishments were introduced for brutalities perpetrated against army recruits. Censorship was eased and religious toleration reasserted. The Society of Sciences which had been founded under Frederick I and had withered in the days of the soldier-king was reconstituted and eventually elevated into an academy. Maupertuis, the distinguished mathematician who had discovered the flattening of the earth at the poles, was called to Berlin to preside over the new body, and other scholars of repute were invited to join it. Christian Wolff, the father of the German Enlightenment, whom Frederick William had chased from his Chair at Halle University because he naively misunderstood his teaching about determinism, was recalled from exile and reinstated.

Plans for building an opera house in Berlin were put in hand. Last but not least, as an earnest of a new beginning, the regiment of tall grenadiers was disbanded. All this was, however, on the surface and deceptive.

In his relations with his ministers the new King made it clear that he was determined to keep all decisions in his own hands and soon he was to decide, contrary to all ministerial advice, on a move with epoch-making consequences, the rape of Silesia. The opportunity came when the Emperor Charles VI of Austria and the Tsarina Anne of Russia died almost simultaneously in the autumn of 1740. In spite of all that the Emperor had done, through the Pragmatic Sanction, to ensure the succession of his daughter Maria Theresa, the young Queen found herself in a highly vulnerable position. The death of the Tsarina made it certain that she could expect little support from a Russia plunged into confusion. This European constellation gave Frederick the chance to seize a territory which would augment and round off the Prussian domain far more effectively than the puny principalities on the Lower Rhine for which his father had struggled so long in vain. It was useful that the House of Brandenburg had long-standing claims in Silesia, but it was hardly very important, as the King himself cynically admitted. When Frederick later wrote his own account of these events, he made much of his desire to cleanse the Prussian name of the reputation of weakness it had acquired in the closing years of his father's reign. But there are also hints in *Histoire de mon Temps,* written by the King in the years of peace after the first two Silesian wars, that he was aware of at least two deeper issues in flinging down his challenge.[2] Prussia had reached a stage where she could not stand still in her development: she must either go up or decline again. If she was to continue on an upward path she must assert her position in Germany against the Habsburg power. The duel with Austria for the soul of Germany, which was to go on for nearly a century and a half until the final Prussian victory, could not be avoided.

The invasion of Silesia was at first only too easy. The Protestants in Silesia had long smarted under the bigoted Austrian regime and welcomed the Prussians. The Prussian tradition of religious toleration ensured that the Catholics in the province were not unduly offended. Having seized Silesia successfully, Frederick offered to defend Maria Theresa in the possession of her other territories and even undertook to cast his vote for the election of her husband as emperor, provided she recognized his conquest. But he had not yet got the measure of his opponent, whose courage, paired with good sense, matched her homely and intensely feminine charm. In

April 1741 the first major battle between Prussians and Austrians occurred at Mollwitz. It was hardly a glorious occasion for Frederick and he preferred to forget about it later. The Austrian cavalry, superior to the Prussian in numbers and training, mounted a devastating attack and the King, advised that all was lost, fled the battlefield. On his flight he had been nearly taken prisoner when he received news from the Prussian commander, Field Marshal Schwerin, that his infantry had restored the situation and that the battle had in fact been won.

In spite of Prussian military weaknesses revealed at Mollwitz Frederick's victory brought the French into the war against Austria. This created a strategic and diplomatic situation of great complexity. The French aim in Germany was to keep a number of powers, Austria, Prussia and to a lesser extent Bavaria and Saxony, in balance. For the moment this meant fighting against Austria, still much the strongest state in Central Europe. The Elector of Bavaria, Charles, became the Franco-Prussian candidate for the imperial throne, instead of Maria Theresa's husband, and was elected Holy Roman Emperor, as Charles VII, in 1742. The French, however, did not desire too decisive a Prussian victory or too much aggrandizement. Frederick for his part, while intent upon asserting himself against Austria and hanging on to as much of Silesia as possible, did not desire too overwhelming a French preponderance in Germany nor did he want to put an end to Austria's independent existence. Such calculations determined the Central European power balance for most of the time till 1870.

At this stage they led to a lot of diplomatic twists and turns which brought Frederick in particular the reputation of fickleness and spread resentment against his upstart country. At the end of 1741 he concluded, with the help of English mediation, a secret treaty with Austria, which he hoped would secure him in the possession of Silesia. Great French and Allied victories, culminating in the occupation of Prague, changed the situation immediately afterwards. Frederick was now faced with the prospect of defending Silesia against his former allies. Thus he broke the treaty with Austria, giving as his excuse the fact that the Austrians had not guarded its secrecy. In May 1742 Frederick decisively beat the Austrians at Chotusitz, the first victory for which he could claim some personal credit. This convinced the Austrians that it was time to get rid of their most dangerous enemy, the King of Prussia, by recognizing his conquest of Silesia, and a separate peace was once more concluded, this time openly. The French were again loud in their accusations of duplicity, but they had themselves toyed with the possibility of a separate peace with Austria. Thus ended the

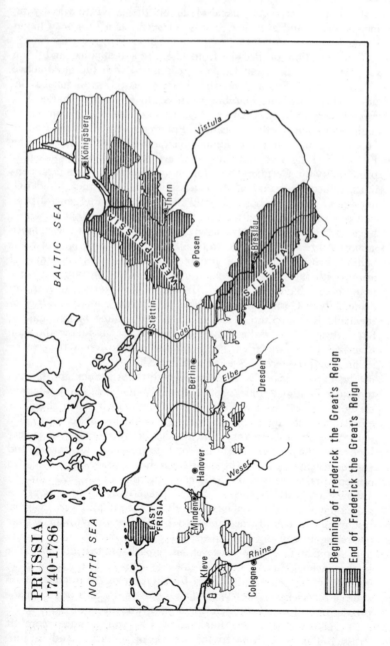

PRUSSIA
1740-1786

NORTH SEA

BALTIC SEA

Königsberg

Vistula

Thorn

WEST PRUSSIA

Posen

Breslau

SILESIA

Stettin

Oder

Berlin

Elbe

Dresden

Hanover

Weser

EAST
FRISIA

Minden

Kleve

Rhine

Cologne

Beginning of Frederick the Great's Reign

End of Frederick the Great's Reign

first Silesian war, yet Prussia's hold on the province was by no means secure and even less so was her status as a European Great Power.

The defection of Prussia from the French alliance and from support for the Bavarian Emperor, combined with the more active intervention of England on the side of Austria, soon turned the tide in favour of the Habsburgs. In South Germany Charles VII was driven from his native Bavaria and became an impotent fugitive. In the North a so-called "Pragmatic Army" under George II of England won the famous victory of Dettingen over the French in June 1743. Saxony, at one time the leading Protestant principality in Germany and far more important than Branden-burg, joined the ranks of Austria's allies. All this made Frederick once more anxious about his hold on Silesia and the general posi-tion of Prussia. He gradually reached the conviction that he would have to fight again for his new province. To redress the balance against Austria he first tried to mobilize German imperial sentiment behind Prussian aims. He proposed the raising of an imperial army, with himself as lieutenant-general under the nominal com-mand of the Bavarian Emperor. It was an early version of Prussian leadership in Germany, which tried to play on the old loyalties to the Holy Roman Empire and owed as yet nothing to nationalism, but it inspired only the Palatinate and Hesse to follow the call. Eventually, by June 1744, Frederick was able to renew the French alliance and the second Silesian war started.

The French gave the Prussian King little assistance and he had to fight his campaign in Bohemia virtually unaided. The limitations of the Prussian army which had been built up by such strenuous efforts became apparent. The King could not force a decisive battle; supply became very difficult and the rate of desertions very high. By the winter Frederick had to retreat into Silesia and confidence in his leadership was severely shaken even among his officers. Fresh misfortunes came crowding in: Charles VII died in January 1745 and Bavaria made her peace with Austria: hopes of a change in English policy were disappointed and the financial resources so carefully accumulated by Frederick William I were beginning to run out. In adversity Frederick rose to more mature and heroic stature, a foretaste of his remarkable feat of endurance in the Seven Years War. Boastfulness and his early quest for glory gave way to more sober concern for the permanent interests of his state. Frederick was determined to hold on to Silesia and made preparations for a last-ditch stand in Brandenburg.

As it turned out, the fortunes of war smiled once more on Prussia. The King restored the morale of his army and in June won the famous victory of Hohenfriedberg over the Austrians and Saxons. For the first time the Prussian cavalry showed itself superior to the Austrian. Even now the situation was still full of perils. Maria Theresa had her husband crowned Emperor in Frankfurt, with the acclaim of the populace, and was henceforth "the Empress" in popular parlance. Austrians and Saxons made plans for a campaign against Berlin and there were sinister threats of Russian intervention on behalf of Saxony. Frederick, however, surmounted all dangers. In September 1745 he won a second major victory over the Austrians at Soor, a battle which confirmed his fame as a general. The Old Dessauer, friend of his father, who had thus far failed to gain the full confidence of the young King, was put in command of an army to invade Saxony and won a decisive victory over the Saxons before the onset of winter. Dresden was occupied by Prussian troops and Maria Theresa at last induced to make peace and acknowledge the loss of Silesia a second time.

This was the end of the war for Prussia and the Empire; the Treaty of Aix-la-Chapelle, which ended the War of the Austrian Succession nearly three years later, set the seal of European recognition on Frederick's conquest. The five years of war with which his reign had opened had increased the population and area of the Prussian countries, as they were usually still called, by nearly a third. They had also established Prussia as a major European power, but the course of events had made the King himself only too well aware of the limits of that power. On his return from the second Silesian war his subjects were beginning to bestow the title "the Great" on him.

Silesia quickly became an integral part of Prussia. The new province fitted admirably into the Hohenzollern heritage; by comparison many later acquisitions, the territories of the third Polish Partition of 1795, for example, or even the Rhine provinces taken over in 1815, had a distorting effect on Prussia. Although a proportion of Silesia's population was Catholic, they became loyal subjects of the Prussian Kings. The aristocracy of the province was a great asset to the Prussian state; it was wealthier and, when industrialization came, more enterprising and outward-looking than the Junker nobility of the older and less well-endowed East Elbian territories. Silesia under Frederick the Great became a showpiece of Prussian administration; to the Habsburgs the loss of this province was a disaster but not fatal, to the Hohenzollern it was an essential step in their rise to greatness.

Ten years of peace, from 1746 to 1756, found Frederick in his prime. He had what was thought to have been a stroke in 1747, an apoplexy, and this made him careful of his health, and addicted to a strict routine which did not overtax his strength. He remained strong enough to survive the great physical endurance test of the Seven Years War and live to a ripe old age. Even before the second Silesian war had quite drawn to a close, Frederick had begun to build himself a new palace at Potsdam, on a piece of ground where his father had grown vegetables for the royal kitchen. It was at the top of a terraced garden, embellished with busts and balustrades, that Frederick built the house of his dreams, Sans Souci, a miniature palace. The centre was an oval dining room; on the left were the King's own apartments, on the right those used by his visitors. The morning was spent reading state papers and issuing instructions to the royal secretaries; other parts of the day in reading, writing and conversation, serious or more light-hearted. Members of the Berlin Academy were often in the King's company. In 1750 Voltaire came to Berlin. He helped the King in his literary activities and took great liberties in correcting the King's poetry. Relations between two such *prima donnas* could never be easy and Voltaire for his part was greedy and abused his privileged position in many ways. The breach between the King and the literary patriarch in 1753 was not final and later they were in correspondence again right up to Voltaire's death in 1778, but they never saw each other again. Frederick continued to be a lover of music and spent much time practising the flute; he was no more original as a composer than as a poet. He brought Johann Sebastian Bach to Sans Souci for a visit, shortly before the great composer died.

Philosophy was still one of Frederick's major interests and to have a coherent view of the universe and man's place in it was a necessity for him. He was now more of sceptic than in his youth : he admitted that the orderliness of nature made the existence of God likely, but beyond this it was unprofitable to speculate about matters which the human intellect could never know. Metaphysics was to be despised; human reason was to be applied to all things which were at all amenable to it. Such ideas were not original and indeed very typical of the Enlightenment : Frederick followed writers like Bayle, Fénelon and Locke. Problems of political philosophy still engaged his attention a great deal : he was now much more aware of the role of power in the essentially lawless relationships between states; but he remained open to the demands of welfare in domestic policy, the application of rational humane rules to the internal government of the state. The King's wide-ranging intellect makes him attractive; but as a ruler he seems infinitely remote from his subjects, contemptuous of them and toiling not so much for them as for an abstraction. The searing experience of the Seven Years War confirmed him even more in his contempt for human kind; his whippets were closer to him than any human being.

Frederick was not an administrative innovator like his father and left the structure he inherited essentially unchanged. His more advanced concept of the state fitted in well with the general trend throughout his reign : Prussia was ceasing to be a collection of territories in the possession of a dynasty and becoming a centralized state. Frederick added to the General Directory a number of new departments, each responsible for a sector of government, which cut across the old provincial subdivisions established in the General Directory of his father. In practice this led to a good deal of confusion and inter-departmental friction which the King ultimately had to resolve. This suited Frederick because as the benevolent despot with unlimited confidence in his own judgement he wanted to have a finger in every pie. In fact he was the exponent *par excellence* of cabinet government in the Prussian style. An endless stream of papers went to the royal closet and decisions came back. Frederick communicated with all parts of his bureaucracy in writing and his political secretary Eichel was one of the most important men in the kingdom. Lack of contact and a "studied pose of infallibility" combined to make the King intensely suspicious of his officials high and low. He called Podewils, his foreign minister of many years' standing, "Monsieur de la timide politique". In describing the behaviour of the average royal official in a Prussian town, he called him "impertinent towards the citizens; he acts the minister; he treats all matters *en bagatelle* and hardly condescends to talk to the mayor, councillors and burghers."[3] Frederick's frequent tours of inspection through his provinces were a method of spying on his bureaucracy, and by means of a system of conduct reports he tried to keep an eye on large numbers of royal officials.

The King's policy in recruiting his civil, as well as his military servants differed somewhat from his father's. He was by predilection more aristocratic and stressed heredity in appointments. The relationship of the Junkers to the dynasty and the state was no longer a problem. Thus the process went on by which on the one hand non-nobles serving in the administration were assimilated to the nobility and often formally ennobled; while on the other hand in many of the Junker families a tradition of holding high office in the state was established. Under Frederick's weaker successors this ruling class, more than the Hohenzollerns themselves, became the decisive factor in Prussia.

Frederick deserves much credit for taking in hand, during this period of peace, the judicial reforms which had come to naught in his father's reign. The man chosen for the task was Samuel von Cocceji, son of an eminent jurist who had himself been ennobled. His career is an example of how a man of non-aristocratic origin could rise to great power in the Prussian service and become in time assimilated to the Junker aristocracy. Cocceji's chequered progress in public life also illustrates the prejudices of the old and established aristocracy which a man of his origins had to overcome. Frederick William I had a passionate interest in the administration of justice and towards the end of his reign entrusted Cocceji with the task of clearing out the Augean stables of the Prussian judicial system. The courts were still an appendage of the old provincial governments; they were corrupt, unprofessional, slow-moving and tied up with local privileges of birth and family prestige. During this first instalment of his career as a reformer, Cocceji found himself completely frustrated. His principal enemy was one of his co-ministers of justice, von Arnim, a grand seigneur who regarded Cocceji as a pushful upstart.

Frederick the Great decided to resume the task of judicial reform and in an interview with Cocceji in 1746 laid down the guidelines for action. There had to be radical changes in the personnel and procedures of the courts, a centralization and unification of the judicial system in all the Hohenzollern provinces, with a proper progression from lower to higher courts. Armed with the King's full confidence and with the title Grand Chancellor, Cocceji travelled through the Prussian provinces, rearranging the hierarchy of courts and weeding out corrupt and undesirable elements from the legal profession. His old enemy Arnim was driven to resignation and withdrew to his estates. Cocceji based his reforms on the provincial Junker-controlled governments which had for so long fought a losing battle against the advancing royal administrative boards, lately unified in the General Directory. He used the surviving judicial functions of the provincial governments as a counterpoise to the judicial functions of the administrative bureaucracy. Had he fully succeeded he would have brought about something like the classical separation of powers between judiciary and executive. In this sense he was one of the progenitors of the rule of law in Prussia. The King made sure, however, that Cocceji could not go the whole way and the royal bureaucracy continued to discharge many judicial functions. The Grand Chancellor himself was by no means concerned to diminish the power and status of the nobility of which he had become a member. His reform in fact gave a new lease of life to the Junker-dominated provincial governments; insofar as they helped the establishment of the rule of law against administrative excesses, they again benefited mainly the nobility. The peasantry continued to receive their justice in the main from the master of the estate to which they were tied. On the other hand the higher professional standards introduced by Cocceji led in time to an infiltration of properly educated non-nobles into the legal profession.

Cocceji failed to introduce a unified Prussian code of law and this task remained to be tackled in the closing years of Frederick. Under the supervision of Suarez, a Silesian jurist with enlightened, humanitarian views, a general code of Prussian law was produced, which after going through various versions finally went into operation in 1794, in the reign of Frederick's successor. Its aim was to be intelligible even to the layman, to remove doubts and conflicts and to supply practical answers. It has always been hailed as a monument to the progressive nature of the Old Prussian State and even as an embodiment of the rule of law. This is true only within limits; this general code is very much a product of the enlightened despotism and the conservative approach to society of the Frederician age. The royal prerogative could still interpose in the administration of the law; the privileges of the nobility and the division of society into estates with different legal status remained fully entrenched. Nevertheless the work of Cocceji and his successors did much to give the Prussia of Frederick the Great the reputation of being a progressive and enlightened state.

When Frederick had entered Dresden at the end of the second Silesian war, he remarked that he would not in future attack even a cat. During the years of peace he can hardly have believed, however, that Prussia would not be put to the test of war again. Indeed much of his work during those years, particularly in the building up of the economy and in the training of the army, was designed in preparation for a trial of strength to come. Prussia's position in Europe continued to be weak and full of dangers. In resources and population she was not the equal of the established Great Powers. This was aggravated by the disjointed nature of her territory, which made areas like East Prussia or the Hohenzollern lands on the Lower Rhine quite indefensible. It remained true that she could only go up or down in the scales of power, but could not stand still. As the upstart among the Powers, on the look-out for gains, she was suspect and unpopular and this had been made worse by Frederick's turncoat policies in the Silesian wars. Two factors in particular presented increasing dangers to Prussia in 1750s: the growth of Russia's power and the leadership of the brilliant diplomatist Kaunitz in Austria. The Empress

Elizabeth of Russia and her Grand Chancellor Bestuzhev regarded
Prussia as the new rival in the Baltic in place of Sweden and had
a violent personal aversion to Frederick. Kaunitz was probably the
Prussian King's superior in cool calculation and in the craft of
diplomacy; he was moreover convinced that Austria's fortunes
could never be retrieved until Prussia was once more degraded to
the status of a minor German principality. The overt hostility of
Russia and Austria was not fully counterbalanced for Prussia by
really friendly relations with France and England. Frederick regarded the Franco-Prussian alignment as a law of nature and did
little to nurture it. In fact he needled the French court, not merely
by his unreliability as an ally, but by his widely reported witticisms
at the expense of Madame de Pompadour. With Britain his relations after 1748 passed through an unhappy phase, when in retali-
ation for the seizure of some Prussian merchant ships, he stopped
the payment of interest and capital on a British loan to Silesia.
Moreover George II, still as much the Elector of Hanover as the
King of England, was traditionally hostile to his Prussian cousins
and suspected them of having designs on his Electorate.

The whole tangled web became more menacing for Frederick
in 1755 when England made a subsidy treaty with Russia. He now
saw the imminent danger of an Austrian and Russian attack,
backed by British resources. He tried to counter this by the Convention of Westminster in January 1756, a treaty between England
and Prussia guaranteeing the neutrality of Hanover. Frederick
considered this a master stroke : it would restrain Russia's aggressive impulses, dependent as her armies were on British subsidies.
At the same time it would not, so he thought, damage his essential
understanding with France, since it in no way inhibited the French
in their fight with the English outside Europe. These were grave
miscalculations : on the one hand the Russians were outraged by
what they felt to be British treachery and British influence declined
in St. Petersburg. The French were equally affronted by Prussian
behaviour and became more ready to accept the design which
Kaunitz had for long harboured : the reversal of alliances. By the
summer of 1756 an alliance of France, Austria and Russia, pledged
to the destruction of Prussia, moved rapidly into the realm of
possibility.

Frederick decided to anticipate the threat by invading Saxony
in August 1756, thus starting the Seven Years War. It was what
modern strategists would call a pre-emptive strike and to some
extent it was a defensive move. Frederick hoped to prevent the
hostile alliance from consolidating before it was militarily ready,
but the desire to gain more territory cannot have been entirely

absent as a motive. The acquisition of Saxony was an obvious step towards rounding-off Prussia and Frederick clearly hoped either to keep it or use it as a bargaining counter. To this extent there was also an element of aggression in his move. Had he held back, the hostile coalition might still have failed to come together; by invading Saxony, whose ruler was the father-in-law of the French Dauphin and a protégé of Russia, he made virtually certain that it did.

Each separate member of the continental coalition was more powerful and strategically better placed than Prussia and together Austria, France and Russia were overwhelmingly stronger. Coalitions, however, can rarely bring their resources to bear as effectively as a single power and in this case Prussia enjoyed interior lines and the monolithic leadership of a man of genius. Moreover, she acquired one very powerful ally, England. Through the Anglo-Prussian alliance two separate trials of strength, the rivalry between France and England outside Europe and the attempt to crush Prussia on the Continent, became merged into a single world-wide conflict. When Pitt came to power in 1757 the decision followed that England must vigorously prosecute the continental war to supplement her fight against France overseas. This in turn sealed the alliance between Austria and France.

At first neither Prussian strategy nor British help were very effective. Frederick invaded Bohemia and hoped to deal a decisive blow against Austria, but he lacked the resources to pursue a successful offensive strategy and had to withdraw to defend his central citadel. British efforts were at first concentrated on safeguarding Hanover against the French and when this failed the convention of Kloster-Zeven, concluded by the Duke of Cumberland, left Prussia's western flank exposed. Frederick escaped from this wellnigh hopeless situation through the two brilliant victories of Rossbach and Leuthen fought right at the end of the campaigning season of 1757. He used the oblique battle order with great effect, a device to overcome the numerical superiority of his opponents. It consisted of a concentrated swift attack on one flank, carried out by the best elements in the army, while the rest of his force was used as a reserve either to exploit the victory or cover a retreat if necessary. When victory was complete at Leuthen, a Prussian grenadier began to sing the chorale "Nun danket alle Gott" and the whole army took it up. Even the King, religious sceptic though he was, felt the emotion of that moment deeply. Prussia was saved from destruction, Frederick's fame as a general established for all time. In Germany the first faint stirrings of national sentiment made him into a hero. In England his birthday became the occasion for popular celebrations and religious sentiment elevated him into a Protestant hero. Even in France the intellectuals, including Voltaire, acclaimed him and poured scorn upon the incompetence of their government and their generals.

The English alliance now became much more effective. William Pitt decided to throw Britain's full weight behind Prussia and as long as he remained in power the alliance was safe. Heavy British subsidies flowed into Frederick's coffers; a mercenary force under Ferdinand of Bevern-Brunswick, the Prussian King's brother-in-law, was maintained against the French in the West of Germany and henceforth safeguarded the Prussian flank. Even so, a long and agonizing war of attrition started for Prussia and her King. Frederick has often been hailed as the precursor of Napoleon in military tactics, but he did not possess the resources which enabled the French emperor to deal annihilating blows against his enemies over and over again. Frederick's battles were never decisive; they were merely tactically offensive incidents in what had to be a long defensive manoeuvre. It remains a wonder how he could stay in the war at all, with his inferior resources and when so often many of his provinces were occupied by the enemy and no longer able to support his war effort. Undoubtedly the personality of the King was a decisive factor. With iron self-discipline and unshakeable determination he carried on, prepared to bury himself under the ruins of his country rather than surrender. The merciless buffetings of the war broke all vestiges of his remaining youthful arrogance and turned him into a wizened, bent, old cynic, careless of his personal appearance. But at night, in his field headquarters, he could still be heard reciting Racine with emotion and playing his flute.

Frederick's fortunes reached their nadir at Kunersdorf in August 1759. "Will not some accursed bullet strike me?" he was heard to say, and he wrote to one of his ministers : "I will not survive the destruction of my country. Adieu for ever."[4] The failure of the Russians under Soltykov to follow up their advantage and their reluctance to pull Austrian chestnuts out of the fire saved him. In the last two years of fighting the war became increasingly one of manoeuvre only, punctuated by battles even less decisive than those of the earlier years. Prussian resources and even those of her enemies were near the point of complete exhaustion. Frederick had always known that Prussia could tolerate only a short war, yet here she was fighting incessantly year after year, with many of her provinces, the Lower Rhine, East Prussia, Silesia, occupied by the enemy. Frederick only managed to carry on because he squeezed the last drop out of the territories he had conquered, especially Saxony, and because he received British subsidies and because, in the later stages of the war, he systematically debased the coinage. From this latter practice Prussia suffered for a long time to come, and Frederick tried to divert the wrath of those defrauded by employing two Jewish financiers to do his dirty work for him.

Frederick moved along the brink of destruction right up to the end. He stood in danger of encirclement and slow strangulation. In a letter to his old friend, the Marquis d'Argens, written in the autumn of 1761, he said, after complaining about insomnia, headaches, depression and his intolerable burden : "I seek escape from all this by looking at the world as if from a distant planet; then everything appears to me very small and I feel sorry for my enemies who take so much trouble for so little."[5] In this situation it seemed a saving grace when one of his arch-enemies, the Tsarina Elizabeth, died in January 1762 and was succeeded by the imbecile but pro-Prussian Tsar Peter III, husband of Catherine the Great. The withdrawal of Russia from the ranks of Prussia's enemies was largely counterbalanced by the loosening of the English alliance. When Chatham fell from power and the direction of British policy passed into the hands of Bute, there was an increasing tendency to disengage from the expensive continental war and to make peace with France. England's major imperial objective had been achieved and Bute and George III had powerful domestic reasons for ending the war. A series of misunderstandings further clouded relations with Prussia. Austria on the other hand, also exhausted by her war effort, now began to recognize that not only the destruction of Prussia, but even the recovery of Silesia was beyond her grasp. The Peace of Hubertusberg, between Prussia and Austria, and the Peace of Paris, between England and France, were concluded separately, but within days of each other, early in 1763. Prussia gained no more territory, but she had maintained herself as a major European power. The furnace of war and the hero-figure of the King had helped the inhabitants of the Hohenzollern territories to think of themselves as citizens of one state. Prussia remained markedly inferior to the other major countries of Europe in population and resources, but the great reputation which her King, her army and her administrative machine had acquired made up for these deficiencies.

After 1763 the diplomatic chessboard on which Frederick had to operate looked different from what it had been before the Seven Years War. The alliance between France and Austria, the product of the diplomatic revolution, proved enduring. For a chastened Austria it secured the safety of her Italian, German and Belgian possessions. For France the advantages were less obvious, but her horizons had also narrowed. In Germany the balance of power between Prussia and Austria, now firmly established, suited French interests. Frederick would have liked to have resurrected his alliance with France, but it was no longer possible. Yet his own feelings about the British alliance prevented him from renewing what would have been an obviously advantageous link. The way in which the Convention of Westminster had exposed him in 1756 had left a deep mark. Britain's callous disregard for Prussian interests in 1762 rankled for ever after; the shifting sands of British parliamentary politics filled the Prussian despot with suspicion. In the American War of Independence he maintained strict neutrality and while not recognizing the colonists obstructed British recruiting efforts in Germany. The antagonism between Austria and Prussia was now built into the structure of Central Europe.

Prussia was thus isolated and there remained available to her only one possible partner among the Great Powers, the Russia of Catherine the Great. The price of the Russian alliance signed in 1764 was Prussian support for Russian aims in Poland. Frederick felt the danger of bringing potentially so great a power as Russia closer to his own territories. In his Political Testament of 1768, drawn up to take account of the new conditions that had arisen since his previous Testament of 1752, he wrote : "How insane and blind is Europe to contribute to the rise of a people which some day may become her own doom."6 That day was still far off. For many generations alliance with Russia remained one of the basic options in Prussian foreign policy. Immediately, the Russian alliance ended Prussia's isolation, brought Russian recognition of the conquest of Silesia and safeguarded East Prussia, which was indefensible against Russia.

In Poland the interests of Russia and Prussia coincided at least to the extent that neither of them wished to see an Austrian or French candidate, nor another Saxon prince, on the throne. For the rest Frederick was aware that the policy his Russian ally required him to follow in Polish affairs carried the danger of replacing a weak neighbour with a very powerful one. For a long time he harboured a plan for the partition of Poland as a means of escape from his dilemma. When the time was ripe in 1772 to put the plan into operation, it was one of Frederick's diplomatic masterpieces. Prussia was the greatest beneficiary of the first partition of Poland. The acquisition of West Prussia was strategically, though not in population and resources, more important than the conquest of Silesia, for it ended the separation of East Prussia from the central tract of Hohenzollern territories. For the first time Prussia acquired a sizeable non-German population. German nationalist historians of the 19th century, like Sybel, claimed a

German mission to overcome the inferior civilization of the Poles. There was no trace of nationalism in Frederick's policy, even if he likened his new Polish subjects to the Iroquois Indians. It seems fair to add that Prussian policy towards her Polish citizens for a long time matched the Prussian tradition of religious toleration. German settlers and administrators moved in and economically the German-speaking population became preponderant; but Polish national sentiment was not as grossly offended by Prussia as by Russia and even when it became fully articulate in the 19th century did not clash as violently with the Prussian as with the Russian administration. Nonetheless the partitions of Poland, which ended in the disappearance of that state in 1795, were a crime against the established European order and the Prussian acquisitions cannot be excused by the fact that most of them had once been under the control of the Teutonic Order. But if there was a crime Russia was no less a perpetrator than Prussia.

In the last decade of Frederick's reign the rivalry with Austria became again the principal preoccupation. The end of the Bavarian Wittelsbach line opened the possibility that Austria might recoup her loss of Silesia through the acquisition of Bavaria. To prevent this Frederick went to war for the last time in 1778. Little serious fighting occurred and because the troops spent much time picking potatoes in the fields the event became known as "the Potato War". Frederick himself called it an "insipid" campaign. By negotiation the rights of the Zweibrücken Wittelsbach line to succeed in Bavaria were safeguarded and Austria acquired only a small strip of territory on the right bank of the Inn. In his efforts to block Austria, Frederick had once again mobilized what loyalties remained to the constitution of the Holy Roman Empire and had used the old cry of "Libertät" to rouse the smaller princes against the Emperor.

The installation of Habsburg princes in some of the German prince-bishoprics caused further uneasiness about the aims of Austria and there was the continuing danger that she might revive her designs on Bavaria. Joseph II's deft policy led to a *rapprochement* between Austria and Russia after 1781 which threatened to leave Prussia once more very isolated. In this situation Frederick was again driven to mobilize the feeling of the smaller German princes against the overpowering position of Austria. His last major act of foreign policy in 1785 was the formation of a Constitutional Association of German princes designed to uphold the constitution and institutions of the Empire. Frederick in truth cared little about the Holy Roman Empire and in his Testament of 1768 envisaged its eventual disappearance.[7] The rise of his star in the European

firmament had the incidental effect of stimulating German patriotic
sentiment, which was usually still imperial, but which now often
became "fritzisch" as Goethe called it.[8] In Prussia the growth of
civic loyalty was entirely "fritzisch" and displaced the old imperial
sentiment.

When Frederick returned to Berlin at the end of the Seven Years
War, prematurely aged and a stranger to his capital, he faced a
formidable task of *rétablissement*. The task of economic reconstruction was made more difficult by the continued maintenance of a
large army and by a general economic crisis, as yet barely understood, in Northern Europe. Frederick's economic policy was mercantilist. He placed greater emphasis than his father on the promotion of manufactures, especially textiles. By 1786 silks and
woollen goods were the chief Prussian exports. Especially after
1763 the state, which meant often the King personally, became
very closely involved in the promotion and financing of economic
enterprises, so much so that private initiative was frequently stifled.
The tradition of state intervention in economic affairs remained
alive into the days of industrial revolution a hundred years later.
Frederick did a good deal to promote better communications and
transport, through the abolition of internal customs barriers, and
the building of canals and ports. A particularly successful aspect
of his economic policy was internal colonization. Through the
clearing of marshes and active agricultural improvement some
300,000 new settlers were drawn into Prussia by 1786. This to a
large extent made good the losses of population caused by Frederick's wars.

Another major part of the post-war *rétablissement* was the reorganization of the taxation system. The King was dissatisfied with
the proceeds of the excise and was suspicious of his officials. In
1766 he set up a new separate department in the General Directory, with provincial branches, for the administration of this tax,
and brought in something like two hundred Frenchmen to run it.
It was accordingly known as the *Regie* and although effective in
raising the revenue became highly unpopular. Equally hated were
the tobacco and coffee monopolies, which raised prices to the sky
in order to yield a massive profit to the state.

Although Frederick had some notion that it was wise to make
the rich contribute more in taxes than the poor, essentially he
viewed the whole population, other than the nobility, as a milch
cow, "the in-filling substance in the state which has no existence
of its own", as one German historian has put it.[9] The exactions of
the military, bureaucratic state weighed heavily on all classes
except the Junkers and bore especially hard on the peasants. They

had to provide the bulk of the army insofar as it was of native recruitment. In order to make sure that they could fulfil this vital function for the state the King had to prevent the alienation of land available to the peasants; but apart from this he did little for them and they remained *leibeigen*. At the other end of the social scale he continued to regard the nobility as the real pillar of the state and made sure that after 1763 all the middle class or foreign elements which had had to be taken into the officer corps in the war were removed as swiftly as possible. At his death some 4 per cent of the population was in the army and it was the biggest in Europe. There was some progress in education, of which Zedlitz, a man with progressive convictions, was in charge after 1770. The educational system was socially divided and highly utilitarian : the King felt that no-one should be educated above his station and that a minimum of reading and writing was sufficient for peasants. Zedlitz had some success in reorganizing secondary education, though even here the teachers were on the whole of poor quality and badly paid. Compulsory primary education, decreed by the King, remained largely a paper obligation, particularly in country districts.

At the centre of the Prussian state was still the King himself and without his ceaseless labours the whole organism could not function. He was increasingly cut off from contact with his officials and communicated with them only in writing. His strictures on those whom he considered failures were biting and not a few of them ended up in Spandau prison. The great masses of his subjects regarded the shabby, hunched figure of their old King, the "Old Fritz", with awe, but the gulf between his world and theirs was enormous. He considered the later French philosophers decadent and the early flowering of German literature passed him by. While the young were enthusing over the early romantic works of Goethe and discovering Shakespeare, Frederick's literary taste remained centred on Racine. The King's reputation as a ruler and soldier was still massive. Prussia was regarded as the most progressive of states : the judicial reforms carried out or prepared during the last few years of Frederick's reign seemed once more to confirm this. The conquests of the King, his efficient administration and sound economic policies had more than doubled the population and almost doubled the area of Prussia and had made her the fourth economic power in Europe, though still a long way behind England, France and Holland. Frederick was regarded as the foremost general of his age and the Prussian army was a model for many others.

Yet some acute observers could already detect signs of decay in the Frederician state. It was obvious that a country so dependent on the ability of its ruler must be in a precarious state. But beyond this the system of enlightened despotism as practised by Frederick had already outlived itself. It was incapable of mobilizing the deeper energies of a whole nation. All but a tiny minority of the community were objects only of state policy and deprived of all means of participation. This weakness was to become a fundamental defect when the French Revolution opened new horizons. For one so well versed in history, Frederick had a very static and mechanistic vision of society. It was a clockwork of which he but no one else held the key and he could contemplate no development that might transcend the situation. Mirabeau thus described the mood on the day of the King's death : "All was silent, but there was no grief. Everybody was busy, but no one was sad. No regrets, no sighs, no praises. They were tired of him—'fatigué jusqu'à la haine'."[10]

CHAPTER IV

The Decline of Old Prussia 1786–1806

FREDERICK THE GREAT was the last Hohenzollern to occupy a central position in the development of Prussia, the last of that remarkable trinity of princes beginning with the Great Elector who had fashioned the Prussian state out of virtually nothing. He left the helm at the very moment when currents of unprecedented complexity and intensity were impinging on the ship of state. The end of the 18th century was a climactic moment in the political and intellectual affairs of Europe. In Germany a sufficiently numerous educated class had arisen to produce and provide an audience for a great blossoming of creative work. The dominant trend in the intellectual atmosphere was changing rapidly : a reaction against Reason and Enlightenment made itself felt and ushered in an age when Romanticism became the prevailing spirit; cosmopolitan humanism gave way to the rise of national consciousness and nationalism. The evolution of ideas was naturally gradual and one intellectual system did not exclude another, but formed a further layer upon it. The link between political events and intellectual fashions was no more direct at this period than at any other, least of all in relation to Prussia, a state so politically distinctive yet fully exposed to all German and European influences. Nonetheless Prussia under Frederick the Great had been the leading example in Germany, perhaps in Europe, of the practical application to government of the ideology of the Enlightenment; as the leading Protestant and in many eyes the most significant state in Germany the movement of ideas was bound to have a profound effect on her.

Under Frederick the Great, Berlin, the Sparta of the North, had become something of a cultural centre in Germany. The King's dazzling personality drew Europe's gaze to his capital, and the relatively tolerant atmosphere of Prussia was inviting for men of intellectual curiosity. Frederick's own orientation was, however, so entirely French, as was also the academy he set up in Berlin, that neither could have much impact on the growth of German culture. The presence of other men in Berlin proved more significant. The great Lessing spent many years in Berlin between 1748 and 1767 and was for a time Voltaire's German secretary. He was the first major German dramatist; his ideas were a product of the Enlightenment, but they were suffused with the deeper and broader insights of genius. In Berlin he started a life-long friendship with Moses Mendelssohn, the sickly Jewish clerk from Dessau who became another of the apostles of German Enlightenment.

Mendelssohn was the first German Jew to leave the ghetto and make a contribution to the German cultural scene. That this should have happened in Prussia is again a tribute to the tradition of religious toleration in the Hohenzollern state. Officially Frederick the Great's policy towards the Jews was still fairly illiberal and the King's enlightened rationalism did not get the better of his ingrained traditional prejudices against the children of Israel. Individual Jews, however, came increasingly to occupy important positions in Prussian financial life and to enjoy commensurate privileges. Mendelssohn, however, was the first prominent Jew in the world of letters, precursor of a long line of German-Jewish writers, artists and academics of exceptional distinction. His standing as an original thinker is but slight, but he scored through his winning personality and as a popularizer of the ideas of the Enlightenment in a balanced and accessible form. Lessing, his greater friend, paid him a tribute by making him the model for the central figure of his play *Nathan the Wise*, written towards the end of his life, when he had left Prussia and settled at Wolfsbüttel in Brunswick. This drama epitomizes many of the positive sides of 18th-century rationalism—toleration, humanity, belief in happiness and natural goodness, and opposition against prejudice and superstition. The third figure in the Berlin trinity of the Enlightenment was Friedrich Nicolai, whose own talents pale into insignificance besides those of Lessing and even of Mendelssohn, but who became a power in the land as a popularizer and fighter against obscurantism. His widely read magazine *Allgemeine Deutsche Bibliothek* did perhaps little to educate the literary taste of Germany, but it fought prejudice, dogmatism and intolerance wherever they were to be found.

The cultural life of Berlin under Frederick the Great, in spite of these beginnings, was sparse and restricted. It began to broaden towards the end of the reign, but it required the stimuli of the French Revolution and the Romantic movement to make it blossom. But Berlin was not the only city in the Kingdom of Prussia where men of the spirit were at work. At Königsberg Kant, Hamann and Herder, three highly significant figures of German philosophy and literature, were at one time or another active and in contact with each other. Kant and his friend and antagonist

Hamann, an enemy of rationalism, known as the "Magus of the North", were natives of the city : the former never left Königsberg throughout his long life and the latter returned to it in early middle age. Herder was also born in East Prussia and spent his student days at Königsberg, but during the rest of his life he lived outside Prussia.

Kant was one of the finest products of the remarkable flowering of German civilization in the later 18th century. In his later works, on which his reputation chiefly rests, and of which the *Critique of Pure Reason* is the most famous, Kant was above all concerned with the theory of cognition, perhaps the central problem of all philosophy. Complete originality is not possible in this field, for all philosophers from Plato, with his cave analogy, down to the modern linguistic philosophers, have wandered round this problem of the relationship between human thought and external reality. There is a certain repetitiveness in the answers which they have given : the idealist solution and empiricist solution keep recurring in various forms and with different degrees of emphasis. Kant's central importance in the history of philosophy lies in the fact that he grappled with the problem of cognition at a time when the pendulum had swung a long way towards pure empiricism. The thinkers of the English Enlightenment in particular, for example David Hume, had denied any *a priori* elements in the process of apprehending external objects and had based it purely on experience. There was also another earlier trend in the philosophy of the Enlightenment of which Descartes was the most prominent representative : this form of rationalism implied a sharp break with all metaphysical thinking and dogmatism, but it did postulate the superiority of certain *a priori* categories, such as the laws of mathematics, over pure experience in the process of apprehending the world external to the self.

Kant came to grips once more with this essential problem. The key question which he asked himself was : how are synthetic *a priori* judgements possible? Or in other words, how do experience and pure reason come together in the process of cognition and what therefore are the limits of pure reason? Kant's treatment of this problem is distinguished by the careful and methodical way in which he builds up his argument while yet letting one sense the powerful intellectual drive behind it. This is indeed the hallmark of his mature work : no argument is burdened with more weight than it can bear, limits are always recognized and no immodest claims are made. The whole edifice constitutes a most satisfying fresh synthesis from which new and divergent schools of philosophy could in their turn grow.

The immediate reaction to the *Critique of Pure Reason* was cool and uncomprehending. It was dedicated to Zedlitz, the minister who was reforming the Prussian educational system in the closing years of Frederick the Great's reign and in whom Kant saw a sympathizer in high places. The dedication remained unanswered. Kant attached great importance to Mendelssohn's reaction to his book. He held the Jewish sage of Berlin in high regard and it was a red letter day when Mendelssohn, having specially made the journey to Königsberg, appeared unannounced in Kant's lecture room at the University in 1777. But Mendelssohn could no longer follow Kant into the higher realms of his critical philosophy and could not bring himself to read the *Critique*. Before many years were out, however, Kant had become famous and his philosophy was the centre of discussion in an age which was unusually addicted to philosophizing.

Epistemology was the first concern of Kant's mature work, but it was followed by a systematic moral philosophy, most fully elaborated in the *Critique of Practical Reason*. Kant had shown the limits of pure reason and demonstrated that rationalist metaphysics was a pseudo-science. But if there are no answers that pure reason can give to problems such as the existence of God or the immortality of the soul, practical reason postulates the existence of a moral law based on freedom of will. Often quoted are Kant's statements that there is nothing which can be thought of as good without reservation except the will to do good; and that nothing filled him with greater admiration and veneration than the starry firmament above and the moral law within him. He built up his ethical philosophy with the same rigid regard to method as his theory of cognition. At the core is the duty which bids us obey that autonomous moral law which manifests itself to us through our reason. This is the categorical imperative. It depends on the existence of freedom, even though this existence cannot be proved or disproved by pure reason. Kant's moral philosophy is far removed from any psychological or utilitarian ethic and has its existence in the rarefied air of rational constructs. Thus it has great power and dignity. Kant's most systematic pronouncement on a political problem, the *Essay on Perpetual Peace,* which appeared in 1795, arises out of his moral philosophy. In it he constructs a theoretical international system, a kind of League of Nations, through which the divergent interests of states could be brought into harmony on a moral basis. It is not a utopia, but an attempt to use the methods of his critical philosophy in the chaotic field of international relations.

The question has often been posed to what extent Kant was a product of Prussia. He himself thought, with some pride, that he was of Scottish origin, but this cannot be proved for certain. The fact was that he was a native of Königsberg and never left that city. He was born of modest respectable artisan parents; the principal influence in his early life was his mother, who in her simple way radiated the spirit of Pietism. The Enlightenment and Pietism were also the chief elements in the school and university education through which Kant passed, and both these movements were typical of 18th-century Prussia. It is tempting to see in Kant's severe and rigorous mental processes, in his sober, cool judgement, in his emphasis on duty and obedience to the moral law for its own sake, a reflection of the Prussian ethos. It would, however, be a mistake to overstress the connection, for nothing is more character-istic of Kant than the timelessness and universality of his thinking. His concern was with humanity in the abstract, his relationship with the existing historical reality of the Prussian state distant and tenuous. With Kant's work, German philosophy was still in com-plete harmony with the main stream of European thought. Soon there was to develop a divergence between German and Western European ideas which was to have fateful consequences in the political field.

The two other men of East Prussia, Hamann and Herder, were of a completely different cast of mind from Kant and are both of them precursors of German Romanticism. Hamann, born in 1730 and therefore six years younger than Kant, was one of those rare swimmers against the tide : while the Enlightenment was at its height he remained a passionate opponent of rationalism and abstraction and an ardent follower of the senses, the emotions and of faith. He did not write very systematically; his life was a grim struggle with adversity; he received little recognition of his work, and was only rediscovered long after his death. A curious friendship tied him to Kant, while a gulf divided their mental worlds. On Hamann's side it was a love-hate relationship. Later generations have seen in Hamann a thinker of depth and great inner tension, like Rousseau an anticipator of the Romantic agony.

Herder's impact was more immediate. He was twenty years younger than Kant and sat at his feet at the University of Königs-berg. He then lived for some years in Riga and it was perhaps his East Prussian birth, reinforced by this period spent at the extreme limits of the German-speaking world, that sharpened his awareness of nationality. He began to investigate the origins of language and saw it linked up with the development of ethnic groups. He saw the connection between nations, their language and their history; he sensed the natural lyricism in the primitive folk poetry of peoples. One of his most influential works was *The Spirit of*

Hebrew Poetry in which he reflected on the development of language and poetry. He shone as a translator, publishing the folk songs of many nations in German. He developed into a passionate, enthusiastic opponent of the Enlightenment, praising faith, sentiment, nature, emotion—and decrying the limitations of rationalism. Herder became a friend of the young Goethe and had much influence on him during his *Storm and Stress* period, though later, when Herder settled at Weimar, Goethe's classical restraint produced a more sober style in Herder. As a philosopher Herder lacked the method and precision of his former teacher Kant. When he published his *Ideas on the Philosophy of the History of Mankind* Kant's review of the book was full of typically gentle reproof which infuriated Herder. The break between the two men was complete. Herder was not a major literary figure in his own right but he prepared the way for the German Romantic movement and for the rise of German national consciousness. He was, however, by no means a nationalist : national idiosyncrasy and the separate historical development of races and nations were to him chords in the greater harmony of mankind's progress. Hamann and Herder represent a tradition in East Prussia different from that seen in Kant : the mysticism which is also to be found in Lutheranism and the Pietist movement. Apart from his birth and education, Herder had no bonds with Prussia and despised the enlightened depotism of Frederick the Great.

In the closing decades of the 18th century the cultural life of Germany reached a peak never attained before or since. The wealth of genius was overwhelming in literature, music, philosophy. It was a phenomenon far transcending the confines of Prussia, but nevertheless Berlin did become an increasingly important focal point, for a time ranking only behind Weimar and Jena as a literary and philosophical centre. In its salons men like the brothers Schlegel, the brothers Humboldt, Schleiermacher, Kleist, Chamisso and many others of note were to be found. In the 1790s Berlin began to acquire a more coherent *élite,* something which could consider itself society. French influence was still strong in it and the new Jewish *élite* played a notable role, in spite of the legal disabilities which still afflicted the mass of Jews.

Two leading salons were kept by two remarkable Jewesses, Henriette Herz and Rachel Levin. The former was the wife of Marcus Herz, a doctor and philosopher, who had gone to the University of Königsberg and become Kant's favourite pupil; our knowledge of the genesis of the *Critique of Pure Reason* derives mainly from the correspondence between Kant and Herz. The prevailing atmosphere at Henriette's salon was still that of the

Enlightenment and of Kantian philosophy, but increasingly its *habitués* fell under the sway of Romanticism. It was here that Friedrich Schlegel met Dorothea Veit, the daughter of Moses Mendelssohn and wife of a banker. He fell in love with her and married her, occasioning one of the great scandals of Berlin society. Wilhelm von Humboldt—Pomeranian aristocrat, thinker, writer, friend of Goethe and Schiller and distinguished public servant of the Prussian state—admired Henriette Herz greatly when he first came to Berlin. His letters to her give the impression of being part of a highly erotic attachment, but in fact the relationship was one of elaborate pretence. Only a few years later Humboldt saw "Jette" in a different light: "... so little true and genuine feeling ... so much self-importance, pettiness, vanity and moodiness and not even much benevolence.... In every relationship the other person has to concern himself with her. She is never concerned with him..."[1] Even more widely influential was Rachel Levin. She had none of the physical beauty of Henriette, but a warm, very out-going nature, a considerable brain and much insight. She inspired great devotion in many of the leading men of Berlin for decades. She knew Goethe and was a great propagandist for his genius. She married the diplomatist Varnhagen von Ense; both she and Henriette were converts to Christianity, the latter only towards the end of her life.

The great issues which concerned the German intellectual world in the 1790s and the early years of the 19th century, in Berlin as elsewhere, were the French Revolution, the conflict between the Enlightenment and the Romantic movement, and the gradual rise of German national consciousness. As in England, the French Revolution was at first greeted with enthusiasm by many in Prussia, while later doubts arose because of the excesses and atrocities of the Revolution. It was a drama which those who lived in Prussia watched with fascination but entirely as observers. The Frederician state appeared still so solidly built that it seemed the French Revolution could not affect it either domestically or from the outside. The aristocracy and the official classes watched without alarm the enthusiasm of the intellectuals for the revolutionary upheavals across the Rhine. Condemned to inaction and deprived of political influence, many Germans admired the dynamism and drama of the Revolution. Fichte, the most significant philosopher in the apostolic succession from Kant, who was soon to proclaim from Berlin the necessity of a powerful state for the Germans, published a passionate defence of the Revolution.[2] Friedrich Schlegel followed in 1796 with his *Essay on the Concept of Republicanism*, enthusiastically endorsing the ideas of Rousseau about the

general will as the only moral basis for a state. Even Schleiermacher, a calmer character, was outraged at the reaction to Louis
XVI's execution which occurred when he was house tutor in the
great Junker family of the Dohnas : his aristocratic masters condemned the execution not because Louis was innocent but because
he was a king. Thus the Revolution was almost universally welcomed by the leaders of German thought in its early years and
even when the Terror came, most of them insisted that the revolutionary ideas were right. The war which Prussia fought against
the Revolution and from which she retired through the Peace of
Basle in 1795 was on principle unpopular amongst the educated
classes.

For those Germans who lived within Prussia, and for most others,
the French Revolution was a stirring but extraneous event. The
Romantic movement was indigenous and was distilled from the
reaction against the Enlightenment. The particular form it took
in Germany and its eventual reverberations in the field of political
thinking began to put Germany out of step with the ideas of the
West where previously she had been entirely in harmony. The
Romantics had no coherent system of thought, for they were react-
ing against systems. Romanticism was a compound of mysticism,
nostalgia, longing for the infinite, fascination with the irrational,
subjectivism—a list which could be lengthened without difficulty.
The Romantics had a high regard for the past, particularly the
Middle Ages, and their historicism contrasts with the primarily
unhistorical, universalist mode of thought characteristic of the
Enlightenment. There was no common political attitude implicit
in Romanticism : it was compatible with revolutionary enthusiasm
as well as with reactionary nostalgia for an idealized past. The
early Romantics in Germany were not in the main politically
orientated and in the 1790s for the most part sympathized with
the Revolution. As a specifically political Romanticism began to
emerge in the early years of the 19th century it became decidedly
conservative and also linked with the rising tide of German
nationalism.

Friedrich Schlegel, resident in Berlin for many years, was typical
of the early Romantics and was their foremost literary theoretician.
His luxuriant, overgrown romantic novel *Lucinde* scandalized his
contemporaries as much as his adultery with Dorothea Veit. His
political views fluctuated and were far removed from the practical.
In the 1790s he was sympathetic to revolutionary ideals and cosmopolitan in his views. A few years later he had become anti-
revolutionary and conservative; the German middle ages cast their
spell over him, he became anti-French and wrote German patriotic

songs. In 1808 he became a convert to Catholicism, moved to Vienna and saw Austria as the real representative of German nationhood. Friedrich's elder brother, August Wilhelm, produced the German translation of Shakespeare, together with Ludwig Tieck, another member of the Berlin circle. It was so effective that it made Shakespeare into a German classic. The philosopher *par excellence* of the earlier Romantics was Schelling, with whom many of the Berlin group were in close contact when they were living in Jena. Schelling's philosophy of nature, with its emphasis on unity and contending forces always striving for equilibrium, appealed to the Romantic imagination. Schelling also anticipated Hegel in seeing history as a manifestation of the absolute. In Berlin Schleiermacher was one of the group round Henriette Herz and the Schlegels. His reaction against the Enlightenment came from the religious angle. He stressed that God was not capable of being grasped by reason, and that in his capacity for religious feeling man was entirely dependent on the infinite, but that through this feeling he was able to restore the lost harmony of his being. It was this longing for unity, for recapturing a lost repose, whether it was given a religious turn as with Schleiermacher or whether it was expressed in poetry, which lay at the root of the Romantic attitude.

The third major intellectual issue of the period was the gradual evolution of German opinion from cosmopolitan universal ideals towards an appreciation of the importance of nationality. The prevalent attitude in the 1790s and beyond was that the German mission was to be a cultural nation rather than a state exercising power. In a sketch for a poem which was never completed Schiller wrote: "At this moment [after the Peace of Lunéville] can the German, who emerges without glory from a grievous war, who has two exultant people with their feet on his neck and whose destiny is determined by the victor, can he feel any pride? ... Yes, he may! He has been unfortunate in the struggle, but he has not lost that which gives him his real worth. The German Empire and the German nation are two different things.... The Germans have acquired their real value independent of the political sphere, and even if the Empire were to perish, German dignity would remain. It is a moral grandeur, which resides in the cultured character of the Nation, independent of its political fate...."[3] This feeling was shared almost universally by the educated classes in Germany, whether they still lived in the intellectual climate of the Enlightenment or whether they had been caught up in the reaction against it.

The prevalent attitude can be clearly seen in the ideas expressed by Wilhelm von Humboldt in the 1790s. Here was a Prussian

Junker, trained to serve his state in the administration of the law and later to become one of its leading political figures. He was a child of the Enlightenment, but the Romantic movement also left his mark on him. Underneath the lofty idealism and classical repose of his personality there lurked dangerous emotional undercurrents. His ideal, like that of many of the great Germans of his day who were his friends, was the free autonomous individual, a citizen of the world, conscious of the bonds that united all mankind, broadly cultivated and sensitive to all manifestations of the human spirit. This idea left little room for the nation, let alone the political nation or state, to play any but a secondary role. Wilhelm von Humboldt was sufficiently influenced by the historicism of the Romantic movement to sense that the national entity to which an individual belongs must shape his character, but he was afraid that the state might make exorbitant demands on individuals and felt that at best it was concerned only with the lesser material conditions of their existence. Humboldt, like so many others, thought that the absence of a national state did not detract from German pride, dignity and cultural achievement, but that this absence positively enhanced the status of the Germans as the standard-bearers of humanity. When he spoke of the Germans he meant the small cultural *élite* within which he lived. The Prussian state within which he was born, and which he began to serve as an official in the 1790s, influenced his thinking hardly at all. He knew it was the most progressive German state; he knew that its inhabitants shared a pride in the achievements of the great Frederick, but beyond this he regarded "the Royal Prussian states" as no more than a piece of machinery.

Some of the writers of the turn of the century formed a more exalted notion of nationality than Humboldt. This was particularly true of Romantics like Friedrich Schlegel or Novalis. The latter, a Saxon nobleman, whose real name was Friedrich von Hardenberg, had a mystical regard for the middle ages, the Holy Roman Empire, the Universal Church, the knights and princes of the German past. For a short time he served as an official in the Prussian mining administration. His view of Prussia is summed up in his remark : "No state has been governed more like a factory than Prussia since Frederick William I."[4] His hopes rose, however, when Frederick William III and his attractive consort Queen Luise, came to the throne in 1797. He saw them as a young, knightly, and pious couple. The political views of Novalis, as of most German men of letters of this period, were incidental, no more than an occasional glance sideways from a romantic view of the world at the centre of which stood the individual in all his glory and despair.

The great intellectual ferment and cultural achievement of Germany in the later 18th and early 19th century had thus only a tenuous connection with the Prussian state in the years after Frederick the Great's death. Prussia's reputation was for efficiency, competent administration, sound finance, and military strength. This reputation carried on until the shattering defeat at Jena in 1806 revealed the weakness of Prussia's central institution, the army, and thereby showed that the reputation was no longer deserved. The Prussian machine could, however, only work efficiently if there was a ruler at the controls who was willing and able to labour day and night at the tasks of government and administration. Even Frederick the Great had found the complexities almost beyond him in his later years and many of his detailed decisions failed to rest on a sound basis. His successors were men of much lesser calibre who could not even begin to master the manifold duties which in theory they should have discharged, while their determination to maintain the outward appearance of absolute rule made matters worse.

Frederick William II was an amiable man, but, unlike most of his predecessors and successors, he had a number of mistresses who exercised much influence over him, even in political matters. His first marriage, to Princess Elizabeth of Brunswick, ended in divorce. Meanwhile, at the age of twenty-three, he began a relationship with Wilhelmine Enke, herself only sixteen and the daughter of a court musician, from which sprang five children. Wilhelmine was genuinely devoted to her royal friend and he often turned to her for advice and comfort even when he was on the throne. She was ennobled as Countess Lichtenau in 1794. Frederick William's second marriage to Princess Frederika of Hesse produced six children; but when he was King he was in addition married morganatically to two ladies of the Court in succession. The Count of Brandenburg, a son of the second of these marriages, to Countess Sophie Dönhoff, became Prime Minister of Prussia during the year of revolution 1848. The subservience of the Lutheran ecclesiastical authorities is illustrated by their willingness to cover the King's irregular liaisons with an air of respectability through these morganatic marriages; as an alibi they cited the precedent of Philip of Hesse during the Reformation. The moral laxity of Frederick William II's court, so out of keeping with the tradition established by his predecessors and soon to be restored again, reinforced the permissiveness in the upper strata of society brought on by the reaction against the austerity of the previous reign and by other tendencies of the period.

Perhaps even more serious was the King's flirtation with Rosicrucianism. Secret societies, with elaborate initiation rites, were a feature of the 18th century. The most famous of these orders were the Freemasons, but in their principles at any rate, if not in some of their ritual, they were dedicated to rationalism and the Enlightenment. The Rosicrucians claimed legendary origins, the possession of all kinds of secrets, such as the transformation of base metals into gold, they indulged in fantastic rites and elaborate hierarchies, in occultism and spiritualism. They had a wide following among the Prussian upper classes. They and other secret societies shared a similar psychological root with Romanticism. Their political influence, and the belief they had in all kinds of conspiratorial theories of history and politics, had a strongly reactionary and virulently anti-revolutionary flavour. When Frederick William was still Crown Prince, he met, during the "Potato War" of 1778, a Saxon officer called Bischoffwerder who introduced him to the Rosicrucian order. Through Bischoffwerder Frederick William met Wöllner, also a Rosicrucian, who gave him instruction in government and political science based on outright opposition to the policies of enlightenment as practised by Frederick the Great. Wöllner was a theologian and had been given a pastoral office through the noble family in which he worked as a tutor. He soon gave up his ecclesiastical office and married the heiress of the family, much to the disgust of all her relations and even of King Frederick, who called him an "intriguing and deceitful cleric".[5] Wöllner and Bischoffwerder became the leading men in the reign of his nephew. The former was the chief adviser of the new King in civil matters. He administered the "Dispositionskasse", yet another revenue-collecting agency instituted by Frederick the Great, and at the personal disposal of the King; this position made him virtually Minister of Finance, though he never attained that coveted title. He also had a seat in the General Directory and in 1788, having been ennobled, he became minister concerned with ecclesiastical affairs. It was in this latter field that he was able to change most decisively the policies of the previous reign which had been guided by the ideas of the Enlightenment. Bischoffwerder became an adjutant of the King and had much influence in military and foreign affairs.

In spite of these influences at the top, which ran right against the Prussian traditions established under the two previous rulers, there was in fact no decisive change of course in the short reign of Frederick William II. There was, however, a slackening of the will, a relaxation of the tautness and tension that had permeated the whole system from the top. This was popular, not only among the

narrower circle of the bureaucracy, many of whom had personally
suffered from the exacting demands of the Old Fritz, but also
among the populace at large. The hated French *Regie* was abolished, much to everybody's relief. It was merely one example of
how Frederick had himself undermined the fairly logical administrative system inherited from his father by creating new authorities.
To some extent the intention had been to ensure his personal control by leaving himself as the only ultimate co-ordinator of conflicting departments. The central intelligence which produced a
coherent policy out of contending administrative pressures was,
however, now lacking. The attempt to bring the General Directory
back to the collegiate principle and to do away with the special
departments created by Frederick, such as the forestry department, were half-hearted and only half successful. In fact major
areas of administration and policy which Frederick the Great had
ultimately supervised in person now fell under the control of really
independent and often competing agencies. Thus many military
functions earlier discharged by the King from his personal cabinet,
such as commissioning of officers, training and command, were now
transferred to a new body, the *Oberkriegskollegium*. Yet this body
proved incapable of effectively co-ordinating even the purely
administrative functions of the army, while the control of actual
military operations remained reserved for the King personally. In
the discharge of this duty Frederick William relied on his General
Adjutants, of whom Bischoffwerder was one, and who had the right
of access (*Vortragsrecht*) to the sovereign. The Oberkriegskollegium
and the Generaladjutantur were rival authorities, which in the
event frustrated the emergence of an effective General Staff.

The role of the Prussian bureaucracy was gradually shifting. In
theory it was still the servant of the absolute monachy, but even
in the latter part of Frederick the Great's reign it was seeking to
throw off the royal tutelage. The heavy pressure to which the
King subjected his administrators forced them to find means of
protecting themselves and of getting their way in spite of the King.
Mirabeau, in his large work *La monarchie prussienne*, published
in 1788, portrayed Frederick as the most deceived ruler in Europe.
When the pressure from above was relaxed the bureaucracy
acquired even more of a will of its own and greater self-confidence
in maintaining it. The administrators began to be influenced by
the neo-humanist ideal of the educated, cultivated individual which
the great men of German literature and thought, from Kant to
Goethe and Schiller, were proclaiming. This ideal was also closing
the gulf between nobles and non-nobles which had had such a
divisive effect earlier. A kind of civil service commission had been

instituted in 1770, when it was a matter of repairing the gaps
made in the administration by the Seven Years War. Frederick's
policy had always been to reserve the higher positions to members
of the nobility, particularly in the officer corps. The greater emphasis on merit which the establishment of the *Oberexaminationskom-
mission* of 1770 seemed to imply did not in fact throw the service
open to talent : it was simply that a higher standard of profession-
alism was needed and the ideal of "Bildung" (education, cultivation) was gradually replacing the notion of mere pedigree as a
criterion. The higher royal bureaucracy thus became a self-confident
élite group, an amalgam of noble and bourgeois elements fused
together by common standards of education. It was jostling for
position with other *élite* groups such as the Junker aristocracy itself,
which was still powerful at local and provincial level, the officer
corps which was almost entirely Junker-recruited, and the intellectual *élite* which was largely alienated from the state and all its
works. The influence of Kantian humanism made for some liber-
alization, as can be seen in Zedlitz's school reforms and in the
introduction of the new legal code in 1794.

For the lower orders, the *petite bourgeoisie* and especially the
peasants, the state was, however, still authoritarian, an *Obrigkeitsstaat,* which treated them as non-participating objects of its actions
and arrangements. For the peasant his Junker master was still
more important than the state. The monarch at the top of the
structure, who had been for so long the central figure in the Prussian drama, became increasingly a tool in the hands of the self-
confident bureaucracy. Great power was wielded by those nearest
his person, such as the favourites Wöllner and Bischoffwerder
under Frederick William II. In his son's reign the cabinet councillors, who under Frederick the Great had been merely secretaries
executing the King's orders, became key figures often exerting more
influence than ministers.

The obscurantist influences round Frederick William II produced
a real change of course in the field of church affairs and education.
Zedlitz, friend and protector of Kant, was forced out of his position at the head of the newly founded supreme education authority
(*Oberschulkollegium*). A more stringent censorship was established
and even the great Kant himself was reprimanded in 1794 for
"having misused philosophy to falsify and degrade many of the
principal teachings of the Bible and Christianity".[6] Kant did not
consider it worth while to make a stand on the matter and undertook to refrain from public pronouncements on religion. An edict
on religion promulgated by Wöllner in 1778, while reaffirming
toleration as a general principle, laid down very narrow norms of

Lutheran orthodoxy to be followed by pastors in church and school. In 1791 a commission was appointed to examine clerics on their beliefs and the men chosen for the task were of the most intolerant Lutheran orthodoxy. Their report disclosed a state of affairs which profoundly dissatisfied the King and he pushed Wöllner into taking stronger action, thus showing he personally was responsible for the anti-rationalist policies. The degree of official intolerance reached alarming proportions in the last two or three years of his reign: for example Nicolai's famous journal *Allgemeine Deutsche Bibliothek* had temporarily to go into exile. It was a blot on the normally tolerant traditions of Prussia and no doubt contributed to the alienation of the intellectual *élite* from all things political.

The domestic affairs of Prussia were dwarfed at this stage by the mighty upheavals which were shaking all Europe. In the years immediately after Frederick's death Prussia continued on a predominantly anti-Austrian course. There was a possibility that the last gambit of the great King, the League of German Princes, might make a permanent impact and bring about the formation of a North German Empire or Confederation under the leadership of Prussia. Men like the Grand Duke Karl August of Saxe-Weimar, Goethe's master, would have liked to have used the League as a means towards a fundamental reform of the Holy Roman Empire. Count Hertzberg, who was in day-to-day control of Prussian foreign policy, was opposed to such ambitions and thought of the League mainly as a device for checking Austria by maintaining the old liberties of German princes against the excessive claims of the Habsburgs. Hertzberg was a scholarly man, very much a product of the Enlightenment, but his conduct of policy was based on theory rather than on a sensitive appreciation of realities. His guiding concept was the formation of a North European Alliance, at the core of which would lie a revived version of the link between Prussia and England, which had been so effective in the Seven Years War. This alliance would counterbalance the Franco-Austrian *bloc*. Hertzberg was successful in promoting a treaty between Prussia and England. He was helped in this by the fact that the interests of both countries coincided in the Netherlands. A revolt by the Patriot party, backed by France, against the Stadholder, William V, who was married to Frederick William II's sister, brought Prussian and British intervention on the side of the House of Orange. Thus the Triple Alliance became a fact but it brought little advantage to Prussia.

In the meantime Prussia hoped to profit from the embarrassments in which Austria found herself at this juncture. These arose from the centralizing policies of Joseph II which had aroused opposition in various parts of the far-flung Habsburg dominions. In addition, Austria was involved with Russia in a war with the Turks. Hertzberg hoped to profit from this situation by acquiring additional territory for Prussia in Poland and began to cultivate his relations with Warsaw and Constantinople. He got little support for his projects from Pitt, who did not want a war over an Eastern European issue, when events in France made the situation look ominous in the West. Hertzberg wanted to acquire Danzig for Prussia, a move which had long seemed contrary to British trading interests in the Baltic. Pitt's attitude and a number of other factors combined to frustrate Hertzberg's Polish designs. The King, who at one time had been eager for war with Austria, lost interest; Joseph II died and was succeeded by the cautious and conciliatory Leopold II. The Convention of Reichenberg, concluded in July 1790, ended the tension between Austria and Prussia, the latter obtaining again little advantage. This Convention can be seen as a fundamental change on the European chess-board. It ended half a century of almost uninterrupted hostility between Austria and Prussia; it ushered in a prolonged period, ending only in the 1850s, when Vienna and Berlin were often in alliance, under the leadership of the former, while the competition between the two for hegemony in Germany was suppressed rather than resolved. Bismarck, commenting on the Convention of Reichenberg in his *Reflections and Reminiscences*[7] considered that the authority of Prussia in the European concert of powers had been needlessly wasted.

The French Revolution was now increasingly preoccupying the makers of Prussian policy. Hertzberg's day was done and Bischoffwerder became the King's most influential adviser on foreign policy. Frederick William II now felt strongly the pull of monarchical solidarity in face of the events in France. He was one of the principal promoters of the policy enshrined in the Declaration of Pillnitz of August 1791—that the position of the French monarch was of concern to all European sovereigns. He believed that the much-vaunted Prussian army could easily overcome the revolutionary rabble. In 1792 the war against France began, precipitated from Paris, and Prussian arms were at first successful. They received a check at the famous cannonade of Valmy in September 1792, of which Goethe was an eye witness. Thereafter the fortunes of war fluctuated and in spite of the growing number of countries that joined the anti-French coalition no decisive victory could be won against the Revolution.

Frederick William, in spite of the anti-revolutionary ideology that enveloped his court, became more concerned with affairs in Eastern Europe, where the opportunity of territorial aggrandisement at the expense of Poland beckoned. Prussia, moreover, had to maintain her stake in the Polish question against her rivals Russia and Austria. Such considerations of territory and power soon took precedence over the ideological and even national German and imperial motives which had inspired the crusade against the revolution. Two further partitions of Poland in 1793 and 1795 brought about the complete extinction of the Polish state. This was a worse offence against the established order and the principle of self-determination, though this was hardly yet an accepted idea, than the first partition perpetrated by Frederick and Catherine the Great. This time the Poles had genuinely tried to put their house in order and they fought fiercely against their final doom under Tadeusz Kosciusko. Catherine the Great took the lead in the extinction of Poland and in 1795 Prussia obtained her share of the spoils only with difficulty. As a result of these partitions Prussia increased her territory by over a third and added 2½ million inhabitants to her population. In 1795 some 3½ million out of her total population of 7½ million were of Polish nationality. Warsaw was now part of Prussia.

These acquisitions in the East contrast strangely with the policy of surrender in the West. Prussia was financially exhausted and her dependence on foreign, particularly British, subsidies had almost reduced her again to the position she held at the beginning of the 18th century. In 1795 Prussia retired ingloriously from the French war. In the Treaty of Basle she withdrew her troops from the left bank of the Rhine and ceded to France those parts of the Cleves-Jülich territories that lay west of the river. The cession was to take effect if France could maintain her position on the left bank of the Rhine and it was understood that in this case Prussia was to be compensated, possibly from secularised ecclesiastical territories. The King of Prussia was called the Judas of the Empire for his surrender, unjustly perhaps, for the Emperor made his own peace with France only a little later. The war against the Revolution had, anyhow, never been popular with the majority of the German educated classes. None could foresee at this stage that the situation would give Napoleon the chance to defeat most of the major powers of Europe piecemeal. The events of the 1790s show to what extent Prussia was still a dynastic state and completely divorced from any national sentiment. There was no doubt some feeling that in fighting the French Prussia was defending the Holy Roman Empire or even Germany, but it was neither widely shared nor clear-cut. The Polish acquisitions, though most of them were

soon to be temporarily lost again, turned Prussia into a bi-national
state and many distinguished Polish or Lithuanian noble families,
like the Radolins and the Radziwills, became prominent in the
service of the Prussian kings. The Polish territories did not become
a source of strength to Prussia : they were economically backward
and in no way helped to stave off the Prussian defeat of 1806.
However, the decade of peace which the Treaty of Basle provided
for north Germany made it possible for the German intellectual
renaissance to continue to flourish uninhibited by immediate political pressures.

The accession of Frederick William III in 1797 brought great
changes at the top. The permissive atmosphere of the Court came
to an abrupt end. The new King was simple, sober and almost
bourgeois in style. He was deeply religious; but he had also imbibed the rationalist and humanist ideas of the Enlightenment. His
tutor in law and politics was Suarez, one of the men responsible
for the new legal code promulgated in 1794. Frederick William
III's weakness was a damaging mixture of diffidence and obstin-
acy : he feared to commit himself and entirely lacked the *élan* to
take great decisions. His wife, Princess Luise of Mecklenburg-
Strelitz, with whom he lived in happy domesticity, was more
spirited and grew to heroic stature in the days of Prussia's defeat
and humiliation. Frederick William, in spite of his weaknesses,
remained, like his father, an absolute ruler. But whereas the result
with Frederick William II had been the predominance of favourites like Wöllner and Bischoffwerder, the son, a man of greater
application, fell under the sway of those officials most frequently
in personal contact with him. These were his cabinet secretaries;
men who in his great-uncle's reign had merely carried out the
King's orders now gained much influence over policy. Among
them were Mencken, Bismarck's maternal grandfather, Lombard,
a son of a French wig-maker settled in Berlin, Beyme, a distinguished
jurist of little political judgement, and Köckritz, the chief of the
King's cabinet. Ministers who had to take public responsibility for
policies and decisions felt affronted by this barrier between themselves and the King. This was the reaction of Hardenberg, the
principal minister responsible for foreign affairs, who became one
of the central figures in Prussian affairs during the Reform era.
Another minister who shared responsibility for foreign policy, Haugwitz, took the opposite line and tempered his course to the prevailing wind from the royal cabinet. The result was the fatal vacillation
that finally led to Prussia's doom.

In domestic affairs the reign of Frederick William III produced
some effort at reform. Many leading officials and to some extent

the King himself were influenced by Kantian moral ideals. The profound changes in France in the revolutionary and consular period also made an impact in Prussia and impressed on many the need for change. There was, however, no presentiment either at court or in the bureaucracy that the Frederician state, was on the verge of collapse. The reason for the collapse was, in the last resort, nothing more nor less than military defeat. Shortcomings in the civil administration or the structure of society could have responded to remedial treatment. The army, however, had always been the central pillar of the Prussian state and when it was shattered all else was called into question. The war of 1792–5 had shown weaknesses in the Prussian military establishment and a Commission to suggest reforms was appointed. None of these were very effective because there were too many obstacles; the King's indecision, the conflict between different military authorities, the powerful vested interests arising from the identification of Junker aristocracy and officer corps, all these frustrated any radical change. In addition, the financial exhaustion of Prussia after the Peace of Basle made it imperative to save on what had always been the largest item in the budget, military expenditure. There were weaknesses in the officer corps itself : the young sons of Junker families, who made up the bulk of it, were utterly uneducated and quite incapable of appreciating changes in the art of war. Senior officers were absurdly over-age : over half the generals in the Prussian army in 1806 were over sixty.[8] The admission of non-nobles to the officer corps was considered, but there was too much resistance to it. The Prussians were proud of the many exceptions to their cantonal system which left large sections of the population unmolested by military service. Those who served were inadequately paid and had to have a lot of time off to follow a civilian calling as well. The Prussians believed they had the best of both worlds, military efficiency and undisturbed trade, but in fact a large part of their army was manned by foreigners and of doubtful reliability. A militia system, which might have been more appropriate to military conditions as they were at the turn of the century, posed insuperable problems for an authoritarian state like Prussia.

Reforms in the civil sphere were hardly more effective. The spur of necessity was lacking and Prussia, sheltered by neutrality, felt herself safe from domestic upheavals of the French kind. Frederick William III, however, was full of good intentions and wanted to carry out in a slow and gradualist fashion some of the changes which had come about precipitately in France. On the royal domain a minor emancipation of serfs was carried out.

Peasants were turned into proprietors and freed from service obligation, in return for the payment of rents, and their hereditary servile status (*Erbuntertänigkeit*) was brought to an end. The King would have liked to have extended the reforms to Junker estates, but the combined resistance of the nobility and officialdom frustrated him. Frederick William I and his son had exerted persistent pressure to improve the treatment and security of tenure of peasants and in their dealings with their own Crown peasants had tried to set an example to the Junkers. Their success was limited and Frederick William III did not fare much better. Moreover, if peasants on private estates had been set free then the "Bauernschutz", the regulations of Frederick the Great protecting peasants against eviction, would also have to go. This in turn would mean fewer hearths to feed the army's cantonal system. Thus one change would have necessitated a fundamental reappraisal of the whole system. The King lacked the force of will to face up to this and when the international situation became menacing again after 1803 the opportunity slipped by. An attempt to improve the financial situation of the state by ending some of the tax exemptions of the nobility came to grief on the same obstacles. The Junkers, like the army, were too deeply embedded in the fabric of the Prussian state to be deprived of their privileges without a major upheaval. In spite of the increasing acceptance of free market and free trade economic doctrines, little change was as yet made in the mercantilist and interventionist policies of the 18th century. The King himself sensed that the whole Prussian system, whether in the military, administrative, social or economic sphere, had become brittle and might not survive another collision. This awareness sapped his ability to act in the swiftly changing and dangerous international scene.

In 1801 the Peace of Lunéville had finally set the seal on the French acquisition of the left bank of the Rhine. Prussia now received the compensation from ecclesiastical territory for which she had been waiting since 1795 : parts of Münster, Paderborn, Hildesheim and some smaller territories. In outward appearance she was now bigger than ever. She had also taken control of the Hohenzollern territories in Franconia, Ansbach-Bayreuth. Under the brilliant administration of Hardenberg these were turned into an important Prussian power base in south Germany. But outward appearances were deceptive : in addition to her internal weakness Prussia found herself in a position of little respect between the growing and militant power of Bonapartist France, the massive Russian colossus, the ubiquitous maritime and financial strength of Britain and the still considerable resources of the Habsburgs.

This was brought home more than ever to the Prussians when after the brief respite of the Peace of Amiens the French occupied neighbouring Hanover in 1803. Opinion in Prussia was now deeply divided and official policy timid and vacillating. On the one hand there were those who approved of Napoleonic France and regarded her as Prussia's natural ally. This view had much support at Court and in the army. Colonel von Massenbach, an influential military figure, consistently held this opinion. The most fully-developed statement of the pro-French position was to be found in the works of Friedrich Buchholz, a prolific writer and journalist. In his *New Leviathan,* published in 1805, he advocated a radical despotism of which he considered Napoleon the most shining practical example. It was up to an enlightened despot, with radical ideas of social reform, to strike a proper balance between individual desires and the common good. Prussia's place was in the universal system of progressive social relations and peace to be established by Napoleon. The real menace, according to Buchholz, came from Britain, a country with an antiquated political system, driven by her own inadequacies and by her mercantilist rapaciousness to impose her hegemony over other nations.[9]

As against the pro-French view, there was a rising tide of opinion in Prussia which looked at her great western neighbour with apprehension. Many of those who had earlier hailed the Revolution were now disillusioned with Napoleon; the ideological opposition to the War of the First Coalition was giving way to fear of the French military menace. The most prominent writer taking a consistently anti-French, anti-revolutionary view was Friedrich von Gentz. He had from the early 1790s conceived a deep loathing of the Revolution as a force disturbing all balance and moderation in human affairs. He had translated Burke's *Reflections* into German. He was an official of the General Directory in Prussia, but much of his energy was devoted to writing. Gentz admired the British constitution and saw in Britain the natural protector of continental nations against French hegemony. He wanted the two principal German powers, Austria and Prussia, to bury the hatchet permanently and stand together against France. In 1801 he accepted a British subsidy, left Prussia in disgust at the policy of neutrality and went to Vienna. Later he became an influential figure in the entourage of Metternich and in the conservative policies of the Restoration period. Buchholz and Gentz stand at opposite ends of the spectrum of opinion after the Peace of Lunéville; the majority of the intellectual community remained indifferent to politics and under the umbrella of Prussian neutrality continued to be detached spectators of the troubled European scene.

The confusion of opinion is reflected in the uncertainties of Prussian policy. There were tempting offers from Napoleon : Hanover was to be handed over to Prussia and Frederick William, who had been quick to recognize the Corsican's imperial title, was to become North German Emperor. Such an arrangement would have left Prussia a French satellite and the King recoiled from so presumptuous yet empty a title. Hardenberg laboured to keep relations friendly with Russia and when the break came between Alexander and Napoleon, he cherished the vain hope of mediation. Yet there were moments in the autumn of 1805 when Russia rather than France appeared more threatening for Prussia. When shortly afterwards Alexander visited the Prussian royal couple at Potsdam, however, and stood at midnight by the tomb of Frederick the Great it seemed the prelude to Prussia joining the Third Coalition. Frederick William was permanently antagonized by the invasion of the Ansbach-Bayreuth territories by French troops on their way to Ulm. But just when he seemed finally inclined to listen to those who wanted war with France, the battle of Austerlitz on 2nd December 1805 smashed the Third Coalition.

Now Prussia was forced into the French orbit after all, under increasingly humiliating conditions. In the Treaty of Schönbrunn Prussia became Napoleon's ally and ceded Ansbach to Bavaria, a French satellite, and Cleves, Wesel and Neufchâtel to France. In return she received Hanover from Napoleon's hand, a country that was not his to give. This inevitably embroiled Prussia with England; previously this relationship had been governed by the strictest neutrality and Prussia had thus saved her maritime trade. Nonetheless the acquisition of Hanover, even under such circumstances, was potentially of considerable importance to Prussia's position in north Germany. The Treaty of Paris of February 1806 made the Prussian situation as an ally of France even more onerous. All Prussian ports had to be closed to English trade. Even now the relations between Paris and Berlin were marked by deep suspicion on Napoleon's side and intense embitterment on the part of Frederick William III. Some of the Prussian King's advisers—for example Lombard and Haugwitz—wanted a genuine collaboration with France. They had some backing in the press and even in the army.

The King and the public generally were increasingly inclined to listen to the war party. The humiliating position into which Prussia had been led was deeply resented by men who were already wielding influence and were to become famous after the collapse. Among them were Scharnhorst and Blücher in the Army; Stein who had made his name in administering territories acquired by

Prussia after the Peace of Lunéville, and Hardenberg who had now withdrawn from his public position—due to pressure from Paris, so it was widely believed. Stein drafted a memorandum in which the blame for Prussia's luckless policies was laid on the Prussian form of government from the King's cabinet, on that division of responsibility between the advisers immediately surrounding the King and ministers charged with the public execution of policies. The memorandum was couched in such strong language that the Queen did not dare to pass it to her husband. A more moderately worded one did reach him and was ungraciously received. In the preparation of it the initiative was taken by Prince Louis Ferdinand. This lively member of the ruling House had taken a full part in the intellectual life of Berlin, had been a frequent visitor of Rachel's salon, and was now filled with patriotic fervour. He was killed in the first few days of the war, towards which Prussia was now drifting irresistibly. In August 1806 news reached Berlin that Napoleon was contemplating an agreement with Britain over the return of Hanover. French troops were still occupying Prussian territory in west Germany and an ultimatum was sent demanding their withdrawal. By September Prussia and France were at war. Yet there had been no diplomatic preparation for this fateful step, either with Russia or with Austria.

It was a war begun under the most unfavourable circumstances imaginable. Had it been fought a year earlier Prussia could have been the member of a powerful coalition. Defeat was almost inevitable and would probably have come even if Prussia had not had the administrative and social weaknesses that beset her. The military backwardness, however, which was now glaringly revealed, made the collapse swift and devastating. Only the German word "Zusammenbruch", so frequently used after 1918 and 1945, adequately describes what happened.

The Prussian armies moved slowly south to meet the French thrust from the strong position which Napoleon had made for himself in south Germany. At first it was planned that the Prussians should cross the Thuringian mountains in separate columns and then converge, but logistically they were no match for their enemy, who moved rapidly to meet them. Even Yorck von Wartenburg, who at this time commanded Prussia's most mobile regiment, the Jäger, began the campaign encumbered with a massive amount of personal baggage which disappeared in the confusion of defeat.[10] A last-minute attempt to bring the Prussian armies together north of the mountains was frustrated by Napoleon's swift manoeuvre and they went to their doom in two separate battles fought on the same day, 14th October 1806, within a few miles of each other : at Jena Napoleon utterly routed a Prussian army under Prince Hohenlohe; at Auerstädt the Prussian main army, at first under the old Duke of Brunswick and then directed by the King personally, was only slightly less severely beaten by Marshal Davout.

The double disaster brought about a complete collapse of morale. The Prussian armies retreated in disorder and dissolution across the Elbe. Formations which had not been involved in the great battles or survived them frequently surrendered without a fight, as did many fortresses (for example, Magdeburg, Spandau and Stettin), and even the redoubtable Blücher, who retreated on Lübeck with the remnants of one army, was able to hold out only a little longer. The King and Queen, both caught up in the head-long retreat, were reunited at Küstrin on the Oder. Most of the King's ministers and officials left Berlin without making any attempt to deny its resources to the enemy, and Napoleon entered the Prussian capital in triumph on 27th October 1806. The governor of the city, Count Schulenburg-Kehnert, was a typical product of the old Prussian bureaucracy and had worked his way painstakingly up the administrative ladder. Before leaving his post to rejoin the King he issued a proclamation which contained a phrase that was to become proverbial : "The preservation of calm is the citizen's first duty". This seemed to sum up much of what the Prussian state stood for.

The war was, however, not yet over. Napoleon's terms were the cession of all Prussian territory west of the Elbe, but he soon changed his mind and, seeing the degree of Prussian disintegration, offered only an armistice. His main enemy was England. To make the Continental Blockade effective he needed the co-operation of Russia; he was about to force Russia to fall in with his design and for this purpose the help of Prussia could still be useful. Napoleon's intention to push Prussia into a war against Russia was more than anything responsible for Frederick William's decision to continue the war against France. He took this decision five weeks after Jena and against the advice of a majority of his ministers, but the link with Russia had been the basis of his policy for some years. If Prussia had not continued the war against France she would probably have passed completely into the Napoleonic orbit and the conditions under which any reform might have been taken in hand would have been very different. As it was, the basis was laid for the survival of Prussia as a truncated buffer-state. In the meantime Napoleon's sphere of power expanded steadily while the Prussian court moved farther and farther east, finishing up in Memel, the most easterly city of the Hohenzollern monarchy. East

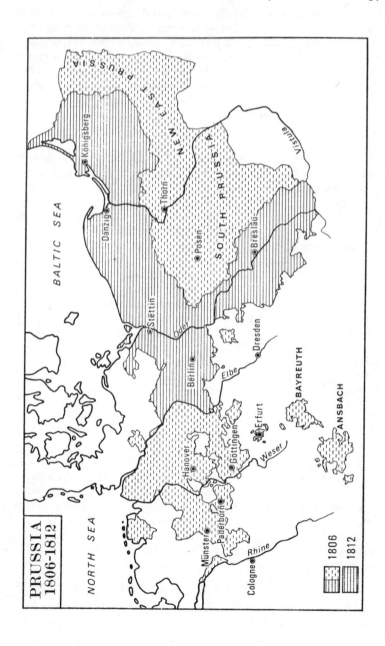

Prussia was becoming the main theatre of operations, though a few places farther west, notably Kolberg in Pomerania, under the command of Gneisenau, held out. The Prussians tried to strengthen their links with Russia. They also made peace with Britain, finally giving up Hanover, but concrete British aid in the form of subsidies was slow in coming. Austria remained obstinately neutral. Napoleon's lines of communication were also dangerously extended, however, and in February 1807 a French military setback at Eylau raised fresh hope that Russia supported by Prussia might yet retrieve the situation.

Hardenberg now again became the King's principal adviser on foreign affairs and he played the leading role in bringing about the Agreement of Bartenstein between Russia and Prussia. The two countries resolved to stand together; they envisaged throwing French power back beyond the Rhine, the restoration of Prussia to the state of 1805 and the creation of a German confederation led by Prussia and Austria to take the place of the defunct Holy Roman Empire. A settlement not unlike this eventually concluded the Napoleonic era, but for the moment these hopes were rudely shattered. After Napoleon's great victory at Friedland in June 1807, Alexander I's will to fight was sapped and he moved to reach an understanding with the French Emperor, largely at the expense of, and certainly without any consultation with, his Prussian ally. This was the Peace of Tilsit, to which Prussia had perforce to agree. Her territory and population were roughly halved : all territory west of the Elbe and Magdeburg were lost and even in the East all acquisitions subsequent to the first Polish partition had to be given up again. It was only Alexander's desire for a buffer state which allowed Prussia to survive; heavy French indemnities weighed on the rump that remained.

Such in bare outline were the course and consequences of Prussia's war against France. It came at the end of a period which from the point of view of power and military prowess was one of decline. "We went to sleep on Frederick's laurels ..." so Queen Luise put it in the days of Prussia's humiliation.[11] But the twenty years that had elapsed since the great Frederick's death were also a time of great cultural enrichment for Prussia as well as for Germany and this provided the main source for the regeneration and reform that were now to follow.

CHAPTER V

The Reform Era 1807–1813

THE years after the peace of Tilsit wrought a deep transformation in the structure and spirit of Prussia and for good or ill set the country in a pattern that remained basically unchanged until the period of German unification. The immediate result of the military collapse was, however, a profound confusion of values, attitudes and ideals. The future was completely uncertain and almost anything seemed possible.

A majority in Germany and even in Prussia probably still felt that the Germans had no particular reason to be concerned about French hegemony in Europe and should accept without qualms the benefits of Napoleon's rule. Many great Germans, from Goethe to Hegel, admired Napoleon : under the impact of the Battle of Jena Hegel called him "the Weltgeist on a horse". In southern and western Germany there was a general predisposition to work within the French system and some states, notably Bavaria, had found their position greatly enhanced by Napoleon. If Prussia had not gone to war at the eleventh hour she might well have taken her place in Napoleon's European scheme without too much strain. There had always been an affinity between Prussia and France and it had been no mere accident that the two countries had so often been in alliance. Now that the opposite course had ended in disaster there were many, both inside and outside the country, prepared to moralize over Prussia's downfall. Von Cölln, a Prussian official and also a prolific writer, wrote copiously about the shortcomings of the Prussian state since the death of Frederick the Great. He made sweeping accusations concerning the military collapse and the premature surrender of fortresses. His view now was that Prussia must seek salvation within the Napoleonic orbit and that domestic reforms to end the predominance of the nobility were necessary. His opinions following the defeat were close to those of Buchholz who had long advocated a new European order under Bonapartist aegis. Buchholz was now at the height of his prestige. He saw the future of Prussia as part of the Napoleonic system, like the Kingdom of Westphalia or Bavaria, which under its reformer Montgelas he regarded as the model German state. He felt that the very idea of Prussia, artificial as it was, should now disappear.

The social structure should be radically reformed along the lines of "la carrière ouverte aux talents". Buchholz was still a man of the Enlightenment, to whom nationality meant nothing and who was looking for a rational, effective system of government. Long ago Prussia was foremost among states in providing it; now Napoleonic France was the leading example and likely to spread it throughout the civilized world. The Swiss historian Johannes von Müller, a man of great reputation throughout Germany and speci-ally in Prussia, was also advocating an accommodation with Napo-leon, but his political position was quite different from that of Buchholz. Before Jena Müller had been a leading promoter of the revival of interest in the middle ages; this in turn had made him into one of those who built up German awareness of their national characteristics and their past. He had advocated an alliance of Austria and Prussia against French hegemony and in his immediate political aims he was close to Gentz. After Jena he lost heart and began to see in Napoleon an instrument of Providence. In a lecture which he delivered in French-occupied Berlin on Frederick the Great he celebrated him as one who had brought together the spirit of France and the glory of Prussia. To Müller the choice for Germany was now between France and Russia and he preferred France.

Views such as those of Buchholz and Johannes von Müller were freely voiced in Berlin, not only under French occupation, but also when the Prussian administration was re-established after the with-drawal of French troops. In the rest of Germany the fate of Prussia did not necessarily arouse sympathy. Even those who felt stirrings of German patriotism and hatred for the French con-queror were not always enamoured of Prussia. In Hanover there was a disposition to welcome the Prussians in 1806 after a period of French control. This feeling quickly evaporated once the Prus-sians had actually taken over and the Hanoverians' long-standing fear of being absorbed into the Prussian military state reasserted itself. There can be no doubt that the majority of the population were proud of the British connection, attached to the Guelph dynasty and believed their relatively free political system to be much superior to the Prussian. Ernst Moritz Arndt, one of the fathers of German nationalism, was another who felt little sym-pathy for Prussia at this stage. He was a Protestant from north Germany, having been born on the island of Rügen off Pomerania, when it was under Swedish sovereignty. Yet he considered that the Prussia created by Frederick the Great had been largely responsible for the disasters of Germany. He felt it to be a creation based on alien principles which had finally shattered the traditional structure of the Holy Roman Empire and its component states.

If North German Protestants could feel like this about Prussia it is not surprising that those whose allegiance lay with the South and Catholicism remained unmoved by the collapse of the Hohenzollern state. The Romantics, insofar as they developed political opinions and interests, tended to look to Austria and the Habsburgs. Friedrich Schlegel had become preoccupied with the problem of nationhood and was extolling the virtues and the harmonies of the German middle ages. He became a Roman Catholic and in 1808 went to Vienna. He spoke of Berlin as the "German Babel". As a man of action he was immensely ineffectual, yet he nursed the ambition of achieving political importance and hoped to do so in the Austrian service. The case of Adam Müller was more complex. This native of Prussia is now regarded as the most authentic progenitor of the Romantic conservatism, the prevalence of which distinguished 19th-century Germany from the liberal West. As a student at Göttingen, situated in the Electorate of Hanover, he had caught something of the Anglomania so common in many quarters on the Continent. The Englishman who influenced him most was Burke; Gentz, Burke's German translator, was his mentor and life-long friend. Gentz, however, although often associated with political Romanticism and catholicizing tendencies in politics, was still a man of the Enlightenment and of 18th-century rationalism. He believed in order, balance and moderation, and abhorred enthusiasm. Müller, on the other hand, evolved a political philosophy in which the mystique of tradition, the instincts of the folk community, the organic nature of the state and the wisdom enshrined in inherited institutions, held a central place. He claimed that he understood the deeper meaning of Burke better than it had ever been grasped in England.

In 1805, at the age of twenty-five, Müller became a Roman Catholic. Between 1805 and 1809 he lived in Dresden, where he wrote and lectured, always against the spirit of French rationalism, the Revolution, and the mechanical and doctrinaire approach to social problems. Many of the twists and turns of his life can only be explained by his desperate desire for position, power and influence, goals which were difficult to attain for a man of relatively humble birth. Thus he returned to Prussia in 1809. He hoped to find employment under Hardenberg, who paid him a retainer for journalistic work. When his hopes of Hardenberg were disappointed he turned to the conservative Prussian opposition, led by Marwitz, who were fighting the reform movement every inch of the way. Müller's rebuttal of economic liberalism and the high role

he allotted to the nobility as the true guardians of social continuity naturally appealed to the Prussian Junkers. Finally, when
Müller realized that his Catholicism would prevent him from ever
gaining a high position in Prussia, he went to Vienna and entered
the Austrian service. The case of Adam Müller, even if vitiated by
mere careerism, shows only too well the great maelstrom of conflicting currents on the German scene : German patriotism flowed
with and sometimes against Prussian, Austrian and other particularist loyalties; all these ties were complicated by the potent
emotions of pro-revolutionary and conservative sentiment; Romanticism clashed with the still powerful forces of rationalism; neo-
humanist German idealism remained essentially cosmopolitan, while
the need to adjust to the stark facts of French power tossed men
hither and thither.

It is hardly surprising that in this welter of opinions, the product
of a historical situation in which an infinity of possibilities seemed
open, one strand has come in for particular attention : the marriage
of rising German nationalism with the Prussian state, reforming
itself and taking the lead in the struggle against France. At the
highest intellectual level this union was accomplished by Fiche.
Born the son of a weaver in Saxony, he had sprung to fame when
his first major work was thought to have been written by Kant.
His own philosophical system evoked enthusiasm by its taut, almost
mathematical construction. Friedrich Schlegel called the French
Revolution, Fichte's philosophy and Goethe's *Wilhelm Meister* the
greatest "tendencies" of the age. At the University of Jena his
compelling personality and great gifts as a teacher brought him a
large following, but he soon made many enemies. He was a man
of steely will, incapable of concession for the sake of peace and
amity, who was relentlessly concerned to press his superior vision
of truth and morality upon the world. Schiller, with whose moral
idealism he had much in common, broke with him; Kant in the
end disowned him. When he tried to reform student life at Jena
the students turned against him; the authorities suspected him of
atheism and with the consent of Goethe he was deprived of his
chair at Jena in 1799. Goethe took offence, not so much at Fichte's
opinions, as at his mode of expressing and conducting himself.
Fichte then moved to the more tolerant atmosphere of Berlin,
but he also toyed with the idea of going to Mainz to accept a post
at a university to be created under French aegis. Fichte was and
essentially always remained universalist and cosmopolitan in his
views. The state was to him an entirely rational construction, the
highest purpose of which was to enable man to function as a moral
being and to educate him to realize his full moral and cultural

potential. Right up to the Prussian collapse of 1806 he continued to feel that revolutionary France came closest to realizing his ideal of a rational polity and that his allegiance lay with the new France. On the other hand he felt enough of an obligation to Prussia as the state within which he lived to flee with the Prussian court to Königsberg after the battle of Jena. He offered to serve with the army as a kind of lay padre. The shattering events of those days and the acute suffering produced by the war and the French conquest disillusioned him with Napoleonic France. More positively he became aware that his idea of the moral, educated man was in fact a national ideal, tied to a particular national heritage and language.

This metamorphosis in Fichte's thinking forms the background to his famous "Addresses to the German Nation" delivered in Berlin in the winter of 1807/08. Here he proclaimed that the full cultural and moral realization of man in his collective nature is only possible on the basis of national independence. The ultimate values, however, which Fichte wanted to safeguard, were universal and he was still far removed from demanding a German national state as a power. Even at this stage he only occasionally gave attention to the role of power in political affairs, for example in an essay on Machiavelli; in general this approach was entirely alien to him. At the time of the Wars of Liberation, Fichte toyed with the idea that Prussia might propel the Germans towards full nationhood; again not in the sense of erecting a German national state, but of enabling them, in the multiplicity of their separate states, to live fully as Germans. His emphasis on the importance of national education as the key to a full life led him to produce plans for a reformed system of higher education in Prussia. It was Wilhelm von Humboldt, not Fichte, who became responsible for the important educational innovations of the Reform era, but Fichte did become the first Rector of the newly founded University of Berlin in 1810. Fichte's writings and speeches were difficult to understand and it is unlikely that many of his contemporaries could follow the elaborations of his thinking. It was, however, significant that a man of his stature and authority should now preach German self-awareness and should do so in Berlin.

A similar contribution to the formation of patriotic opinion, not less than Fichte's, was made by Schleiermacher's sermons delivered at the Church of the Holy Trinity in Berlin in 1808. Schleiermacher went to Berlin when the French authorities closed the University of Halle and he refused to return to Halle when the University was reopened under the auspices of the Kingdom of Westphalia. He had for long been in fundamental opposition to the prevailing current of cosmopolitan rationalism and in his Berlin sermons he re-emphasized the Romantic view of the state as an organism and its deep roots in nationality and history. He regarded the Prussian defeat as an opportunity for the Germans to become fully conscious of themselves. Schleiermacher was, like Fichte, at too exalted a level to be understood by many : one sarcastic comment was that he was heard only by some Moravian brothers, some Jews, baptized or otherwise, some philosophers and philologists and a few elegant ladies.[1] Even if Fichte's and Schleiermacher's direct impact was confined to certain select intellectual circles, the views of these prestigious personalities could not but have wider reverberations. It is, however, noteworthy that while both of them advocated German patriotism, they did so from very different fundamental positions. Schleiermacher was part of the reaction against rationalism; his religious views were in the Pietist tradition which had been so important in Prussia and had never been entirely eclipsed by the Enlightenment. This Pietist feeling now became an increasingly important ingredient in the recrudescence of nationalism, especially among conservatives. Fichte on the other hand remained in the cosmopolitan, rationalist, pro-revolutionary stream even when he proclaimed German national consciousness : his ultimate values were universal and transcended nationality.

At a much lower intellectual level than Fichte or Schleiermacher, but of more direct political influence, was Friedrich Ludwig Jahn, better known as Turnvater Jahn. Of the many men who nurtured German nationalism, he was one of the few who was a Prussian patriot before he became a German patriot. A native of Brandenburg, he was proud of his Prussian birth and felt that the Prussians, conscious of the traditions of Frederick the Great, were apart from and superior to other Germans. The events of 1806, the influence of Arndt and of Fichte's *Addresses* turned him into an ardent German patriot. Like Arndt, but with less balance and more aggression, he developed a mystical attachment to the German Volk which had many of the overtones of modern racism. His virulent attacks on French and other Western influences in Germany helped to give German nationalism its anti-Western twist. In his invective Jahn often descended to a deplorable level and revealed his intellectual poverty, but did give emotional drive to the nationalist movement. Jahn's practical importance lies in the fact that he advocated the formation of free corps of nationalist volunteers, and such corps fought in the Wars of Liberation in 1813; he formed gymnastic associations, to which he gave the name "Turnerschaften", to train nationally minded youths and develop their will power and discipline; and after 1815 he played a leading role in the nationalist student associations, the "Burschenschaften", which kept nationalism alive in the Metternich period. Many nationalist movements of the future made use of such devices.

The patriotic movement in Prussia had growing literary backing. The greatest of the literary men who were seized by patriotic fervour after 1806 was Heinrich von Kleist. He came of a Junker family distinguished in the annals of Prussia before and after him. He was caught up in the Romantic movement, fired by Kant's philosophy and plunged into despair by the gulf between Kant's ideal morality and the corruption of real life. Rousseau was always on his lips, yet he came to see France, when he lived there for a while, as a corrupt nation. He acquired education relatively late in life and began to write. He made little immediate impact, but after his death he came to be recognized as the greatest dramatist among the Romantics. Kleist did not concern himself deeply with politics until he lived in Dresden in 1807. The city was at this time a centre of anti-French sentiment: Kleist acquired a fierce hatred of Napoleon and passionate German patriotism. His feeling for Germany made him regard loyalties to particular German states as of secondary significance, but he was by birth and background so much a Prussian that his German and Prussian sentiments often became inextricably intermixed in his creative work. This is very evident, for example, in his play *The Prince of Homburg* which deals with the Great Elector's famous victory at Fehrbellin. At Dresden Kleist fell under the spell of Adam Müller and he later collaborated with him in editing a newspaper in Berlin, the *Abendblätter*, which expressed the conservative, romantic, anti-French point of view. Kleist and Müller were in fact men of a very different kind and outlook; the latter was a subtle political thinker, but also a time-server and careerist; Kleist on the other hand was a creative genius, courageous to the point of recklessness, but not a systematic political theorist. Kleist was by no means committed to the conservative political Romanticism of Müller and of many of his literary colleagues. In some of his writings he had been strongly anti-authoritarian and he was quite prepared to accept liberal reform in Prussia, if this would contribute to strengthening the country against France and Napoleon.

Both Kleist and Müller were members of the *Christlich-deutsche Tischgesellschaft*, which was founded in Berlin towards the end of 1810 and met weekly. It was conservative and patriotic in attitude and formed a link between the politico-intellectual Romantics and the Prussian aristocracy. Twenty, even ten, years earlier the

salons of Berlin had still been dominated by the ideas of cosmopolitan Enlightenment; now conservative Romanticism, buttressed
by revived Pietist sentiment, was in the ascendant. It was also
significant that earlier the salons of rich, emancipated Berlin Jewry
were in the lead; Jews, unless baptized, were expressly barred from
the Christlich-deutsche Tischgesellschaft. All members of this group
were German and Prussian nationalists; but most of them were so
conservative and committed to a restoration of the *ancien régime*
that they could not stomach liberal reforms, especially those brought
forward under Hardenberg, even though these reforms were also
largely inspired by patriotic, anti-French motives. The Christlich-
deutsche Tischgesellschaft included some of the Romantic writers
and poets of the Heidelberg school, notably Arnim and Brentano.
The Heidelberg Romantics, among whom the brothers Grimm and
the poet Joseph Görres are also to be counted, had put special
emphasis on the folkloristic aspect of Romanticism, the poetic
collective heritage of a people with all its legendary and mythical
overtones. Arnim and Brentano had brought out the famous collection of German folksongs "Des Knaben Wunderhorn". Arnim was
a member of a well-known Prussian Junker family and returned
to live on his estate; Brentano, his brother-in-law, also lived in
Prussia for a time.

No less important than the literary members of the conservative,
nationalist, Romantic movement were those whose main interest
lay in history and law. The Romantics had stressed the intercon-
nections that exist in the cultural life of a nation and how the
totality of cultural manifestations both constitutes and is inspired
by the national spirit. An awareness of history was one of the
principal attitudes distinguishing the Romantics from the rational-
ists of the Enlightenment. Historians and lawyers thus had much
to contribute to arousing nationalist emotions and the foremost
among them were Niebuhr, Savigny and Eichhorn. Niebuhr was
both man of affairs and academic. He was called into the Prussian
service by Stein in 1806 and stayed till 1810 and later he was
Prussian ambassador to the Vatican. As a historian his most famous
work was his Roman history. He admired Rome in its heroic age,
when it was a peasant republic, before commercial sophistication
brought about decadence. He approved the Roman balance between the patricians and the masses and for the same reason he
was drawn to the British Constitution. He was a Romantic in that
he derived from the past an attachment to conservative values
and opposed the destructive power of progressive ideas. On the
other hand the mystical element in Romanticism repelled him and
he had no sympathy with the many unbalanced personalities

among the Romantics. He was a Prussian rather than a German patriot: at the time of the Wars of Liberation he advocated the aggrandisement of Prussia at the expense of minor states like Saxony.

Savigny and Eichhorn were both historians of law and stressed that the legal order grew out of the spirit and the customs of a nation. This view of law as a product of history ran right counter to the concept of natural law which had bulked so large in the age of rationalism and among the ideas of the French Revolution. Savigny had many links with the Romantic movement; during two years as a professor at the Bavarian University of Landshut he had acquired a sympathetic understanding of Catholicism and in Berlin he was a member of the Christlich-deutsche Tischgesellschaft. His views were profoundly conservative in the Burkeian sense and he had a keen feeling for German traditions. He was opposed to the adoption of what he considered alien principles, such as those enshrined in the Code Napoléon and to the very idea of codification. The influence of Savigny and the many literary and academic men associated with the political side of Romanticism reached its peak in Prussia only after 1815. As long as the hegemony of Bonapartist France remained unbroken they strengthened the stream of patriotic opinion, Prussian or German, even if they were often opposed to the reform movement in Prussia.

Thus patriotism, even if not universally shared, was yet broadly based in Prussia after the catastrophe of 1806. A multitude of associations, best known among them the radical Tugendbund, disseminated nationalist sentiment among the more educated classes. Whether the patriotism was German or Prussian or a mixture of both varied from one individual to another. There were periods when the Napoleonic system appeared so firmly based, for example in 1809 after Wagram, that accommodation with it seemed the only realistic policy and at such times patriotism was under a cloud. The most serious complication was that the reform movement in Prussia had on the whole to take a liberal direction and ran into conservative opposition. This alienated the conservatives among the German patriots. Conservatives and liberals each had their dilemma. The conservatives looked forward to a rising against the French oppressor, but what they really wanted was a return to the *ancien régime* and what they most feared was a revolution. The liberal reformers had to regard revolutionary and Napoleonic France both as a model and as an oppressor. Nevertheless the desire to strengthen Prussia and with it Germany against French domination was the main driving force behind the reform movement. Underlying it there was also a widely accepted analysis of what had been responsible for Prussia's defeat and humiliation. The blame was laid on the mechanistic nature of the state founded by the great Hohenzollern rulers. It had failed to enlist, so ran the analysis, the participation of the broad mass of citizens; when the bureaucratic and military machine was crushed the event evoked nothing but apathy among the people. It was certainly true that there had been little resistance to the French invaders and that many state officials had hastened to show subservience to their new masters. The more immediate blame for the Prussian catastrophe was laid upon the misconceived system of responsibility at the top under Frederick William III, in consequence of which Prussian foreign policy had been so disastrously conducted; but the decline of the Prussian military machine since the days of its glory under Frederick the Great was the most glaring defect exposed by defeat.

The more generalized criticisms of the old Prussia could no doubt have been equally well levelled against almost any state in Europe other than revolutionary France, but the "contrived" nature of Prussia as a country made these shortcomings more damaging in her case. On the other hand, reform which was taking place in all parts of Germany directly or indirectly under French influence was now inevitable for Prussia also, but it was more significant there because of the modicum of independence which the country, truncated though it was by the Peace of Tilsit, still retained. The ideas which shaped the Prussian reform movement were still derived in part from the Enlightenment : rational social arrangements, efficient government and humanitarian considerations were the guiding lights. The movement also reflected the idealist philosophy of Kant and his successors : the cultivation of the morally responsible individual was seen as the highest function of the state. The French Revolution itself, its theories and practices, had a deep influence on the Prussian reformers. All of them were members of the Prussian high bureaucracy, some of them natives of Prussia, others long in the Prussian service, and yet others drawn there by German patriotism and anti-French feeling. The process by which non-noble and noble elements had become fused in this bureaucracy had progressed further since the days of Frederick the Great. By the turn of the century the criterion of selection for civil servants was no longer birth so much as "Bildung", that ideal of the educated man which had such a hold on the articulate classes of Germany. Reform was a movement from the top and could not have been effective without the support of the King. Frederick William III remained indecisive and timid, but the defeat had convinced him more than ever that reform was necessary and as long as he clung to that conviction it could proceed. The opposition to the reform movement frightened him, however, and he faltered; this was one of the reasons why the movement was only partially successful.

The three principal civilian figures of the reform era were Stein, Hardenberg and Wilhelm von Humboldt. Of these, Stein has always been considered the most significant in spite of the fact that he was in power only for a short time. The attitudes and ideas which inspired his work in Prussia were of great complexity and cannot be easily classified as liberal or conservative, rationalist or Romantic, German or Prussian. He was not of Prussian birth. His family had for generations been imperial knights and most of their possessions were situated in the area of Nassau and the valley of the Lahn. This is where Stein passed his youth, while his student days were spent at the University of Göttingen. Here he was much influenced, like so many others, by the study of English history and institutions. He made the deliberate choice of entering the Prussian service, rather than work for the Empire or the Austrians. This is perhaps a good indication of the hold which Frederick the Great had on the imagination of young Germans in the 1770s and '80s. Stein was a young man of high and progressive ideals : he wanted to improve the lot of his fellow Germans in a modern and humane manner and he thought he could best accomplish something worthwhile in the Prussian service. After completing his apprenticeship, he spent the first twenty years of his service in Prussia's western provinces.

The process of assimilating the administration of all Prussian territory to the general pattern, dictated in the main by military needs, had progressed less far in the West than in the rest of the Hohenzollern dominions. Vestiges of the old territorial estate governments remained effective and there was some participation in the administration at least by the nobility and the more substantial citizens of the towns. These western provinces had more affinity with neighbouring Holland than with the rest of Prussia. Stein's first few years in the Westphalian provinces were spent in the administration of mines and manufactures. Through practical experience he learnt to combine faith in economic liberalism with belief in the virtues of state action to promote welfare and social responsibility in economic affairs. This combination of individual enterprise tempered by state control was characteristic of the essentially ethical inspiration of Stein's work as an administrator and statesman : he wanted to cultivate the integrity of the self-reliant individual while ensuring that devotion to the general good would drive out personal egotism.

As Stein rose in the administrative hierarchy he became *Ober-präsident* (superior president) of all Westphalian War and Domain Chambers. In this capacity he had to meet and consult regularly with the provincial assemblies, mainly representative of the nobility, which in this part of Prussia had retained some powers. He valued these links between the bureaucracy, ultimately responsible to Berlin, and the local population. Stein regarded them as living symbols of a deeply rooted German tradition of representation which he did not want to see confined to the nobility. He thus believed in representation and participation, but from a point of view quite different from that which inspired the French Revolution. During the last two years of his provincial service, Stein was in charge of incorporating the two bishoprics of Münster and Paderborn into Prussia. They were part of the compensation Prussia received under the Treaty of Lunéville for the loss of her territories on the west bank of the Rhine. Stein tried to develop loyalty to their new country in the mainly Catholic populations of these two territories by acclimatizing them slowly to the demands of the Prussian military state. He wanted to preserve the local assemblies, free the peasants, and promote ambitious education reforms centred round the University of Münster. The Prussian bureaucracy paid little attention to his recommendations and he did not hold the appointment long enough to fight for his schemes.

In 1804 Stein was made a minister in the General Directory in Berlin. He became one of the ministers whose responsibilities were not for one particular province but extended over all Prussian territories except Silesia. Excise and manufactures, the bank, the salt monopoly and maritime affairs were under his direction. In modern parlance Stein discharged some of the functions of a minister of finance and trade; he became, within the limits set him, something like a Prussian Turgot. He accomplished distinguished work in rationalizing the administration of the salt monopoly, the excise tax and the tariff structure, and in rooting out inadequacies in the national bank. He had not been in office long before Prussia was sucked into the maelstrom of events from Austerlitz to Jena. As a German patriot and imperial knight, Stein felt strongly the humiliation of Prussian policy and the dismemberment of Germany. Yet at times he was inclined to make allowances for Prussian vacillations and to excuse the desperate attempt of the Prussian monarchy to survive amid the Napoleonic hurricane. He continued to be willing to serve Prussia provided she worked for her own and for Germany's regeneration. Thus he became one of that distinguished band of men who rebuilt the Prussian state. A first step was that audacious memorandum, drafted by Stein himself, on the reform of the King's Cabinet which even the Queen did not dare to hand to her husband.

Stein's background and development had made him into a German patriot, deeply conscious of his country's rich past, with which the destinies of his own family had been linked for so long. In his attitude there was however, also a strong element of that cosmopolitanism characteristic of the Enlightenment and of German humanist idealism. He believed in Germany because in his view the Germans were most likely to realize his ideal of the free individual who together with his fellows shapes his actions to an ethical code and subordinates narrow self-interest to the wellbeing of the community. In this Stein had much in common with Fichte. If the German states, foremost among them Prussia, were not able by their own exertions to recover their freedom, Stein was quite prepared to see foreign powers, Russia and above all Britain, assume the role of guardians of German integrity. When in the closing years of the Napoleonic era he was grappling with the problem of rolling back Bonapartist France and establishing a new European order, he frequently voiced the view that England should take over large parts of Northwestern Germany and become the leading power there. Even a liberal German historian like Meinecke, writing before 1914, considered such opinions on the part of Stein, Gneisenau and others, evidence of a yet insufficiently developed national consciousness.[2] In our own day, when the ultimate validity of national values has become more doubtful, we can well understand that the ideological conflict between tyranny, as represented by Napoleon, and freedom was more important to Stein than the strict assertion of national sovereignty.

Towards Prussia Stein's feelings were even more ambivalent. The Prussia of Frederick the Great attracted him because it was the most progressive and the most active German state. But his frequent struggles with the Prussian bureaucracy convinced Stein that Old Prussia was a machine state. Much of his activity as a reformer was directed towards making the Prussian state a living organism by going back to older German traditions of representation and participation. Stein had Prussian loyalties, but these could be overridden by his German sentiments; his ultimate ideals were ethical and universal. He was profoundly conservative, influenced by Burke, and had never any sympathy with the French Revolution or the ideas which inspired it. Yet as a reformer he was quite radical: he wanted to bring all classes of the community into an organic relationship with the state through representative institutions, and fought fiercely against the attempts of the nobility to monopolize these institutions.

Stein was so much a seminal figure in the reform movement that the paucity and unfinished nature of his practical achievements have hardly detracted from his standing as the greatest German statesman in the nineteenth century before Bismarck. By comparison Hardenberg's role has perhaps been underestimated. He again was not a Prussian, but a Hanoverian who had made his reputation in the 1790s in the administration of the Ansbach-Bayreuth territories after their incorporation into Prussia. He was far more than Stein a typical aristocrat of the *ancien régime,* thoroughly at home in the absolutist system of government of Frederician Prussia. He was sufficiently a man of the world and eclectic enough to be open to many influences. Thus he completely absorbed the ideas of the French Revolution and the practical lessons to be learnt from the post-revolutionary and Bonapartist methods of government. He did not hesitate to recommend their wholesale acceptance in Prussia after 1807. He was in this respect more radical than Stein, who harked back to older traditions. He was also thorough-going in his adherence to economic liberalism. Consequently Hardenberg was more hated by the conservative Junker opposition to reform than Stein. Yet Hardenberg was far more diplomatic and pliable and could often get his way, particularly with the King, where his more forthright colleague failed. Niebuhr said of Hardenberg that if he had thrown a man down the stairs one day he would let him get back through the window the next. Thus Hardenberg was able to hold office under the *ancien régime* in Prussia, become one of the principal reformers, and yet cling to power well into the period of Reaction. He identified himself with the Prussian governmental machine far more than Stein, for whom German sentiment or his universal ideals often took priority. Hardenberg was really at home in diplomacy and foreign affairs : the detailed work of domestic administration bored him. He certainly lacked Stein's moral fervour and reforming energy. Perhaps this is why, in spite of his considerable achievements in practice, he has always seemed a lesser figure of more short-term significance.

The third civilian reformer of outstanding stature was Wilhelm von Humboldt. Since the early 1790s when he had briefly held an official position in the Prussian judiciary, he had moved about the world a great deal. More than anybody he was on terms of friendship and familiarity with the great literary and intellectual men of Germany. In spirit he was perhaps closest to his friend Schiller, the poet of the classical age of German humanist idealism. As a personality, Humboldt was difficult to grasp.[3] Many regarded him as cold, detached, even ironical—a mere spectator. Others saw this detachment as a form of selflessness and Humboldt as a sensitive idealist too pure to be a man of action. His understanding of his many brilliantly creative friends was deep, but he himself lacked artistic creativity. As a philosopher and political thinker he was, however, signficant : the pillars of his thinking remained the Enlightenment and Kantian and post-Kantian idealism. Humboldt spent some years in Paris at the turn of the century and then moved to Rome, where he was Prussian representative at the Vatican from 1802 to 1808. His official duties burdened him little and he was able to live the life of a leisured aristocrat and writer. There was an element of self-indulgence and dilettantism in him. Power, the state, and nationality meant little to him, the self-perfection of the individual remained all-important. His appreciation of the languages and culture of the different peoples amongst whom he lived did, however, sharpen his understanding of national characteristics. A mixture of motives brought him into the reform movement in 1809 : the French occupation of the Papal States was threatening to end his diplomatic career in Rome and the Prussian catastrophe after Jena had aroused in him a sense of obligation to his native country; he who had been so much a spectator now felt the urge to take a hand in shaping the course of events. The brief period which he spent in charge of the Prussian educational system was in its way as important as Stein's brief tenure of power and its effect was felt for a long time to come. It was perhaps an indication of the metamorphosis which the Prussian state was undergoing that it could enlist the services of a man so lofty and spiritual in outlook as Humboldt.

The era of civil reform got properly under way when Stein took office as minister in principal charge of domestic and foreign affairs in October 1807. A previous attempt, a few weeks after Jena, to give him a place in the central direction of affairs had miscarried. Stein had insisted that ministers should communicate direct with the King, the chief point of the earlier memorandum which he had drafted. Frederick William could not bring himself to do without his one remaining cabinet councillor, Beyme. Finally, the King dismissed Stein with a letter couched in the language of an absolute ruler to his servant, accusing him of disobedience. Stein retired to Nassau, but if he was to resume his work for German regeneration and for his moral ideals the Prussian service remained his only opportunity. So great was his reputation that Frederick William for his part had no alternative but to turn to him a second time. Beyme very nearly proved an obstacle again, but the Queen's passionate entreaties convinced Stein that he must assume the burden even if the constitutional position was not all that he would have liked. Curiously enough Napoleon, who had earlier pressed for the dismissal of Hardenberg, favoured the appointment of Stein, assuming that the situation of his Nassau estates within the French orbit would provide a means of putting pressure on him. Within days of taking office Stein published the edict on the liberation of the peasants which, along with the reform of the towns and attempts at constitutional change, represents the major achievement of his ministry of fourteen months.

The liberation of the peasants was a matter which could brook no delay. On the royal domain the King had already set the peasants free before 1806. In neighbouring countries, for example in the Grand Duchy of Warsaw which included many of the Polish territories that had been acquired by Prussia in the Partitions, the peasants were being emancipated. The war itself, and particularly the Continental Blockade, had created such economic havoc that there was urgent need to modernize agricultural conditions. Thus the emancipation edict had already been prepared before Stein took office and his chief contribution to it was to extend its application to all Prussian provinces instead of only to East and West Prussia. The concomitant of declaring the peasants free was to end the regulations chiefly prompted by Frederick the Great which had hitherto protected the peasant-serfs against eviction. It was all-important how the general principles of the edict were to be applied in practice to the highly complex and infinitely variable relationships between the peasants and their lords. Stein's own view was that a happy mean should be struck between leaving the old ties between master and serfs intact, on one hand, and creating an entirely free market in land on the other, thereby removing all protection from the peasants. He was also not inclined to give way too much to the demands of the nobility that they should be compensated to the hilt for the loss of rights to land and to services from the peasants.

It took many years for new conditions to establish themselves in the various Prussian territories and Stein had by then long ceased to hold office. The regulations for East Prussia, issued in 1808, became the model for most subsequent edicts covering the rest of Prussia. They were the work of Shön and Schrötter; Schön particularly was an outstanding civil servant destined to play a great role in Prussia's most eastern province for many years to come. He was, however, far more than Stein, a wholehearted adherent of *laissez faire* economics, a true disciple of Adam Smith. Schön laid it down that the more recently created peasant holdings should be available for purchase by the manorial lord without restriction. In the case of older holdings, the estate owner could compensate himself for loss of peasant services by taking over up to half the holding; the remainder would be consolidated into viable allotments. Stein declared himself satisfied with these arrangements and shortage of credit made aggressive expansion of their estates by the Junkers impossible at that stage. But in course of time this type of settlement worked greatly to the advantage of the nobility.

Hardenberg, who held office after 1810, was much more of an economic liberal than Stein, but he was progressively more open to pressure from the Junkers who were rapidly recovering their power and confidence. An edict of Hardenberg's of 1811 applying general principles similar to those of the East Prussian regulations was never fully put into practice. Under it certain classes of peasants, in return for becoming freehold owners, had to surrender to their lords a third of their holdings. This was favourable enough to the nobility, but if it had been carried out it would have created a numerous free and economically viable peasantry. It was, however, Hardenberg's edict of May 1816 which really governed the conditions of most of the peasants for a long time to come. All smaller holdings created after the 17th century now retained their service obligations. Since the protective regulations no longer applied and the peasant was no longer personally tied to his lord, many of these small owners preferred to give up their holding rather than render services and the estate owner could simply take over their land. This meant that large numbers of peasants either became agricultural labourers or drifted into the towns, while large Junker estates could be created, particularly east of the Elbe.

The original intentions of the emancipation edict of 1807, particularly those of Stein, were thus largely falsified by the course of events. The nobility emerged greatly strengthened. The Junkers were so vital an element in Prussia that no reform could have been carried out against their interests but it should not have been necessary to load the dice quite so much in their favour. The edict of 1807 and other measures effectively brought to an end a society divided into Estates and substituted a society divided into economic classes, but the topmost of these classes was left in a very powerful economic, social and political position. Non-nobles were now entitled to buy noble land; given the weakness of the middle classes, however, this simply mean that those wealthy enough to become landowners were absorbed into the aristocracy and accepted their values. At the other end of the social scale, the opportunity was, nevertheless, used to create a quite significant independent peasant class.

The central idea animating Stein's reforms was to give the state greater organic life by securing the participation of the citizens at every level and by educating them to the tasks of self-government and responsible citizenship. Thus he outlined in his famous Nassau memorandum, composed in 1807 between his first and second ministry, a series of administrative and constitutional reforms designed to put these principles into operation from the local through the provincial to the central Government.[4] Only one of these, the reform of city government, was eventually put fully into practice and it represents Stein's greatest triumph. Cities and towns had always been weak in the Prussian territories with the possible exception of the western provinces; and only two or three cities, Berlin, Königsberg and perhaps Breslau, developed any vigorous life. Owing to the weakness of the municipal spirit it had been easy for rulers like the Great Elector and Frederick William I to subject the towns to central government control. This was done through the *Steuerrat* (tax commissioner) and the local garrison commander. The tax commissioners were now swept away and power was handed over to elected bodies. Deputies were elected from wards and from the assembly of deputies the executive members of the magistracies were in their turn chosen. In the bigger cities candidates for the post of burgomaster had to be presented for royal nomination. The number of salaried members of the magistracy was restricted and the burgomaster's term of office was limited to six years. Thus the scope for professional bureaucrats was deliberately reduced; on the other hand the ordinary elected town deputies were themselves associated with municipal administration. The privilege of municipal citizenship, and with it the vote, was not automatic, but had to be acquired; property qualifications were, however, fairly low. Another important aspect of this municipal reform was the separation of the judiciary from the administration. The dispensation of justice remained with the state and was thus independent of those holding executive power in the towns. Stein had many helpers in drafting his municipal reform edict, notably Frey, who was Director of Police at Königsberg, a post of wider significance than the modern meaning of the term would imply. Frey was one of the many high Prussian officials who had felt the influence of Kant. Frey introduced into the Prussian municipal legislation some clauses taken straight from the post-revolutionary French municipal laws. The lessons of France were inevitably never far from the minds of the Prussian reformers, but it remains true that Stein was harking back to older German practices of representation rather than looking to revolutionary France which he abhorred. The Prussian municipal reform was imposed from above with the aim of educating the urban middle class to self-government and civic pride. The Prussian cities became, and in spite of some later restrictions remained, islands of autonomy in a bureaucratic state.

Stein's other constitutional reforms were less completely successful. He had insistently demanded that the King should end government through cabinet councillors and this had been the cause of his brusque dismissal early in 1807. It was Hardenberg, thanks to his more diplomatic methods, who had induced the King to make these changes and to communicate direct with his ministers. When Stein resumed office it was in practice as Prime Minister : Hardenberg on his return to office in 1810 occupied the formal position of State Chancellor. Stein wanted to bring in something like cabinet government and would have liked the King to govern not with one predominant minister but through a "state council" of ministers. This did not suit the personality of Frederick William. Nevertheless, the central government was strengthened by the abolition of the General Directory, with its provincial division of work, and the appointment of five ministers dealing with the major aspects of government, foreign affairs, war, finance, justice and internal affairs.

Reorganization at the centre entailed changes in provincial government. Here the War and Domain Chambers were abolished as well as the old "Regierungen", the governments of the provincial diets whose functions had become mainly judicial. As in the towns, administration was now separated from judicial functions. The latter were vested in provincial courts, while administrative tasks were distributed round a number of departments all of them under a President, the so-called "Oberpräsident". The office of Oberpräsident became general in all Prussian provinces after 1815 and formed the link between provincial and central government. These positions came to be occupied by a number of outstanding public servants, such as Schön in East Prussia and Vincke in Westphalia, who enjoyed great prestige and loyalty in their own provinces as well as general recognition throughout Prussia. The Oberpräsident was not a despot, but merely the first in a collegiate system of departmental chiefs. This was a safeguard against arbitrary government, but it also led to much delay and bureaucratic red tape.

Stein would have liked to build into his new system of provincial government some kind of representative institution, through which the more substantial citizens and not only the nobility as in the existing diets of a province could have become associated with its administration. In this he failed, as well as in his plans to set up some kind of national assembly. These plans were all tied up with Stein's foreign policy and were an attempt to rouse the national spirit of Prussia against Napoleon. It was this policy which caused his downfall in November 1808 and it was later left to Hardenberg to realize plans for national and provincial representation but in a very modified form. Stein was equally unsuccessful in bringing in the representative principle at the grass-roots level, in the village communities and in the counties (*Kreise*). In view of the servile habits of the peasantry this was perhaps hardly surprising. The failure to prepare the way for constitutional government, particularly at the central level, was the most serious omission of the reform era and had fateful consequences for Prussia and for Germany in the long run.

Stein's energies as a domestic reformer were constantly drained by his negotiations with France over the size of the French indemnities. Napoleon's demands did, however, also act as a spur on Prussia's reorganization at home. If his exorbitant demands were to be met and Prussia was to regain some room for manoeuvre, then there simply had to be reforms to improve the social and economic health of the rump that remained. Stein was not suited to the task of conducting foreign policy in the very restricted circumstances in which Prussia was placed. His hopes, encouraged by the Spanish insurrection against French rule, that Prussia could put herself at the head of a similar popular uprising in Germany were unrealistic and premature. Many of the opponents of Stein's reforms preferred acquiescence in Napoleon's system to a policy which toyed with the dreaded spectre of revolution. Stein was seriously compromised by an indiscreet letter of his, mentioning plans for an anti-French rising, which fell into French hands in August 1808. His days in office were numbered, especially when it became apparent to the King that Alexander of Russia would do little to use his influence to ease the terms of the indemnity which France had imposed upon Prussia. In November 1808 Stein resigned. It was a personal tragedy. He had embarked upon reform but had to leave his task unfinished. In his long negotiations with the French over the indemnity he had tried to co-operate with the conquerors but had failed. When he turned to desperate plans of insurrection he again failed, and lost the chance of directing events. He was never fully to recover it. Perhaps Stein's ill-judged attempt to involve Prussia in a rising and new war against Napoleon was the first indication that German nationalism and the interests of the Prussian state could not always be easily harnessed together.

Stein was succeeded by the short-lived Dohna-Altenstein ministry which accomplished little. Hardenberg was waiting in the wings.

Napoleon had forced his dismissal in 1807, but once Stein had gone the King turned to him increasingly for advice. As was the case with Stein, the influence of Queen Luise, herself much more firmly on the side of reform than her wavering husband, finally paved the way for Hardenberg's return to office. Hardenberg had laid down his own view of what was needed to reform Prussia in the Riga memorandum, composed in 1807 after his dismissal, a document analogous to Stein's Nassau memorandum. In it Hardenberg used the phrase "democratic principles in a monarchical government".[5] In practice Hardenberg was prepared to be more radical than Stein in the economic field, but in general he was far more sensitive to what the King and the Junkers, with growing self-confidence, wanted. His foreign policy was dictated entirely by Prussian considerations, it showed the caution and time-serving appropriate to a country in a very weak position.

The severity of the French financial demands had been the immediate cause of the Dohna-Altenstein Ministry's resignation and Hardenberg had to consider as a first priority how he could improve the financial state of the country. He proposed extensive tax reforms of which a principal feature was the abolition of the nobility's tax exemption. This caused an outcry and greatly reinforced the Junker opposition from which Stein had already suffered. To strengthen his hand Hardenberg summoned, in February 1811, a national assembly of notables, a pale reflection of the national assembly which Stein had earlier proposed. This device could not, however, break the opposition of the Conservative Junkers, which took its constitutional stand on the rights of the old provincial diets. A memorandum to the King from nobles in the province of Brandenburg complained that Hardenberg's new taxes violated the contractual rights of the nobility and that the provincial diets were the established means of representation in Prussia. All land would soon fall into the hands of the Jews, the memorandum stated, and "our venerable Brandenburg-Prussia will become a new-fangled Jew state".[6]

The Junkers found an able leader in Marwitz, a man who really wanted to undo much of what had been done in Prussia for a century or more to create a centralized state. Marwitz was well aware that many of his followers were not interested in long-term principles, but merely wanted to preserve their economic position from attack. The Junker opposition was strengthened by the fact that it had intellectual support from the circle round Adam Müller, from the Christlich-Deutsche Tischgesellschaft and from Kleist and the *Berliner Abendblätter*. From these quarters came a reasoned attack on the whole liberal philosophy of Hardenberg and his economic advisers, Thaer and Kraus, both of them disciples of Adam Smith. In consequence, Hardenberg met the opposition with firmness : Marwitz and another leader of the Junker opposition, Finckenstein, were for a time imprisoned. But many of the tax reforms were withdrawn and in particular the tax exemption of the nobility was restored. This has to be set alongside Hardenberg's moves in the field of agrarian reforms. Here too, in the edicts of 1811 and 1816, Hardenberg gradually retreated in face of the Junker opposition. But the final effect was to create something like a free market in land, a situation damaging to the peasantry but on balance favourable to an economically efficient agricultural industry. Economic efficiency according to *laissez faire* doctrines was Hardenberg's real concern in his domestic policy. This can also be seen in the measures he promoted, soon after his return to office in 1810, to complete the steps taken by Stein to break down the old guild-regulated form of trading and manufacture in favour of a free market and competition. Hardenberg's reforms in this field were far-reaching and the old concepts of a fair price, regulated entry to trades and professions and sharp distinction between town and country rapidly vanished. It was a change entirely imposed from the top, like so many measures of the reform era, and caused much resistance and friction.

The emancipation of the Jews in 1812 was inspired by similar motives : Jews had for a long time played an important role in the economic and latterly also in the intellectual life of the country so that it was out of keeping with the concept of a modernized state not to admit them to full citizenship. Neighbouring states, above all France and French-dominated Westphalia had emancipated the Jews. The events of the war had caused a considerable influx of Jews into the remaining Prussian provinces and one way of controlling this movement was to treat the Jews as citizens whilst also imposing on them the obligations which went with these rights, notably military service. Stein had wrestled with this problem, but he had strong anti-semitic prejudices and hoped to deal with the situation through the old regulations of Frederick the Great, under which foreign Jews without permission to settle could be expelled. Hardenberg's further moves towards economic liberalism made the conferment of full citizenship on the Jews living in Prussia a logical and useful step. The Jewish Community of Berlin, under the lead of David Friedländer, a man not unlike Moses Mendelssohn in significance, pressed for emancipation and had many contacts with the State Chancellor. Hardenberg had no prejudices; he had frequented the Jewish salons of Berlin and was accustomed to working with Jewish bankers and financiers. The

emancipation edict, like so many of his economic measures, was
not popular. Opposition did not come only from the obvious
quarters, like Marwitz and his Junkers or the Conservative intellectuals. Anti-semitism, based on a variety of motives and rational-
izations, could be found in men as different as Stein, Buchholz,
Jahn and Kleist. The edict of 1812 conferred full citizen's rights
and obligations, including military service on the Jews, but it was
so phrased that it was made to appear an act of grace, possibly
capable of revocation, rather than a natural right. Given the fact
that Prussia was still a long way from becoming a modern secular
state, this was perhaps hardly surprising. The extent and way in
which Jews would actually serve in the army was not settled and
the question of their admission to other offices of state was left
studiously vague. The emancipation ushered in a period when
individual Jews, many of them baptized, frequently played a
crucial role in the affairs of Prussia. Yet in the mass the Jews
continued to suffer from handicaps and discrimination, right down
to the end of the Hohenzollern monarchy, which made their position often ambivalent and their relationship with their fellow
citizens rarely quite free from inhibiting undercurrents.

By 1812 Hardenberg found himself blocked and frustrated in
many of his domestic reforms and it was fortunate for him that
the conduct of foreign affairs, much closer to his heart, increasingly
claimed his attention. The State Chancellor had succeeded in
modernizing Prussia in many respects, particularly in her economic
life, but the Junker opposition had led him to abandon the ideals
of Stein for training men at all levels to be responsible citizens
through the practice of self-government, ideals which Hardenberg
never really shared. The Assembly of Notables of 1811 had not
been a success. An interim assembly which sat from 1812 to 1815
consisted of eighteen representatives of the nobility, twelve representatives of the towns, including one each from Berlin, Königsberg
and Breslau, and nine representatives of the peasantry. In spite of
the preponderance of the nobility and the fact that the election of
deputies unacceptable to the central government could be invalid-
ated by the provincial authorities, this assembly was kept on a
very tight leash by Hardenberg and in no way allowed to develop
into anything resembling a parliament. The so-called "Gendarm-
erie" edict of 1812 attempted to supersede the Junker controlled
Kreis or county administration by a directorate similar to the
French prefecture system. It was a measure conceived in a centralizing bureaucratic spirit, very different again from Stein's concepts of self-government but the opposition of the Junkers made it

impossible to put it into practice. What remained was a modernized police force.

Education was the only aspect of civil reform which was making steady progress all these years before the Wars of Liberation and the changes here were of the greatest future importance. Wilhelm von Humboldt had become Chief of the Section for Cultural Affairs and Public Education at the Ministry of the Interior in 1809, a post which ranked him just below that of a full minister. He had with great reluctance abandoned his freewheeling existence as Prussian envoy to the Vatican, which suited his aesthetic tastes and detached idealism so well and had answered the call of his sorely-pressed country. Like Stein his term in this office lasted not much over a year, but his work was seminal and carried on by his two main assistants, Nicolovius and Süvern. These two officials, like so many members of the high Prussian bureaucracy at this time, were imbued with the ideas of the Enlightenment and lived in the mental and moral climate of Kantian idealism. Humboldt himself had often expressed his suspicion of the state and of its tendency to invade the sphere that was properly the individual's, but he now practised a vigorous intervention in a field of particular concern to the development of the individual person.

The most spectacular achievement of his short period in office was the foundation of the University of Berlin. Plans for this had been in the making for some years, particularly since the University of Halle had been lost to Prussia. Fichte, Schleiermacher and Stein had all contributed ideas, but in its final shape the institution owed much to Humboldt, who also showed previously unsuspected energy in providing the resources for it. The ideas behind the new University were the pursuit of pure knowledge, the unity of knowledge, freedom to teach and pursue research and the interaction of teaching and research. Such ideas were not new and had been cherished in the later 18th century at a number of German universities, notably Göttingen. It was at this university that many influential men of the period, including Humboldt and Stein, had spent some of their student days. Berlin, however, now blazed the trail for much that was typical of German academic life for the next hundred years or more : impressive and securely based contributions to the advance of knowledge, a large output of efficiently trained public servants, but also remoteness from the ordinary life of the community and from real concern for the political destinies of the state. Humboldt succeeded in drawing to the new University an array of outstanding talent, including Fichte, Schleiermacher, Neibuhr and Savigny. Subjects such as history, linguistics, a particular interest of Humboldt's, natural sciences, and above all philosophy now held an equal place with the traditional faculties of theology, law and medicine. Humboldt took much care to preserve the independence of the university against the state; yet a large proportion of the students were destined for the public service and had to take state examinations to start their careers, with the result that the Government inevitably came to have much influence over the shape and content of courses. It cannot be laid at the door of Humboldt that many of the assumptions on which his idea for a university was based were undermined by developments. The theory of the unity of knowledge became progressively more difficult to maintain; the liberalism of the majority of German academics withered in the Bismarck era; the interaction of teaching and research bore little fruit for the majority of average students, who preferred to spend their time drinking and duelling. It remains true that the Prussian universities, remodelled on Berlin, became a principal element in the high reputation German learning enjoyed in the 19th century.

Humboldt and his assistants gave new impulses to all parts of the educational system. In spite of earlier attempts to make elementary education general, it had reached the humbler levels of society only intermittently; at the other end of the social scale the wealthier classes availed themselves of a variety of special schools such as knights' academies, as well as private tutors. Humboldt laid the ground plan for a universal system of education divided into three stages: elementary, "higher" or secondary, and the universities. He tried to do away with all special schools, even the cadet schools, if he could have had his way, and provided for everybody a general, non-vocational education. The educational theories of Pestalozzi, of allowing the natural gifts of the child to flower, had gained wide currency in Germany: Fichte for example, had taken them into his plan for national education. There was a general disposition to turn away from the mechanistic approach to learning that prevailed in the 18th century. The work of Humboldt and his helpers in the field of elementary education was carried out in the spirit of Pestalozzi.

Their greatest concern was, however, with the Gymnasium, the highest form of secondary education. Humboldt and Süvern developed it into a school providing a ten-year course, starting at the age of ten, through which all had to pass who wanted to go on to a university. The course was based on the classical languages and on German, with some mathematics and (in the higher classes) a study of classical and German literature. The Gymnasium was staffed with university-trained teachers enjoying high academic and social prestige; indeed it became one of the major tasks of the universities to produce these teachers. The Gymnasium provided for many Germans a highly disciplined, efficient general education. It had on the other hand many weaknesses : it created a rigid division between the academic *élite* and the masses at the early age of ten and was also socially divisive, though considerably less so than the English public school system of the 19th century. There was too much reliance on examinations, while the emphasis on the classics produced a conflict between the training of scholars and education for the practical skills useful to society. Humboldt's humanist idealism was basically pagan and religion occupied a minor place in his plans for the Gymnasium—this also created tensions and conflicts. Nor must it be supposed that so far-reaching and all-embracing a scheme of education could come into existence from one moment to the next : it took many years for Humboldt's ideas to come to full maturity, particularly in elementary education. When they did so much of the idealism had evaporated. Nevertheless, as a result of his work Prussia acquired a highly developed public education system ahead of other nations. She became a country of schools as well as of barracks. Humboldt's stature as an educational reformer contrasts strangely with his inability as a politician. He was dissatisfied with his non-ministerial status; yet the very fact that he belonged to the second tier enabled him to get on with his work without too much opposition or distraction. He campaigned for the realization of Stein's proposal for a State Council to which all ministers and higher officials would have belonged; alternatively he wanted his own position raised to ministerial status. When he came up against obstacles he quickly lost patience and resigned. He went back into the diplomatic service, became envoy at Vienna and played an important part at the Congress in 1814. Later he returned to the centre of affairs in Berlin.

Humboldt, Hardenberg and Stein were the great names of civil reform in Prussia. Alongside them worked the military reformers— Scharnhorst, Gneisenau, Boyen and, on a more theoretical level, Clausewitz. Scharnhorst came of quite humble Hanoverian stock. He was educated at the Military Academy of the Count of Schaumburg-Lippe, who stood out from among the unedifying host of minor German princelings as a man of principle and public spirit. Scharnhorst was ennobled just before entering the Prussian service as Director of the newly founded War Academy in 1801. He was a reflective man who arrived at decisions by ceaseless intellectual analysis, a scholar as much as a soldier. The American War of Independence, of which he knew only at second-hand, and the Revolutionary Wars, of which he had personal experience, made a deep impression on him and he thought and wrote much about the lessons to be drawn from them. He was the moving spirit in a Military Society of progressive officers who met in Berlin in the years of Prussian neutrality to consider how the Prussian army should respond to the new conditions of warfare. At Auerstädt he was Chief of Staff, but neither the aged Duke of Brunswick nor the King made much use of his services. He helped Blücher's retreat after the disaster and in 1807 Napoleon's setback at Eylau owed much to the advice which Scharnhorst gave the Prussian commander L'Estocq. Thereafter it was never Scharnhorst's fate again to play a major role in battle, although his premature death in 1813 was due to a wound which he received at the Battle of Gross-Görschen and which he neglected. He had had to stomach many slights in the Prussian service on account of his foreign origin and humble birth, so that it was a token of the change of spirit in Prussia after the disasters of 1806 that Scharnhorst was allowed to assume the role of leading military reformer between 1807 and 1812. He became the real partner of Stein on the military side, because his fundamental concept, an army composed of participating, intelligent citizens, was the counterpart of Stein's work on the civil side. The contrast between the personalities of the two men was, however, startling : while Scharnhorst was withdrawn, cool and intellectual, Stein was emotional and impetuous. They were at one in their German patriotism which transcended their Prussian loyalties.

Gneisenau was also not a native of Prussia. He came of a recently ennobled Saxon middle-class family. He became famous in 1807 when he defended the fortress of Colberg in Pomerania, long after the French tidal wave had swept farther east and when many other Prussian fortress towns had been surrendered with hardly a fight. He became Scharnhorst's closest associate on the Military Commission concerned with the reform of the army. He lacked his Chief's power of sheer intellect, but was often more revolutionary in his thinking. As a passionate German patriot he hated French rule in Germany, but he was at the same time fascinated by the dynamic force unleashed through the French Revolution and by the arresting figure of Napoleon. He wanted a German Bonaparte and it almost seemed that he would not have been averse to playing that role himself, for he was something of a soldier of fortune. When Prussia failed to promote an anti-French rising in 1809, Gneisenau resigned from the army, but continued to serve as an intelligence agent on missions to London and St. Petersburg. In 1811, he addressed a memorandum to the King advocating that Prussia should take advantage of the growing friction between Russia and France and rise against Napoleon. All men capable of bearing arms should be enlisted. Frederick William's marginal comments were "Nobody would come" and "Good —as poetry".[7] Gneisenau represented more than anybody that jacobinical streak among the reformers which made them suspect to the King. When Frederick William came down on the side of Napoleon in 1812 Gneisenau left the Prussian service altogether. Not only were his loyalties German rather than Prussian, there was also in him an element of the cosmopolitan aristocrat which made him at one stage look to the erection of a new Anglo-German Guelph state as a bulwark against France. When he returned to the Prussian army the Wars of Liberation gave him a chance to show his mettle as a general. Gneisenau proved himself almost the equal of Napoleon as a strategist and as Blücher's Chief of Staff he restored the European reputation of the Prussian army. When Blücher received an honory doctorate at Oxford he said that Gneisenau should at least have been made an apothecary.

Among the major military reformers Boyen was the only genuine Prussian. His early military career was like that of any Junker who entered the Prussian officer corps but his intellectual stature and ambition were greater. Boyen was brought up in the traditions of the Prussia of Frederick the Great and the Enlightenment; and he took part in all the intellectual movements of the 1790s. He welcomed the French revolution, he sat at the feet of Kant, he worked hard at his own literary education. From the ideas which came to him through Kant and the German humanists he became an advocate of more humane treatment for soldiers, particularly in matters of punishment. He was thus very receptive to the concept of a citizen army put forward by Scharnhorst and Gneisenau and supported them vigorously on the Military Commission. He became Prussia's first Minister of War and it fell to him to put into execution the plans for a conscript and reserve army made earlier. His resignation, along with that of Humboldt, in 1819, marks the final end of the reform era.

The most important military reforms were concerned with recruitment, composition of the officer corps, education of officers, administration of military discipline and with the reorganization of the central military administration. In addition those who by their dereliction of duty had made the defeats of 1806 and 1807 so humiliating had to be punished or at any rate weeded out. The Military Commission left the long task of investigating the record of accused officers in detail to another body and concentrated on the more important problems of reorganization. Foremost among these was the replacement of the cantonal system by one of universal service. Under the cantonal system there were so many exemptions that in practice only the peasants served in the army as common soldiers. This ran completely counter to Scharnhorst's concept of bringing the army into a close union with the nation. The injustices of the system had produced the apathy which led to the collapse of 1806. France had shown the power of a citizen army, although, as the opponents of Scharnhorst were quick to point out, Napoleon had by this time allowed the more affluent members of society to buy themselves off.

At this stage, in 1808, it would, however, have been impossible to have organized a universally conscripted army, with a reserve linked to it, in what was left of Prussia. French pressure was too strong, the army no longer large enough, and the process of creating reserves would have taken too long. Scharnhorst therefore recommended that the poorer members of the community should continue to serve in the standing army, while those who could equip and feed themselves would serve in a kind of militia. This plan was brought to naught by the fears of the King and the more conservative members of the bureaucracy as well as by French pressure from without. Frederick William and the conservatives feared not only the French reaction to any obvious move of rearmament, but also the social implications of a broadly recruited militia. Even a man like Niebuhr regarded conscription as a threat to liberty and tradition while the educated middle classes despised military service. When Napoleon in the Treaty of Paris of September 1808 imposed a limit of 42,000 on the size of the Prussian army, the plans of Scharnhorst and his colleagues finally became impossible. The cantonal system remained in operation and was supplemented by the "Krümper" system. This was a method of sending a small proportion of longer-serving soldiers on leave and calling up fresh men from the cantons to take their place. It became a widely accepted myth that the Krümper system created large trained reserves for the Prussian army in readiness for the Wars of Liberation. Even those who framed the provisions for the Reichswehr under the Treaty of Versailles were still affected by this myth. In fact the Prussian army and its reserves numbered only some 65,000 men by the spring of 1813.

At that very moment the movement of liberation changed the situation decisively in favour of the reformers. Under the influence of Stein a "Landwehr", or militia, was called into existence in East Prussia, the province which had always remained least affected by French pressure. The King by this time had left Berlin, which was still in the French sphere and had moved to Breslau. He was

now at last prevailed upon to extend conscription to the Landwehr throughout Prussia. It quickly reached a strength of about
120,000 men and without such an addition to the regular army
Prussia could not have made so great a contribution to the war.
The principle of a *levée en masse* was even further extended by the
"Landsturm" edict of April 1813, which raised a force of all remaining able-bodied men, to be used for home defence and haras-
sing the enemy. This proved shortlived, for it created grave fears
of a jacobinical rising among the conservatives at court, in the
bureaucracy and among the nobility. By July 1813 the Landsturm was virtually disbanded again.

The principle of universal service was, however, maintained and
in 1814 was put on a permanent basis by Boyen, who had now
become Minister of War. In his conscription law of September
1814 he created an army of four distinct grades. There was the
regular army consisting of volunteers, supplemented by men between twenty and twenty-five who were conscripted by lot for three
years. Young men "from the educated classes who can provide
their own stabling and weapons" had to serve for one year only.
These so-called *Einjährigen* later provided most of the officers for
the reserve army. The Landwehr provided the second and third
grades of Boyen's scheme. There was a "Landwehr des ersten
Aufgebotes", a first reserve army, selected from men between twenty
and twenty-five not conscripted into the regular army and from
all men between twenty-five and thirty-two. The second reserve
army, "Landwehr des zweiten Aufgebotes", consisted of veterans
of the regular army and all others under forty. The Landsturm
was envisaged as a fourth grade, to be called up in case of emergency. Boyen's law of 1814 passed with relative ease, considering
the passionate resistance such proposals had always evoked from
the anti-reformers. It may have been due to the fact that the idea
of reviving the Landsturm was pushed into the background. Boyen
tried to turn the Landwehr into a genuine citizen's army tied to
localities and with an officer corps open to the middle classes. This
involved him in renewed clashes with the reactionaries after 1815
and led to his resignation in 1819. Enough of his system survived,
however, to make a profound change from the old methods of
recruiting the army. On this point, a matter crucial to the structure
of Prussia, the reformers had got their way to a large extent.

They also had some success in reforming the regular officer
corps. The aim of Scharnhorst and his colleagues was to end the
aristocratic monopoly in the corps and to base promotion on education and achievement rather than on birth. The low ebb which
the prestige of the Junker officer had reached after 1806 weakened

the resistance to such changes. The officer aspirant could no longer enter the army at fourteen, as had been the habit of the Junkers. The future officer now entered the army as an ensign at seventeen, having given proof of his education and ability through an examination. The system of military schools was reorganized and only the Kadettenhäuser of Berlin and Potsdam remained; schools offering courses for candidates for commissions were set up. A higher military academy, later to become the *Kriegsakademie*, offered more advanced courses. The old ideal of the mindless drill-square officer began to retreat. The engagement of foreign officers was discontinued and it would have been in any case difficult to obtain them under the conditions prevailing after 1807. Notwithstanding all these changes, the character of the Prussian officer corps remained essentially aristocratic. In spite of examinations, selection by character and direct appointment to commands by the King continued. This ensured the predominance of the nobility. Their position in the social structure remained too powerful for their hold on the army to diminish substantially.

The reform of military punishment was a matter of real as well as symbolic importance. Barbarous penalties like running the gauntlet had always been considered necessary for the maintenance of discipline in the old Prussian army. It consisted, after all, of the lowest orders of society and its ranks were made up by the recruitment of foreign riff-raff. Now the peasants were no longer *erbuntertänig* (hereditary serfs) and had the rights of citizens; recruits from abroad were no longer available and the growth of national spirit made their use inadvisable. Thus a more humane approach to crime and punishment in the army was an essential part of creating that closer union between nation and army which the reformers had so much at heart. It was also a matter which aroused strong emotions and the conservatives on the Military Commission fought a fierce rearguard action. The King, however, was squarely with the reformers on this point and Boyen had devoted much study to the reform of military punishment even before 1806.

The changes in the higher military organization were not radical. A Hohenzollern ruler still felt that the army was very much his personal concern and Frederick William was not to be deprived of his Military Cabinet in the way his Civil Cabinet had disappeared. It was, however, a step of great importance that Scharnhorst was appointed General-Adjutant in 1808. It was even more significant when, as part of Stein's plan for five central ministries, a Ministry of War was created. It was divided into two departments, a General Department of War and a Military Economy Department.

Each of these had a number of divisions dealing with personnel, training, weapons, finance, supply and all the other concomitants of an army. Scharnhorst became head of the General Department, into which the office of General-Adjutant was incorporated. The King could never bring himself to appoint him Minister of War and this office remained vacant until Boyen filled it in 1814. Since many of Scharnhorst's fellow reformers were in key posts this did not matter very much; the reform party could get its way on many questions of detail even if it failed to reach all its goals on the big issues.

The difficult and uncertain course of the civil and military reforms took place against a background of dramatic events in Europe. Three times it looked as if Prussia might join or take the lead in a general uprising against Napoleon. The first occasion was in 1808 when Stein hoped to bring about such a movement, but instead prepared his own downfall. In 1809, by which time the peasant peoples of Spain and the Tyrol had shown the way of resistance, the moment seemed to have come once more. It seemed on the cards that Prussia would join Austria in the renewed war against Napoleon, but Frederick William would not move as long as Russia remained on the sidelines. High hopes were raised by Aspern, only to be dashed again by Wagram. In 1811 the patriotic reformers were again pressing the King to take advantage of the growing friction between France and Prussia to start the fight against Napoleon. Neither Frederick William nor even Hardenberg judged the moment ripe; the King indeed seemed to be convinced of the invincibility of his hated adversary. The result was the Franco-Prussian treaty of March 1812, which made over three hundred officers leave the Prussian army. Among them were Boyen and Clausewitz; Gneisenau now left the service of Prussia altogether.

The King looked at the situation from a different point of view from those who were primarily German nationalists or opponents of Bonapartist world domination. To Frederick William the first priority was the future of his state and of his dynasty and he was not prepared to jeopardize these by a premature heroic gesture. Inveterate opponents of the reformers like Marwitz, or on the military side Yorck von Wartenburg, were also patriots; but their first loyalty was to the House of the Hohenzollern, to Prussia, and beyond that even to the separate territories, Brandenburg or East Prussia or Silesia, where they had their roots. As for the general population their mood was remote from that of the Spanish masses rising against Napoleon. For one thing they were too much accustomed to the regimentation of the Obrigkeitsstaat to have become

successful resistance guerrilla fighters. Sullen resistance against
French arrogance and exactions was quite common but it did not
lead to action; and there were still many prepared to receive calmly
the benefits of French rule. An adventure like Major von Schill's
rising in 1809 evoked little response and was severely frowned
upon by the King and those in authority. Nonetheless, when the
moment of truth came in 1813 the mood was quite different from
the apathy of 1807 : to this extent the reformers had succeeded in
turning Prussia from an administrative mechanism into a country
capable of rousing the loyalty of its inhabitants.

Yet many commentators consider the reform movement to have
been a failure. This may be true if one judges it in the light of
Prussia's more distant future as an industrial mass society. The
failure to develop the representative institutions so ardently desired
by Stein was reinforced in the years immediately after 1815 and
all vestiges of reform finally vanished in 1819. This and other
failures were most damaging for the future of liberal attitudes in
Prussia and in Germany. But the reform era cannot be entirely
judged in the light of what happened later. That Prussia survived
at all was a mark of vitality; the country could never thereafter
be seen as a mere quirk of dynastic accident. The reform party
had an ideology, born out of the age of Enlightenment, the moral
philosophy of Kant, Fichte, Schleiermacher and others, the humanism of Goethe and Schiller, the national spirit first cultivated by
Herder and more fully distilled by the Romantics. No doubt the
reform movement was imposed from the top, not demanded from
below; its ideas could find a home in the Prussian bureaucracy,
because of the peculiar composition of that bureaucracy at the
time, half noble, half bourgeois, half Prussian, half foreign. Even
if it came from the top the reform movement recreated Prussia as
a state which could impose a strong imprint on all its citizens.
Some of the virtues of the Old Prussia were saved and new ones,
such as civic pride and a high level of public education, were
added. In spite of the grave failings which the future was to
reveal, Prussia remained most formidable.

CHAPTER VI

Liberation, Reaction and Revolution 1813–1849

PRUSSIA joined the fight against France only when there was clear evidence that Napoleon's spell was broken. The King and Hardenberg were understandably anxious to avoid a premature break with Napoleon. Public opinion among the articulate classes and even among the masses, however, was pushing the Government towards war with France. If the King and his ministers had not taken the plunge in the spring of 1813 there might have been, in the view of some contemporary observers, something like a revolution. The mood was very different from the apathy of 1806 and this was an indication of the transformation wrought by the reform era. It is unlikely that the austere humanist ideals of Stein or Humboldt's liberal doctrines of individual self-fulfilment penetrated beyond a limited circle of educated people. The masses were moved by more primitive emotions: sullen resentment of French pressure and heavy-handed financial exactions, love of country and loyalty to the House of Hohenzollern. Not that there was anything like a general uprising in Prussia or Germany. There was a certain amount of enthusiasm, especially among the young and the more educated, and a readiness to get into the fight; this showed itself in the formation of a number of free corps, of which the most famous was Lützow's, and in a disposition to join the colours in the Landwehr or the short-lived Landsturm. The mood was expressed by patriotic writers and poets, foremost among them Ernst Moritz Arndt. Theodor Körner, another young patriotic poet, fought in Lützow's Corps and met his death early on in the war. It was noteworthy that the desire to fight against Napoleon was much stronger in the provinces that had remained to Prussia after 1807 than further west—again perhaps a tribute to the reform movement. In the countries of the Rhineland the population was on the whole passive and content to wait until their traditional ruling houses judged it opportune to switch sides. Only the King of Saxony proved unable to execute this manoeuvre in time and paid dearly for his mistake in loss of territory at the final settlement

Two men played a crucial role in prising Prussia from the Bonapartist embrace and bringing her into the war on the side of the allies, Yorck von Wartenburg and Stein. The former signed the famous Convention of Tauroggen on 30th December 1812, neutralizing his Corps which had been sent to fight the Russians at the side of the French. This move was of great strategic significance, making it more difficult for Napoleon to use Germany as a base for recovery and at the same time facilitating a Russian countermove beyond her western frontier. The Convention of Tauroggen weakened the influence of the French party round Frederick William and enabled Scharnhorst, who now hurried to the King's side at Breslau, to persuade his master that it was time to switch alliances. Yorck had no definite instructions from the King to act in the way he did and Frederick William's immediate reaction was to disown the Convention; his attitude to Yorck always remained ambivalent and Tauroggen was never accorded full recognition as an act of state. Yorck has often been depicted as a thorough-going opponent of reform and lumped together with Marwitz and the Junker opposition. It is true that he greeted Stein's dismissal in 1808 with the frequently quoted remark: "One mad head is already severed; the remaining nest of vipers will die in its own poison."[1] He was also strongly opposed to the admission of non-nobles to the officer corps. In the reform of military tactics and training he was, however, entirely with the progressive party. His own background and somewhat dubious claim to nobility makes it impossible to regard him as one of the old-established and proud Junkers of Brandenburg or East Prussia who rallied behind Marwitz. He was an ambitious and independent man who at all times played a lone hand, never more so than at Tauroggen.

Yorck's move enabled Stein to fill once again a major role on the stage of history. Up to this time Stein's efforts to rally the Germans against Napoleon had been relatively ineffective. He had been summoned to Russia in May 1812 to become the Tsar's adviser on German affairs. He founded a German Committee and later a German legion, steps which were re-enacted in a different context 130 years later in the Second World War. With the help of Arndt, who joined him in Russia, he directed a stream of propaganda towards Germany designed to stimulate an insurrection. The tone was radical and republican, but the German population showed little response. Stein and Gneisenau hoped to induce the British Government to land a force in North Germany to support an uprising. They were quite prepared to see Britain, in return, becoming the leading power in North Germany. All these initiatives, however, were somewhat remote from reality until the Convention of Tauroggen enabled Stein to appear as the Tsar's plenipotentiary in East Prussia. Now he was able to persuade Alexander not to stop his forces at Russia's western perimeter but to take the plunge into a general war of liberation. On Stein's initiative the Estates of East Prussia met and called out the Landwehr and the Landsturm; their example was soon to be followed in the rest of the kingdom. Although Stein acted discreetly his appearance in East Prussia as the Tsar's representative aroused suspicions that the Russians were intending to take over the province. Thus Prussia appeared once again to be confronted, at least potentially, by a choice between French and Russian predominance, a dilemma she had had to face so frequently for at least a decade.

The Convention of Tauroggen and the events in East Prussia at last forced Frederick William's hand. The formation of free corps of volunteers, the Jäger, was now authorized and this was quickly followed by the call-up of Landwehr and Landsturm, thus virtually introducing universal conscription. The Treaty of Kalisch of 27th February 1813 tied Prussia to Russia. Three weeks later appeared the King's famous proclamation "An mein Volk" (To my People).[2] It contained a short apologia for the King's vacillating and unheroic policy in the past. He had hoped thereby, so the proclamation says, to secure relief for his people and to convince the French Emperor that it was in his own interest to respect the independence of Prussia. These hopes having been disappointed, the King now appealed to the old traditions of Prussia, going back to the Great Elector, and reminded all the separate peoples of his state—the Brandenburgers, Silesians, Lithuanians—of the heroic deeds of other European nations against French oppression. He called for a common effort and for sacrifices from all. Such accents would never have been used in a royal proclamation in Prussia before the reform era. The influence of Stein was also apparent in the provisions that were now made for the government of the territories liberated from the French. A Council of Administration, composed of Prussian and Russian officials and those of other states as they came into the war, was to assume authority in the non-Prussian areas of Germany. The support of the smaller German princes was to be sought and they were threatened with loss of territory if they did not respond. All this reflects Stein's distrust of the minor German rulers and his desire to create a larger national unity. When Austria joined the war in August 1812 Metternich insisted that, with the exception of Saxony, the authority of the traditional rulers should be respected. Stein's policy was thus on the way to being nullified.

The course of the War of Liberation and of the attendant political events is part of the broader picture of European history. Prussia made a contribution to the military effort against Napoleon which was large in relation to her size. The battles of the spring and early summer of 1813, for example Gross-Görschen, where Scharnhorst received the wound that was to prove fatal, were indecisive or even favourable to the French, but the Prussians became conscious of a new-found strength and were confident that there would be no repetition of Jena and Auerstädt. When the war was resumed in August 1813, after the armistice to which Napoleon had agreed, Prussia had raised some 270,000 men and by the end of the year this had been increased to 300,000, some 6 per cent of the population. Admittedly these forces ranged from the relatively well equipped free corps, recruited largely from the educated classes, to the virtually untrained formations of the Landwehr. In Blücher and Gneisenau, Prussia provided the allied forces with two notable generals, the former a leader of men whose presence boosted the morale of his forces, the latter a first-class military brain. Both played an essential part in the Battle of Leipzig in October 1813, perhaps more than Waterloo the decisive confrontation of the war. Other Prussian commanders—for example, Boyen, Yorck, Grolman and Kleist—established their reputation during the war. It was their determination which at various points in the pursuit of Napoleon was decisive in carrying the allied troops through to Paris. The Austrians under Schwarzenberg might well have left the task half-finished.

Prussia's achievements in the field could not disguise the fact that she was the least powerful of the Great Powers. Men like Stein and Gneisenau, when from their Russian exile they had tried to rouse the German spirit of resistance, had hoped to produce a new German order, with Prussia setting the example and taking the lead. These hopes were doomed. Austria, under the leadership of Metternich, was determined to restore in Europe the balance of power and the concert of the Great Powers. Metternich would have been quite willing to leave Napoleon in control of a France confined to her natural frontiers. Nothing was further from his thought than to concede to Prussia a leading position in Germany. Bavaria, for so long a client of France and beneficiary of the Napoleonic system, switched sides in the autumn of 1813. At once this step was rewarded by the recognition of her sovereignty and eventually by a most generous territorial settlement. This was the signal that the smaller German states were to be fully restored. Room would have to be found in Germany for Austria, for the medium and small powers, as well as for Prussia. These unavoidable consequences of the distribution of power in Europe and in Germany evoked reactions ranging from utter disillusionment to realistic acceptance. Ardent German nationalists like Arndt and Jahn were driven into opposition both to the international and domestic aspects of the Vienna settlement. Their fight against the Metternich system was of one of the major developments after 1815. The Prussian reform party—particularly Gneisenau, Boyen, and Grolman—went on toying with the idea of a people's war led by Prussia which would produce a new German order. Most of them became resigned to the impossibility of such a solution and hoped that Austria and Prussia would find a way of collaborating in the German interest. Stein and Gneisenau were still sufficiently cosmopolitan in outlook to envisage Britain or Russia playing a major role in German affairs. Some of the domestic opponents of the reform party, for example Marwitz, had been sufficiently roused in their Prussian patriotism by the War of Liberation to demand for their country a predominant position at least in North Germany.

The men responsible for the practical conduct of Prussian policy, the King and his two plenipotentiaries at Vienna, Hardenberg and Humboldt, had to take a realistic view. Their concern was to secure the best possible terms for Prussia. Their main demand was for the annexation of Saxony. This would have rounded off Prussia's territory most admirably and would have fulfilled the aim of generations of Hohenzollern rulers. The Prussian case against Saxony was eloquently put by the historian Niebuhr. He stressed the great service which, as he saw it, Prussia had always rendered to the German cause, most recently in the Wars of Liberation. He seemed oblivious of the fact that the annexation of Saxony would have been an act of aggrandizement by the Prussian state, which at this stage could do little to advance the German national cause. In his pamphlet on the Saxon question, Niebuhr became a forerunner of those historians who, like Treitschke later on, saw the progress of Prussia as synonymous with the advance of Germany towards modern nationhood.[3] Prussia was only partly successful in her designs on Saxony, mainly because of Austrian and French objections and because Prussian annexation of Saxony would have entailed Russian demands for more territory in Poland. At one time it was thought that the King of Saxony would be compensated for the loss of his country by being made the ruler of the Rhineland. Instead, the Rhineland was now transferred to Prussia. This had, in the eyes of Austria, England and others, the advantage of strengthening the barriers against renewed French expansion. The Prussians, on the other hand, were reluctant to accept territories which would fundamentally alter the character of their country; but they were left with no alternative.

As a result of the territorial changes of 1815, Prussia became once more an overwhelmingly German state. More than ever she straddled the whole of North and West Germany. Few people

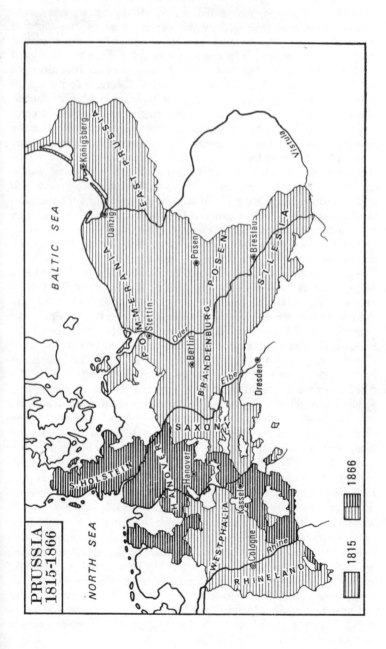

realized fully in 1815 the extent to which this settlement would involve Prussia increasingly in the development of the German question. This tendency was soon to be reinforced by economic factors, the improvement of communications and the beginnings of industrialization. No one foresaw that this reluctant acquisition of the Rhineland would, in the not too distant future, give Prussia an economic preponderance in Germany which would put Austria entirely in the shade. Austria, on the other hand, withdrew completely from her former position in West Germany and thereby became, from the German point of view, more peripheral. Only a section of the Habsburg Empire lay within the boundaries of the German Confederation of 1815. What lay outside was almost entirely non-German. Prussia's eastern provinces, East Prussia and Posen, also lay outside the German Confederation, but the majority of the population was German. It was ironic that at the very moment when Prussia was ceasing to be the torchbearer of German national feeling the ground was prepared for a resumption of this role under very different circumstances.

The constitution given to Germany at the Congress of Vienna was not out of keeping with the spirit of the age. The Confederation was like a revived Empire, but without an Emperor and with the number of separate states drastically curtailed. This draconian operation had been conveniently performed by Napoleon. The Prussian state of the Restoration period fitted into this arrangement without strain. The crucial question for Prussia was how much further the domestic reform movement would go, and in particular whether any form of national representation would be established. Frederick William's decree of May 1815 seemed to leave the answer beyond doubt; provincial estates were to be restored where they survived and to be established where they did not exist, and from these provincial estates an assembly of national deputies was to be elected. The national assembly was to be consulted on all legislation concerning the personal and property rights of citizens, including taxation. This promise of a constitution was limited : there were to be no direct elections to a national body and its role was in any case to be consultative only. Nevertheless it would have represented a big step towards a constitutional monarchy and would have gone some way towards realizing the ideas put forward by Stein seven or eight years earlier. If Prussia was to maintain the image of progress which the reform era had given her in Germany such a step was necessary. Without it the incorporation of the new and more advanced provinces on the Rhine would prove difficult; many of the south German states were adopting constitutions in the years immediately after 1815.

The obstacles, however, in the path of genuine progress towards constitutional government in Prussia were formidable and in the end proved too strong. There was still the Junker opposition to reform. It wanted to preserve what remained of the old provincial estates, but only in order to buttress the privileges of the nobility. Round the King, the influence of reformers declined rapidly once the war was over. Instead those who saw the spectre of Jacobinism behind all the demands for a constitution and who regarded the spirit of nationalism as a conspiracy began to set the tone. Prominent among the anti-reform advisers of the King were Ancillon, the Huguenot tutor of the Crown Prince, later Frederick William IV, and Prince Wittgenstein, the Minister responsible for the Court and for police matters. Ancillon was earlier one of those who had advised the King to be cautious before committing himself to the anti-French course. This influence of the Junkers and of anti-liberal courtiers and officials might not have counted for so much had it not been reinforced by developments which went beyond Prussia. The witch-hunt against liberals and nationalists gathered pace under the guidance of Metternich. The disillusionment of the German nationalist movement was evident particularly among students and in the universities. It took institutional shape in the founding of "Burschenschaften", nationalist student associations, formed to keep alive the spirit of the heroic years of liberation. This idea owed much to Jahn; Arndt remained the most eloquent spokesman of German nationalism. The Wartburg meeting of October 1817, when five hundred students gathered, ostensibly to celebrate the anniversary of Luther's Reformation, and ended up by burning anti-liberal books in effigy, seemed to show the Burschenschaften acting on a national scale. This strengthened the forces of reaction and repression.

Thus it was not surprising that proposals for a representative system made little headway in Prussia. Hardenberg was virtually the only man left in a position of power who was prepared to forward this cause. Even he was by no means a convinced adherent of constitutional government, but merely a liberal bureaucrat with reasonably modern ideas. In 1817 he managed to put into practice the proposal put forward in 1808 by Stein of creating a Council of State. Stein had conceived this as the supreme collegiate executive body in the state; Hardenberg realized it in the form of a consultative body only. It was in no way a parliament, but consisted only of princes of the blood, ministers and high officials. It was this body, however, that at last took up again the problem of creating representative institutions at national, provincial and local level, a matter which had been left in abeyance since the promise made in

May 1815. A commission of inquiry was appointed which travelled
round the provinces and consulted local notables about problems
of representation—chiefly, however, at the local and provincial
rather than at the national level. By this time the enthusiasm of the
King for any move towards constitutionalism had been decidedly
dampened by the reactionary influences around him. He was confirmed in his attitude by an address which the poet Joseph Görres
handed to Hardenberg during the latter's visit to Koblenz early in
1818. Görres, a Rhinelander, was now a Prussian subject; his hopes,
like those of many others, that Prussia would lead a cohesive, constitutionally governed Germany had been disappointed after 1815.
He now demanded that the constitutional rights and liberties of
his fellow Rhinelanders should be secured. He pointed out that the
King of Prussia had not conquered this province but that it had
been handed to him as a trust and he claimed that the Rhineland
had nothing to learn from any country, not even France, in the
degree of liberty it had long established for its citizens. The peremp-
tory tone of these demands shocked the King and the poet soon had
to leave Prussian territory. He was not really a liberal in the
abstract sense, but believed, like Stein, that there had existed in
the past a German communal spirit which it was possible to rebuild
in the present. His attachment to medieval values was soon to lead
to his conversion to Catholicism.

The growing influence of Metternich over Prussian policy was
even more important than the Görres case in hardening the anti-
constitutional attitudes at the top. Metternich's case was greatly
strengthened when a young student assassinated the writer Kotze-
bue in the spring of 1819. This seemed to show the conspiratorial
side of nationalist associations like the Burschenschaften in a lurid
light. Hardenberg was compelled to agree to the Teplitz Protocol
in August 1819 : he undertook to proceed only by slow steps on the
question of representation, from local to provincial assemblies and
after that no further than a national body made up of deputies
from the provincial assemblies. A few weeks later Prussia undertook to enforce the famous Carlsbad Decrees—repressive measures
adopted by the whole German Bund against the nationalist agita-
tion. Jahn now went to prison for a spell; Arndt, whose appointment to a chair at Bonn University had earlier caused much
controversy, was suspended from his teaching activities and Schleiermacher was placed under surveillance. Repressive action of this
kind became common in Prussia for years to come.

Even at this stage progress towards some form of constitutional
government in Prussia need not have been entirely halted. Early in
1819 Wilhelm von Humboldt had returned to Berlin as Minister

with special responsibilities for constitutional affairs. The man who had spent so much of his early life in the quest for individual self-fulfilment had become completely absorbed in great affairs of state. He played no mean role in the events which shaped the fate of Europe, Germany and Prussia between 1812 and 1815. He came to feel increasingly that Germany, which he still conceived essentially as a nation of the spirit, had to acquire enough weight in the scales of power to safeguard her integrity. He saw it as the function of Prussia to lead Germany by her example; the moral force of her progressive institutions would lend her a weight greater than her natural power. Humboldt was not prepared to go all the way with some of the military leaders, like Blücher and Gneisenau, who would have liked Prussia to continue the fight on her own to achieve the kind of German settlement they wanted. Humboldt, however, was deeply disappointed by the loss of momentum that occurred in Prussia after 1815. He understood, though he could not fully share, the more narrowly nationalistic feelings of the Burschenschaften, of Jahn and of Arndt. All this might have marked him out as a potent alternative leader to Hardenberg. His relationship with the State Chancellor was ambivalent. They had worked together for many years and on a personal level Humboldt found it easier to live with Hardenberg than with Stein. As a man of the world he found it easier to understand the realism of the State Chancellor and to forgive his worldly peccadilloes than to accept the impetuosity of Stein, however much he might respect his ideals. Hardenberg may have sensed that Humboldt was a potential rival, for he kept him from the centre of affairs, until early 1819. Humboldt's entry into the Ministry was set about with difficulties, because he wanted to take office as a responsible minister under a Chancellor who was *primus inter pares,* while Hardenberg insisted on the supremacy of his office over all other ministers.

The brief period which Humboldt now spent in office in Berlin was one of constant in-fighting between himself and Hardenberg. In this encounter Humboldt was easily worsted, for he was still an intellectual in politics and at heart an amateur, while Hardenberg was a pure politician and entirely professional. Yet at this point both men had very similar aims, though for different reasons. Hardenberg still wanted a national assembly, for he saw the administrative and financial need for it, to pull together the separate provinces, to integrate the new and more advanced Rhine provinces, to go some way towards meeting the spirit of the age. For the moment Hardenberg was not prepared to advance beyond a national assembly chosen from the provincial estates, rather than directly, and he had agreed to this limitation at Teplitz. Humboldt

wanted a directly elected national assembly, though he was in
favour of a fairly limited franchise. His reasons for wanting constitutional government for Prussia were, however, much broader
than those of the State Chancellor : he saw this as a way of
maintaining Prussia's moral leadership and he was still completely
committed to his old ideas of individual self-fulfilment. It was a
tragedy for Prussia and for Germany that these two men, who
could at this point have collaborated in their aims, wasted their
energies in a futile power struggle. Humboldt left office at the end
of 1819 and with him went Boyen and Grolman, the last representatives of the military reform party. Gneisenau had resigned in
disillusionment in 1816; Boyen had fought a losing battle to keep
his Landwehr independent of the standing army and its professional aristocratic officer corps. The Landwehr survived, but it no
longer represented the close union of army and nation which the
reformers desired. If at this stage Prussia had really adopted a
constitutional form of government it would have amounted to a
breakaway from the system which Metternich had established in
Europe and Germany. It may be doubted whether such a breakaway was practicable for Prussia. In terms of maintaining international order and peace Metternich's system had much to commend it, but its interventions in the domestic affairs of states on
the side of established authority were doomed to failure in the long
run.

The sequel to the resignations of 1819 and to the acceptance of
the Carlsbad Decrees was that Hardenberg lost almost all his influence, though he remained in office until his death in 1822. A new
commission to deliberate on the constitutional question was formed
in 1820 under the chairmanship of the Crown Prince. The future
Frederick William IV was much under the influence of political
Romanticism, as developed by Adam Müller and others and of
the Pietist revival increasingly evident amongst the nobility. Romantic conservatism idealizing old-established communal institutions
combined with the party fighting to retain Junker privileges and
for good measure there was the Court party of Wittgenstein, Ancillon and others, who were anti-constitutional altogether. The outcome was an edict of 1823 which called for the creation of provincial diets in all parts of Prussia. They were to be elected on the
basis of three estates (nobility, towns and peasants) but representation was overwhelmingly weighted on the side of the nobility.
County (*Kreis*) constitutions, where they were introduced, were on
a similar basis. Thus there might be sixty-five votes representing the
big estates of a Kreis on the basis of one vote each, and three town
and three peasant votes representing respectively several tens of

thousands of urban and rural inhabitants. Prussia thus remained entirely an Obrigkeitsstaat, in which only a very small élite participated in the process of government. Authority was no longer concentrated in the monarchy but resided in a bureaucracy recruited from the educated classes, noble and non-noble, with the Junker element predominating in the higher positions. The officer corps remained the preserve of the nobility; the small number of non-noble officers adopted the outlook of the Junkers. The bulk of the middle classes remained unaccustomed to and untrained in any public functions, except insofar as the surviving elements of Stein's municipal reforms allowed them to do so on a rather restricted stage.

Some liberalism survived in the bureaucracy, particularly among the Oberpräsidenten, the heads of provincial governments. This office was now introduced into all Prussian provinces. Theodor von Schön, the Oberpräsident of East Prussia, was a particularly striking example of an official who came to occupy a quasi-monarchical position in his province. Schön was a survivor from the reform era during which East Prussia had occupied a key position. Liberal tendencies remained stronger there than almost anywhere else in Prussia except in the Rhineland. Under Schön there was an exceptionally high proportion of non-nobles in the East Prussian administration, nine-tenths instead of an average of three-quarters, as in the rest of Prussia. In the 1840s Schön was still leading the pressure on the new monarch for a fulfilment of the constitutional promise of 1815 and it was over this issue that he finally resigned.

The Ministry of Education, instituted as a separate entity in 1815 and headed until 1840 by the same Altenstein who had led the Government briefly in 1809, was another place where some of the liberal educational ideas and administrative practices of Humboldt survived. Altenstein, a Franconian nobleman, belonged to the reform generation but he possessed enough adaptability to survive in the period of reaction. He was familiar with the ideas of Stein, Fichte and Humboldt and shared them, but he had none of their idealistic drive. During his long tenure of the Ministry of Education much was done to put into practice the plans of Humboldt and Süvern. A general system of elementary education was created which spread amongst the whole population a high level of literacy and other basic skills and aptitudes. In this respect Prussia was amongst the most advanced countries. On the other hand, the loss of the idealistic impetus of the reform era meant that Prussia acquired a school bureaucracy which dispensed formal skills with great efficiency but neglected the education of the whole personality and the development of civic virtues. In secondary schools

Humboldt's ideal of general education was retained, but again the formal aspects of learning began to predominate. The teacher, like a drill sergeant, put his students over the assault course of Latin and Greek philology; the wider civilizing benefits of a classical education were often lost. Altenstein hovered uneasily between his own ideas and past work as a reformer and his dutiful acceptance of the prevailing politics of reaction. His Ministry was closely concerned with the application of the Carlsbad Decrees in spite of the fact that the Minister himself had considerable reservations about them. Altenstein also bore some personal responsibility for barring Jews from academic posts. The Edict of 1812 emancipating the Jews allowed them to hold such posts, but the relevant section of it was revoked in 1822.

The union of the two major Protestant denominations had seemed attractive to several generations of Hohenzollern rulers. Their position as members of the Reformed Church governing the Lutheran Church was somewhat anomalous. In 1817 Frederick William III carried into effect a Union of the two churches, a matter close to his heart. It was a union of ritual and liturgy, rather than of creed, and Altenstein's new ministry became the instrument for dealing with ecclesiastical affairs. For the first time Prussia acquired a national church rather tightly controlled by the state which made some attempt to impose uniformity on the religious life of the country. Even episcopal titles came into use under Frederick William III. The new liturgy like the closer state control of the Church aroused a good deal of resistance particularly among orthodox Lutherans. Some orthodox Lutheran pastors, especially in Silesia, were removed from their livings in the 1830s and even imprisoned. A more conciliatory policy was pursued when Frederick William IV came to the throne in 1840, since it was one of his main aims in life to create a close union between Church and State. Even so, a small number of orthodox Lutherans seceded from the unified Church in 1841. There was also resistance to control by a royal national church in the Protestant communities of the Rhineland and Westphalia. Here a more democratic church government based on elected synods was the norm. The idea of union between the two Protestant denominations was, however, more acceptable in the West where they had always lived closely intermingled. The question of state control of the Church in the West was in the end settled by a compromise between the synodal system and royal control through superintendents and consistories. In spite of all difficulties the Union and the national church, "evangelische Landeskirche", helped the religious revival that developed in reaction to the Enlightenment and to rationalism.

The Prussian bureaucracy was perhaps most successful in the field of economic policy where the liberal line initiated by Hardenberg continued to prevail. The creation of a widening free-trade area in Germany was not so much the work of Friedrich List, whose ideas, although usually regarded as the origin of the *Zollverein*, were not capable of being immediately put into practice, but of two Prussian administrators, Motz and Maassen. By a customs law of 1818, for which Maassen as Director of Customs was chiefly responsible, the whole of Prussia was turned into one customs area. This did more than anything to undermine the separatism of the various Prussian territories on which the privileged position of the Junkers was based. An even more important consequence was that it gradually forced many of the small German states, particularly those which formed enclaves within Prussian territory, to come to terms with Prussia economically. For a long time they resisted the logic of events, but in 1828 Motz, as Minister of Finance, succeeded in making a customs treaty with Hesse-Darmstadt. The South German states, Bavaria and Württenberg, formed a counter union, and a certain number of the smaller Central German states tried to protect themselves through yet another union. Motz undermined this second union by making arrangements with the South German states; Maassen who succeeded him as Minister of Finance brought off a general German customs union which went into operation in 1834. By 1836 it included most of Germany except Mecklenburg, the Hanseatic towns, Hanover, Brunswick and Oldenburg. These states had a considerable degree of free trade and were therefore not hostile to the Prussian customs union. The union had a population of 25 million within frontiers more manageable than those of Prussia herself. All this was bound to strengthen the position of Prussia in Germany enormously : indeed, of itself, it made some form of political union under Prussian rather than Austrian leadership a likely outcome in the long run.

The removal of internal trade barriers in Prussia together with Zollverein gradually altered the social structure of the country. The middle class was weak except in the newly acquired Rhine provinces. Economic liberalism and the growth of capitalist enterprise strengthened the bourgeoisie and made it more self-confident. On the other hand a genuine proletariat, unprotected against the cyclical movements of a free economy, began to appear. The vast majority of the population continued to earn its living from the land, but here too the changes of the reform era, coupled with the effects of a freer economy, were producing a great deal of movement. Many peasants left the land and their holdings were amalgamated into the larger estates. Large-scale estate farming, for sale on the open market, became prevalent east of the Elbe and particularly east of the Oder. Such large-scale farming was, however, exposed to the fluctuations of the market. Estates changed ownership frequently and it was now perfectly legal for wealthy non-nobles to acquire them. Junker families of declining fortunes often sought refuge in the civil service, the *Beamtenstand,* whose prestige now stood so high, where formerly they would have found official employment mainly in the army. Access to the civil service was through the universities, but this avenue was also open to the middle classes. There was in consequence much competition for positions in the civil service and a degree of tension between higher and lower officials. All this forms the background to the ideological tension in Prussia which finally culminated in the Revolution of 1848.

The prevailing mood in Prussia in the reform era had been liberal; between 1815 and 1848 it became conservative. But Prussian conservatism was not of one variety, any more than Prussian liberalism. Conservatism stretched from the simple, patriarchial, medievalist, hierarchical social theories of Karl Ludwig von Haller to the all-embracing, closely organized and highly intellectualist philosophical system of Hegel. Religion was a complicating factor in the conservative situation. Haller, Adam Müller and many others converted to Catholicism. The Prussian Junkers were in the grip of a Pietist revival, a new and more powerful wave of the anti-rationalist feeling observable in the late 18th century. Their Protestant conservative Romanticism tried to find common ground with the Catholic variety—for example, in their newspaper *Berliner Politisches Wochenblatt* which began to appear in 1831. But Protestant Prussia sometimes clashed with Catholicism, particularly in the newly acquired Rhineland. In 1837 the Catholic Archbishop of Cologne, Droste-Vischering, was arrested and imprisoned in the fortress of Minden. He had refused to allow his priests to give the blessing to mixed marriages. This famous incident ended Protestant-Catholic co-operation.

Even more complex was the relationship of conservatism to German nationalism. During the Napoleonic period a patriotic circle like the Christlich-deutsche Tischgesellschaft had been typical of Prussian conservatism. The brothers Gerlach had been in touch with it; a generation later they were at the core of the Prussian Conservative Party and had great influence on Frederick William IV. But it grew increasingly difficult to combine German nationalism and conservative principles. Nationalism tended to become the cause of liberals, and of even more extreme radicals; it inspired the Burschenschaften and many of those who rebelled against the Metternich system. The break between liberalism and Prussia was almost complete at times between 1815 and 1848. The liberals put their hopes in the South German states or looked to France, England or Poland; they hated the repressive, bureaucratic Prussian state. Prussian conservatives, on the other hand, cultivated mainly a Prussian loyalty; hence they could not allow Prussia to assume a German role in 1848, least of all at the behest of the revolutionaries, and some of them, like the Gerlachs, would not fully accept Bismarck's handiwork. In spite of their Prussian loyalties, the conservative Junkers round Frederick William IV, before and after his accession, did not think of expanding Prussian power. The Christian-German order of their dreams assumed the continued existence of separate German states and the leadership of Austria, rather than Prussia in Germany affairs. To have smashed up this natural order would have been a moral offence. There was concern in conservative circles that the powerful emotion of national feeling should not be left entirely to the opposition; but, when the conservatives spoke at all of Germany they thought of a cultural rather than of a political nation.

Haller was the patron saint of Prussian conservatism in its earlier phase. There was a robust old-fashioned air about the ideas of this man who came from one of the patrician families of Berne and even rationalist overtones were not lacking in them. He regarded the many gradations of society as divinely ordained and considered them no bar to the personal happiness of even the lowliest individual. The strong were ordained to rule, the weak to obey and society consisted of an infinite variety of personal, feudal ties. Haller was suspicious of large states and praised periods of history in which small states predominated. Haller did not really belong to the Romantic movement, but like many Romantics he regarded the medieval social order, in which every man had his allotted place, as his ideal. It is not difficult to see why Haller's writings appealed to the Prussian Junkers. Their strong "awakened" religious feeling demanded a Christian society; they had to justify their class privileges and the concept of society ordered in estates did this for them; and above all they had to fight the enemy, liberalism and revolution.

In the 1840s Friedrich Julius Stahl became the leading ideologue of Prussian conservatism. He was a Bavarian Jew who had become a Lutheran. He taught at the University of Erlangen before being called to Berlin by Frederick William IV. Stahl's conservatism was of a more modern kind than that of Haller. The state to him, as to Luther, was a necessary consequence of man's sinful nature. In a state ordered according to Christian principles there was room for constitutionalism and there was no need to leave this idea to the liberals. The monarch would continue to hold executive power, but at his side there would be a Parliament able to vote the Budget and interrogate ministers. In order to keep this arrangement in due balance, society had to be imbued with the Christian faith through and through, and this was the task of the Church. The Church was to enjoy a wide liberty within the state and by this means its influence was to become pervasive. Stahl's historical view of the Church gave due weight to Protestantism as well as Catholicism and left room for freedom as well as for authority in religious matters. It was a corollary of Stahl's views that those who did not share the Christian beliefs—the Jews, for example—could not be functionaries of a Christian state, though their faith might be tolerated. To Stahl liberalism was a religious as well as a political aberration. On the national issue he asserted the rights of Prussia against the revolutionary national movement in 1848, though he claimed that he was not opposed to the German national idea as such but only to its appearance in revolutionary form. Stahl's influence in Prussia was at its highest after 1848.

Another trend of conservatism was represented by the great historian Leopold von Ranke. In the years between 1832 and 1836 he edited, with official encouragement, the *Historisch-Politische Zeitschrift* in which he explained the spirit which animated the Prussian bureaucracy. This was to be distinguished from Metternich-style reaction, from the conservatism of the Gerlach circle as well as from the different brands of liberalism. Ranke was one of the founders of modern historiography, widely receptive to all intellectual, national and social currents. He greatly developed the technique of historical research, making thorough use of original sources, but he also had the artistic perception necessary to recreate personalities and situations. As a historian he was not without his limitations, relying too much on official sources and tending to underestimate the influence of material as against spiritual factors. A man like Ranke could never be partisan, but his attitude was nevertheless broadly conservative. His historical sense and quest for understanding the past put him almost automatically in opposition to the abstract judgements and demands which came from the liberal-rationalist camp. He deliberately refrained from the construction of general theories of history, but if there was a general thesis running through his work it was that of the primacy of Europe and the States-System in European history. The great nations of Europe, to which most of Ranke's historical writing was devoted, could not be viewed in isolation but only in relation to each other. Their domestic development was to a large extent conditioned by the facts of external power. The thesis of the primacy of foreign policy had a great hold on German thinking, especially after 1870; it was an axiom for Bismarck. In the light of it liberalism and constitutionalism might appear luxuries which a country could ill afford. The thesis could explain many features of Prussia, her authoritarian system, her large army, her powerful bureaucracy. Ranke's ideas brought reinforcement to the traditions of the Prussian state, stretching from Frederick the Great through the Reform era to the "Beamtenstaat" of the 1830s. His conservatism was more subtle and less blatant than the romantic and emotionally inflamed attitudes of the men around the Crown Prince.

Hegel represented a conservatism of yet another kind. He was called to the University of Berlin by Altenstein, the Minister of Education, in 1817. A man of great industry, he became a famous teacher and drew to Berlin a great crowd of students and followers. He came to be regarded as the official philosopher of Prussia, whose all-embracing philosophical system supplied the justification for the Prussian state and for its conservative, anti-liberal reactionary policies. Hegel was undoubtedly always to be found on the side of established authority during his years in Berlin. His pronouncements on current political problems were always conservative in tone, whether he was speaking of the constitution of his native Württemberg or of Germany, or of the first Reform Bill in England, the subject of the last article that came from his pen.[4] Even in his writings concerned with questions of the day he was, however, by no means one-sided. On the Reform Bill, for example, he did not commend the outright opposition of English Tories; he wanted organic change and criticized the bill because he regarded it as a mixture of organic change and assertions of abstract principles of representation. Hegel's philosophical system was in all essentials formed long before he came to Berlin. It sanctioned with the approval of the "Weltgeist" any power structure or established order which the historical process might throw up, but in the dialectic it also left infinite room for movement. If it hallowed the state as the ultimate institution through which the historical process achieved its purposes, it was not necessarily the Prussian state that was so sanctified. Hegel's concept of religion was highly rational, it was a form of pantheism that could not be fitted into any received religious dogma. It was far removed from the emotional pietism of the "awakened" Junkers who belonged to the conservative group most typical of Prussia. In Hegel, official Prussia had captured a prestigious intellectual personality, at a time when its reactionary policies had antagonized the liberal German intelligentsia which had been its friend in the days of reform. State worship and the cult of power were aspects of the Hegelian philosophy which were emphasized later, when Germany came under Prussian leadership.

Soon after Hegel's death in 1831 his followers began to divide into a Left and a Right Wing and for a time the Left Wing made more of the running. A major sensation was caused when in 1835 a follower of Hegel, David Friedrich Strauss, published his book *The Life of Jesus (Leben Jesu)*.[5] Through textual criticism of the New Testament Strauss tried to show that Jesus was not a historical but a mythical figure. This book was a milestone in the 19th-century attack on orthodox Christianity; Darwin's *Origin of Species* a quarter of a century later was another. In Prussia the publication of Strauss's work heightened the suspicion which orthodox Protestants had for some time harboured against Hegel's school. The *Evangelische Kirchenzeitung,* edited by Hengstenberg, the ecclesiastical counterpiece to the *Politisches Wochenblatt,* became the spearhead of the attack against neo-Hegelianism. The organ of the Left Hegelians was the *Hallische Jahrbücher,* appearing first in 1838; here Strauss, Arnold Ruge, Bruno Bauer and Ludwig Feuerbach, a forerunner of Marx, published their articles. The *Deutsche Jahrbücher,* published in Dresden, and finally the *Deutsche-Französische Jahrbücher,* appearing in Paris, continued this school of thought into the 1840s.

Liberalism was as varied in its groups and attitudes as Conservatism but in the 1820s and 30s it had almost a monopoly of the German national idea. In the Rhine provinces there was a liberal *bourgeoisie* which for a long time remained antagonistic to the Prussian connection. The austere spirit of the Prussian military state was not in harmony with the mellow, expansive civilization of the Rhineland. The commercial classes thought the Prussian connection a poor bargain. "We're marrying into a poor family", remarked a Cologne banker in 1815. Their attitudes to Prussia gradually changed, particularly when the Zollverein began to promise a bright commercial future. David Hansemann, a manufacturer from Aachen, expressed himself in favour of Prussian hegemony in the whole of Germany as early as 1830. These men kept up pressure for constitutionalism in Prussia. Another young manufacturer from the Rhineland, Gustav Mevissen, founded a liberal newspaper, the *Rheinische Zeitung,* in 1842, which grew increasingly radical in tone. For a short time, before it was forced to cease publication by the Prussian censorship, the young Marx was its editor. Another of the group of Liberal Rhenish manufacturers was Ludolf Camphausen, who became Prussian Prime Minister in 1848. At the other end of Prussia, something survived of the East Prussian liberalism which went back to Kant and the reform era. Here the *Königsberger Zeitung* was the organ of those who were hoping for a realization of the political promises made in 1815. The repressive nature of Prussian official policy, particularly in the 1830s could not, either in Cologne or Königsberg, entirely dim the belief in the liberal and in the German mission of Prussia.

A more radical, democratic liberalism was put forward by a group of writers and poets known as Young Germany, of whom the only one of great genius was Heinrich Heine. This Rhinelander of Jewish birth defies categorization; almost like Shakespeare, he had the negative capability of sympathizing with and understanding the most diverse attitudes and beliefs. He was a passionate German, who lived most of his life in Paris but was unable to get acclimatized to French life. Yet, in a famous passage about Thor leaping to life with his giant hammer and smashing the Gothic cathedrals, he warned the French against the dangerous proclivities lurking beneath the German surface. He fought for Jewish emancipation but cursed his Jewish origin as a plague brought from the ancient Nile. He was accounted a liberal and radical and his sarcastic wit left nothing sacrosanct; yet he feared democracy and the masses and thought that in the slums of the great European cities there lurked a force which could destroy civilization. As a poet and writer, Heine could like no one else express the purity and simplicity of German Romanticism; yet much of his output must rank as shallow journalism and he was not innocent of gross lapses of taste. Heine was not typical of the radical writers of the 1830s; more characteristic was the novelist and playwright Gutzkow, who in his works proclaimed the gospel of reason, democracy, social and sexual emancipation. This radical liberalism, attacking many established values and institutions, seemed to many of its opponents an emanation of the French and the Jewish spirit, running counter to the Christian-Germanic ethos to be found in the Burschenschaften as well as among the conservatives. Wolfgang Menzel, a follower of Jahn and Arndt who lived to see the unification of Germany in 1871, attacked Gutzkow as immoral and impudent. There were a number of Jews among the radical liberals and the Left Hegelians and this fed the anti-semitism to be found both in the conservative and national camps.

Amid the conflicting ideological cross-currents of the "Vormärz", as the whole period before the revolution of March 1848 is often called in Germany, the official policy of Prussia remained tied to the system of Metternich, under whose sway it had fallen with the adoption of the Carlsbad decrees in 1819. The fear of revolution was intensified by the repercussions in Germany of the French July Revolution of 1830. Prussia adopted the police regulations which the German Confederation had decided on in July 1832, following the Hambach celebrations, a great demonstration in favour of liberalism and democracy staged by Burschenschaften and other bodies, supported by Polish and French sympathizers.[6] Persecution of students and liberals reached a fresh crescendo after an abortive attempt by radicals to seize the city of Frankfurt in 1833. By 1836, thirty-four students had been condemned to death in Berlin alone. Liberal administrative practices and the presence of the rule of law in the Prussian bureaucracy could do no more than alleviate the repressive atmosphere. It was the tragedy of German liberalism that it was thus driven into fruitless opposition. The only German state where it could have found a stage sufficiently large to be significant was Prussia, but the Hohenzollern monarchy was barred to the liberal movement once the last reformers had been forced out of the seats of power in 1819. The more radical liberals were driven underground and dissipated their energies in hopeless conspiracies; the moderates, for example, the Rhenish *bourgeoisie,* were deprived of the opportunity to acquire political experience. Thus the seeds were sown for the failure of German liberalism in 1848.

In her foreign relations Prussia continued to throw in her lot with the conservative countries of Europe. The July Revolution had finally split the concert of powers into two camps, Britain and France, the liberal countries of the West, and Russia, Austria and Prussia, the conservative powers of the East. The consequences of the July Revolution had also opened up external dangers to Prussia and Germany, the Belgian question in the West and the Polish revolt in the East. The second of these events affected Prussia very directly. Down to this time Prussia had, in her treatment of her Polish population, continued in the tradition of a non-national state. Every facility had been given to the use of the Polish language and to the development of Polish culture. In the so-called Grand Duchy of Posen Prince Radziwill, a member of one of Poland's great aristocratic families and related by marriage to the House of Hohenzollern, was installed as Regent. From 1831 a more deliberate policy of Germanizing this province was pursued, although the use of Polish in schools was reaffirmed again in 1842. As Prussian official policy began to move against Polish nationalism, so the German liberal opposition began to sympathize with the Polish patriots. From 1832 to 1837 Ancillon, the inveterate anti-Jacobin, was Prussian foreign minister and his policy was more than ever under the spell of Metternich. It may well be that from the point of view of Prussia's strategic position such a policy was a necessity, for the events in the Low Countries and in Poland in the wake of the July Revolution had shown how exposed was

Prussia militarily. Such considerations certainly seemed more important to the makers of Prussian policy than the capture of German nationalism which would have entailed a much more liberal course in domestic affairs. Such a course seemed precluded by the traditions of the Prussian monarchy, the Junkers, the bureaucracy, the army, in fact by the whole structure of the Prussian state which the reform era had failed to alter fundamentally.

Yet there were hopes in Prussia and in Germany that things might change. These hopes centred on the Crown Prince who after a long period of waiting came to the throne as Frederick William IV in 1840. Never was there a greater misunderstanding. He was certainly cast in an unusual mould for a Hohenzollern ruler. The gulf between his mental world and reality was so wide that it amounted to neurosis and ended in complete mental breakdown. He was of the stuff artists are made of, but without the inner compulsion that makes the great artist. His temperament was wholly unsuited to the fulfilment of a political role or to the exercise of political judgement. He had undoubted intellectual gifts, was idealistic and full of ideas and, unlike any of his predecessors, fond of making public speeches and not interested in military affairs. His mental furniture came from the medievalistic, patriarchal ideas of Haller, his vision was of a harmonious realm, in which a benign king ruled over loyal subjects. It was a vision absurdly remote from the reality of the 1840s and when the real world broke through, as it did dramatically in 1848, the King was thrown into a paroxysm of remorse, depression, elation and indecision.

Frederick William had an ear for the German national idea, but he was really looking to a resurrection of the Holy Roman Empire. It was inconceivable to him that a new Germany should not be led by the Austrian Emperor—the King of Prussia might become his hereditary Field Marshal. Thus Frederick William had really a defective perception of the true interests and power of his own country in an age of growing industrialization. At the same time he took a very high and legitimist view of his office when it came to liberal demands for a constitution. The Prussian court before and after the accession of Frederick William IV was full of members of the "awakened" nobility. Neo-Pietism could easily become facile religiosity; the privileges of the Junkers and the social status quo were hallowed as part of the divine order and this convenient if sincere belief was accompanied by a great deal of religious observance, prayer, Bible-reading and visiting of the poor. Alexander von Humboldt, the great scientist and brother of Wilhelm, talked of the "whining" that went on at Court. Frederick

William's religion went rather deeper; like so many Hohenzollerns he dreamt of uniting all denominations. One of the first acts of his reign was to try and repair the breach with Catholicism caused by the "Cologne Incident", the arrest of the Archbishop Droste-Vischering.

It was perhaps significant that the King's closest friends were two non-Prussians, Radowitz and Bunsen. Radowitz was partly of Hungarian origin and was a Catholic. He was one of the editors of the *Politisches Wochenblatt*—his ideas, like those of the Crown Prince, had been formed by Haller. He occupied the important position of Prussian plenipotentiary for military affairs at the Bund in Frankfurt. He shared Frederick William's idea of a "grossdeutsch" solution to the German problem and his opinions on the constitutional issue were also remarkably close to those of his master. He had perceptive ideas on how the problems caused by the rise of an industrial proletariat might be cured. At crucial moments, Radowitz had great influence and after the revolution of 1848 he became a major figure. Bunsen, a man of much personal attraction and an independent mind, was married to an English-woman and spent many years as Prussia's ambassador in London. He was responsible for making the King feel that English conditions, which Bunsen interpreted in a High Tory sense, could be a model for Prussia. Frederick William came to regard the Church of England, which he saw in the kind of light that the young Gladstone did in his early work *The Church in its relations with the State*, as the ideal ecclesiastical settlement. One practical result was the foundation of the Bishopric of Jerusalem, the incumbent of which was to be appointed alternately by the King of Prussia and the King of England. The brothers Gerlach, particularly Leopold and Ludwig, also belonged to Frederick William's inner circle. These men and the King were too intellectual and too much under the sway of ideas to have much in common with the robust and instinctive conservatism of the country Junkers. Thus Frederick William IV, for the moment Prussia's and soon to be Germany's man of destiny, added yet another and unpredictable factor to the complex knot of Prussian and German problems. As a private citizen he would have been interesting, unstable and on the verge of mental illness, but not without attractive qualities and to be respected for his idealism; as a public figure exercising great power he could be disastrous.

At first the hopes that the King's accession would usher in a new era seemed destined to be fulfilled. There was a general amnesty for political offenders. Arndt, a very old man now, was again permitted to give lectures at Bonn; Jahn was released from police supervision; Dahlmann, who had left Hanover in protest against the withdrawal of the constitution in 1837, was given a chair at Bonn. He was one of the Göttingen "Seven" whose resignations had evoked a nation-wide echo in Germany. Yet all these actions were mere gestures; Frederick William liked to move in an atmosphere of approval and adoration. His real views were seen in the summons of Friedrich Julius Stahl to Berlin. More important and equally characteristic was his relative inaction in the crisis which shook Europe in 1840. The crisis arose out of Mehemet Ali's designs on Turkey. French public opinion, thwarted in the Near East, appeared to be seeking compensation by reviving French claims to the west bank of the Rhine. This stirred opinion in Germany deeply and something of the feeling that swept through Germany at the time of the Wars of Liberation came back. Even those liberals who had, especially since the July Revolution, looked to France for inspiration now saw in her again the national enemy. Patriotic poems like Nikolaus Becker's "They shall not have him, the free German Rhine" and "Watch on the Rhine" were written. Prussia might have used that moment to assert her leadership of the German national movement. Frederick William preferred to go with Austria in strengthening the military posture of the German Confederation. In return for Austria's agreement that the North German military contingent should come under Prussian command he gave the assurance that Prussian and German federal protection would be extended to Austria's possessions in Lombardy. That national considerations were not Frederick William's highest priority was shown by his attitude towards his Polish subjects. It was he who reversed the Germanizing policy which had been initiated after the Polish rising of 1830. He believed that such an attitude of trust by the ruler towards his subjects would counteract the spread of revolutionary and jacobinical tendencies in Poland.

The constitutional question became again the crucial issue in Prussia in the 1840s. The expectations aroused by the new King's accession and his first acts, the patriotic upsurge in Germany in the crisis of 1840, developments in other German states, as well as social and economic conditions all conspired to make the promises given as long ago as 1815 to introduce constitutional government again a matter of immediate concern. Schön, the East Prussian Oberpräsident, sent a memorandum to the King entitled "Whence and Whither" which quickly became public knowledge.[7] He took up Stein's demands for self-government and showed how the bureaucracy had failed to meet them. He called for general estates to deal with national and communal affairs, to control finance and influence military affairs. Another East Prussian, Johann Jacoby, a Jewish doctor, in a widely circulated pamphlet *Four Questions, Answered by an East Prussian*[8] stressed even more strongly the legal right of the Prussians to representation, based on the promise of Frederick William III and the constitution of the German Confederation.

Frederick William IV had no intention of giving way to such demands. When he spoke of estates and representation he thought romantically of traditional German models. Anything he granted would not be based as of right on a written constitution, but given by the King's grace and favour. He implemented a plan to create standing committees of the existing provincial estates and these were called together in Berlin in 1842 as "United Committees". They were allowed to discuss some matters of taxation and the question of guaranteeing a loan for railway development. In all it did not amount to much more than information about actions which the Government had already taken. The King made it clear that he regarded the meeting as consultative and based on the estates and not as representative of public opinion at large. After 1844 the King developed plans for a United Diet consisting of all the deputies of the eight existing provincial diets. It was not to meet regularly but only on rare special occasions. The United Committees should continue to be called into existence every four years. These were plans only and aroused expectations; even if they had been immediately implemented they could by this time hardly have succeeded in meeting the demands of a growing section of opinion.

The pressures for change were multiplying. The leaders of the Rhenish liberal *bourgeoisie*, men like Camphausen, Hansemann and Mevissen, were becoming more insistent in their demands. They were spurred on by the example of the more liberal South German states, particularly Baden. The moderate liberals throughout Germany were becoming a more coherent force and breaking down the barriers which had kept them confined to the separate states. These men did not want a revolution, but they wanted progress towards constitutional government and towards more effective institutions to pull Germany together as one country. On their left a more revolutionary note was being sounded: it came partly from the neo-Hegelians, partly from the influence in Germany of Saint-Simon and other French socialist thinkers. Lorenz Stein and Wilhelm Weitling made French socialist thought known in Germany. Ludwig Feuerbach and Moses Hess were the neo-Hegelians who directly influenced Marx. Revolutionary socialist theories had as yet little concrete material to work upon in Germany. The industrial proletariat was numerically still insignificant but there was enough distress and hardship to make the political climate more extreme. The real sufferers were the workers in domestic industries, like the weavers of Silesia, displaced master craftsmen and journeymen and the poorer and more insecure sections of the peasantry. The economic liberalism which had survived in the Prussian bureaucracy since the reform era and existed elsewhere in Germany left these classes exposed to the forces at play in a free market economy. The position was aggravated by the economic depression which affected Europe between 1844 and 1847. The eastern provinces of Prussia were afflicted by specific disasters, such as the Austrian annexation of Cracow in 1846. This tiny republic had afforded a contraband outlet by which Silesian textiles could overcome the tariff barriers round the Habsburg Empire and Poland : the Austrian annexation caused a severe fall in Prussian textile exports. On top of all this Europe, from Ireland to Silesia, experienced famine and a steep rise in the cost of basic foodstuffs following the failure of the potato harvest in 1845. There were food riots in Berlin in the spring of 1847. The grievances of the masses had little in common with the political demands of middle-class liberalism, but they lent substance to the theories of the revolutionary intellectuals.

Frederick William's plans for a United Diet were at last unveiled in February 1847 and the Diet was opened in April of the same year. It consisted of two chambers, a house of nobility and a house representing knights (i.e. manorial lords), burghers and peasants. The lower house had the three estate division normal in the provincial diets. The Diet was not to meet regularly and it was to have consultative functions only. In his opening speech from the throne the King once again denied any intention of introducing a formal constitution : "Never will I permit a piece of paper to come between our God in heaven and this land, as if it were a second providence, to govern us with its paragraphs and supplant the old sacred loyalty." The United Diet was nicely calculated to create the maximum of political excitement and to unsettle conservatives at home and abroad, while failing to meet liberal aspirations. It was in session for two months during which the King was overwhelmed with demands for regular meetings, participation in legislation and written guarantees. The Diet refused to agree to a loan for the building of a railway between Berlin and Königsberg, thus foregoing clear economic advantage for the sake of principle. In the debates party lines and issues between liberals and conservatives were clearly drawn and the leading figures on both sides began to emerge. The leaders of the liberal opposition included the Rhinelanders, Camphausen and Hansemann, Georg von Vincke, the son of a highly respected Westphalian Oberpräsident, and from East Prussia Count Schwerin and the future Minister of the Interior, von Auerswald. The leading conservatives were Count Arnim-Boitzenburg, von Manteuffel, another future Minister, and last but not least Count Otto von Bismarck-Schönhausen, who made his debut here on the national scene. Bismarck made a speech in the Diet on the Jewish question which was very much in line with the Christian-German ideology of the Court and of the conservatives. He revealed, however, something more of his own headstrong and unconventional character when he admitted that his reluctance to bend the knee to a Jew holding an official position was due to prejudices imbibed with his mother's milk. On general questions, Bismarck was an impetuous defender of the King's divine and legitimate rights against the national rights claimed by the constitutionalists.

The United Diet did nothing to resolve the domestic situation in Prussia. The King went on dreaming his dreams of an episcopal National Church with the apostolic succession for Prussia, while the conservative order in Europe was rapidly breaking down. The Austrian annexation of Cracow and the Swiss Civil War, which led to the absorption of the Prussian principality of Neufchâtel, showed that the international order established at Vienna was collapsing. The demand for change in Germany became more vehement. The radicals met at Offenburg in September 1847 and called for sweeping political and social reforms, not only the safeguarding of civil rights, but primary and secondary education open to all and measures to assuage the conflict between capital and labour. This was primarily a South German meeting, but when at Heppenheim the moderate liberals met a month later Hansemann and Mevissen, the leaders of Rhineland liberalism, were present. Here the demands were much more realistic; at their core was the proposal to extend the competence of the Zollverein in a political direction by the creation of a Parliament of the Zollverein countries. This meant the leadership of Prussia in Germany.

Prussian officialdom was not entirely oblivious of the movement that was going on all round and made some attempt to utilize it in a sense that was both conservative and in the interests of Prussia's position in Germany. Radowitz, the King's friend, prepared a memorandum in November 1847, proposing a reform of the German Confederation to obtain greater military cohesion, a better protection of civil rights and a more effective economic policy for the whole of Germany. All this was to be done with the co-operation of Austria, for both the King and Radowitz were "grossdeutsch". It was realized, however, that Austria might be reluctant to co-operate and special treaties between Prussia and other German states were considered as an alternative. The dichotomy between *Grossdeutschland* and *Kleindeutschland,* Germany with or without Austria, became one of the crucial issues of the revolutionary year 1848 and henceforward. In March 1848 Radowitz was in the midst of negotiations with Metternich about reform of the Confederation when the Austrian Chancellor was swept from office.

The February Revolution in France which toppled the Orleanist Monarchy speeded the pace of events in Germany. A meeting of liberal politicians at Heidelberg in early March 1848 called for a German constituent assembly and to prepare the way for this a so-called "Vorparlament" was summoned to Frankfurt. At the Federal Diet itself a number of liberal decisions were taken; a commission of seventeen distinguished men was set up to make plans for an elected assembly within the framework of the Confederation. These events, the growing unrest throughout Germany, the beginning of demonstrations and popular activity in the streets of Berlin, finally the news of revolution in Vienna, all this persuaded Frederick William that reluctantly he must take further steps to meet the situation in Prussia and to assert Prussia's position in Germany. On 18th March a new patent was published calling an early meeting of the United Diet; it promised a constitution for Prussia and full freedom of the press; for Germany it envisaged the creation of a genuine federal state in place of the loose confederation. These major concessions came just too late to save the King from a humiliating confrontation with open revolt. The events of 18th March and the following few days have often been described and all the evidence has been examined by historians in minute detail. It is unlikely that the King now took his decisions on very rational grounds. The shock to his neurotic mind had been great; the tension between his dreams and an ugly reality was too overwhelming. The decision to withdraw the troops from the Royal Palace in Berlin was probably taken in such a mood and was compounded by misunderstandings. The spectacle of the King honouring the dead of the revolution in the courtyard of the palace and his ride round Berlin draped in the black-red-gold colours of the revolution were deeply resented by all conservative elements at Court, in the army and among the Junkers.

The further evolution of events in Prussia in 1848 saw on the one hand the fulfilment of the constitutional promises of March, on the other the gradual recovery of the conservative forces and their final victory. In May a National Assembly, elected by universal suffrage, began to meet. A few weeks earlier a liberal

Ministry had been formed. It was led by Camphausen and contained most of the opposition leaders from the United Diet of 1847—Hansemann, Auerswald, Schwerin. In the Assembly, however, a much more radical tone prevailed. Men like Waldeck and Johann Jacoby, who believed in full political democracy, played an important role : they were often in alliance with men of the Centre Left, like the economist Karl Rodbertus. Radicalism was stronger in Berlin than it was at Frankfurt. A long wrangle ensued over the constitutional proposals, and the demands of the radical democrats grew more and more extreme. The influence of the revolutionary mob on the assembly, as seen in incidents like the attack on the Arsenal in June, was considerable. The Camphausen Ministry was succeeded by a number of other short-lived governments which tried to cope with this dangerous situation.

In the meantime, the King was biding his time and relying much on the advice of Radowitz. He hoped to use his liberal ministers to take the wind out of the sails of the radical democratic movement in the country and in the assembly, and thereby to allow time for the conservative forces to rally. He also maintained contact with conservatives of the Stahl persuasion, like the Gerlachs, and these men, who were suspected by the liberals of constituting a kind of kitchen cabinet, came to be known as the Camarilla. Frederick William left his liberal ministers in no doubt that he did not feel himself bound by any constitutional or parliamentary system. In due course the conservatives did rally and organized themselves into a more coherent party than previously. The country Junkers, stung by the Assembly's attacks on their privileges and taxation immunities, founded an "Association for the Protection of Property" which held a large meeting in August, the so-called Junker Parliament. Bismarck, aged thirty-three and still an impetuous counter-revolutionary, was a leading figure here. The intellectual conservatives, under the lead of Leopold von Gerlach, founded a newspaper, the *Neue Preussische Zeitung*. It became the organ of the new Conservative party which now had an agrarian and a Christian-German wing. The paper used the Iron Cross as its symbol and became known as the *Kreuzzeitung*. This party, with its associations in the country and supporters at Court, quickly regained influence.

In the meantime the King and his ministers found the Assembly increasingly uncomfortable to live with. The demand was made that the Minister of War should order army officers to refrain from anti-revolutionary activities or else leave the army. This was quite unacceptable to the King and over this issue the Auerswald-Hansemann Government, which had succeeded that of Camphausen, had in its turn to resign early in September. General von Pfuel, who had just suppressed a Polish rising in Posen, headed the next Ministry and was still trying to seek an accommodation with the Assembly. The Government's constitutional proposals were considered in the Assembly from 12th October onwards and a number of radical, democratic amendments, unacceptable to the King, were passed. Things came to a head when it became apparent at the end of October that Windischgrätz was about to crush the revolution in Vienna. An attempt was made, in the Assembly and in the streets, to force the Prussian Government to come to the aid of the Austrian Revolution against the Austrian Government.

The King now took steps to restore his authority against the Assembly and the radical party. He took courage from events in Vienna and the Camarilla had succeeded in stiffening his resolution. The attempt to compromise along liberal lines and with liberal ministers had failed. Pfuel resigned and among the successors suggested by the Camarilla was Bismarck. The King felt that the wild Junker could be used as minister only "when bayonets rule without restraint" and Count Brandenburg, Frederick William II's natural son, became his new minister. Military force was used to restore order in Berlin and other centres of unrest. The Assembly was adjourned and its seat moved to Brandenburg. A call by some of its more radical members that payment of taxes should be refused as a protest proved a vain gesture. Finally, on 5th December 1848, the Assembly was dissolved. At the same time the King announced the grant of a constitution, always referred to as the *Oktroyierte Verfassung* (imposed constitution) because it was prepared by the royal ministers and given by the King as an act of grace rather than passed by a constituent assembly. It was still a surprisingly liberal document, because Frederick William and his ministers had recovered their confidence through the successful restoration of order and also because they realized that the liberal *bourgeoisie* had become too powerful in Prussia to be ignored. There was to be a bi-cameral parliament, with the second Chamber indirectly elected by the people. Admittedly even the first elections in 1849 were held on a restricted franchise and later the three-tier electoral system was introduced. Such bastions of Junker privilege as patrimonial justice and the police power on noble estates were for the moment abolished. In its main framework this constitution remained in force until 1918.

All these events in Prussia were overshadowed by the drama of the National Assembly at Frankfurt. The tragedy of the Assembly was that it had not merely to cope with the conflicts between

different shades of liberalism and the more extreme radical, democratic, revolutionary and even socialist doctrines. This might have
proved easier at Frankfurt than it did in Berlin, for the moderate
liberals were well in the ascendant in the National Assembly. Far
more difficult was the task of forming a German state and it was
on this rock, the continued existence of separate German states and
especially of the two Great Powers, Austria and Prussia, that the
Assembly came to grief. The most fundamental problem was
whether the German state to be created was to include or exclude
Austria. Events made it clear that a reasonably cohesive Grossdeutschland could only be formed if German-speaking Austria
could in some way be separated from the rest of the Habsburg
dominions and that such a separation was in fact not practical
politics.

This left only the possibility of Kleindeutschland, Germany with
Prussia but without Austria. Even before the revolution this solution had been widely advocated, but it could, theoretically, be
realized in a number of different forms. Prussia could be merged
into Germany, or Germany could come under Prussian leadership.
It could be done under a monarchical or a republican regime and
in a federal or a unitary state. All this gave endless scope for dis-
agreement. In the first flush of the March Revolution Max von
Gagern, one of the Gagern brothers who played so prominent a
part in the events of 1848, went to Berlin, hopeful that the eight
Prussian provinces could separately become constituents of a
unitary German state and that Prussia as such would cease to
exist. The Prussian Government was at that moment at a point
of extreme weakness. The King, in a desperate effort to ride the
revolution, had processed round his capital donning the German
colours and proclaiming that Prussia was henceforth merged in
Germany. Gagern was soon disillusioned. He realized that Prussia
would not without further ado give up her separate identity and
that pronouncements by her King could not always be taken liter-
ally. The idea of Prussia genuinely merging into Germany remained
strong, however, and even a Prussian patriot like Droysen, the
historian, held it. He thought it an advantage that Prussia had not
yet acquired a new centralized constitution and proposed that
Prussia should become *unmittelbares Reichsland,* an immediate
part of the new German Empire to be established, without a
separate centralized Government of her own.

Throughout 1848 there was a complex interaction between
Frankfurt and Berlin. The moderate liberals at Frankfurt wanted
the Prussian monarchy and government to be sufficiently chastened
to fall in with their plans for a monarchical, liberal and reasonably

cohesive Germany. But if the established Prussian state was too much weakened it would dangerously increase the power of the radical democratic forces, not only in Berlin but also at Frankfurt. Such a moment appeared to have come when Prussia, under pressure from the Great Powers, concluded an armistice with Denmark in September 1848, at the end of the short war over Schleswig-Holstein. The majority of liberals at Frankfurt did not want to accept an end to this war so unsatisfactory to German national aspirations, yet they had no alternative. The demonstration of their impotence strengthened the revolutionary elements in Frankfurt and elsewhere. The liberal majority at Frankfurt was running a desperate race against the increasingly restored power of the separate monarchical governments of Germany, particularly that of Prussia, and at the same time against the rising tide of revolutionary radicalism.

The left-wing elements in Berlin, for example the East Prussian radical Johann Jacoby, started off by attacking their own government for their refusal to give up the Prussian identity. As the Assembly in Berlin fell more under the influence of the radicals, however, men like Jacoby and others reversed their position. The Berlin Assembly appeared now a much more promising platform for the realization of their social and political aims and they began to emphasize the autonomy and importance of Prussian developments. On the conservative side there was always much more reluctance to forgo the Prussian identity, but on the other hand the Junkers had, for centuries, seen their privileges anchored in the provinces and the provincial diets and had often regarded the central aspects of the Prussian state as their enemy. To this extent the conservatives might have welcomed the dissolution of Prussia into Germany, but hardly as part of a strong liberal and national movement.

The imposed constitution of December 1848 changed the position once more. Whatever they might have hoped earlier, the Frankfurt liberals now had to accept the continued existence of Prussia. The victory of counter-revolution at Vienna made it imperative to come to terms with Berlin. The imposed Prussian constitution, with its relatively liberal slant, and the frequent declarations in favour of the German idea that had come from the Prussian King appeared to make possible a constitutional, federal Germany, without Austria and under the hereditary leadership of the King of Prussia as emperor. This became the programme of the so-called *Erb-Kaiserliche* (hereditary imperial) party at Frankfurt and it was in this shape that the imperial crown was offered to Frederick William IV in April 1849. His first declaration on the offer was that he would accept provided the other German rulers accepted; his final refusal at the end of April was due to the strong Austrian opposition, to the refusal of the German kings, as opposed to the lesser rulers, to accept and finally to renewed revolutionary risings, for example, in Saxony. There were also domestic reasons for the King's attitude: the newly elected Second Chamber had again clashed with his ministers. Frederick William had never wanted a Germany without Austria and he had put forward a number of schemes, with the help of Radowitz, to create a relationship between Austria, on one hand, and a closer German union under Prussia on the other. He was certainly not prepared to go against Austria. His legitimist principles would not allow him to accept a crown proffered by an assembly based on the representative principle. Sometimes his Prussian, Hohenzollern ambition was tempted by the wider prospects before him. He called Heinrich von Gagern, who was negotiating in Berlin at a crucial moment in November 1848, his tempter. But, as he told another of the Frankfurt ministers, he was no Frederick the Great. Considerations of foreign policy were also involved in bringing about the refusal, though they need not be overemphasized. Austria and Russia would have opposed the new German state strongly. With Frederick William's refusal of the imperial crown the German Revolution was virtually at an end. Prussia helped to mop up revolutionary risings in Baden, Saxony and elsewhere. The National Assembly at Frankfurt withered away ingloriously. It had lacked the solid foundation of power necessary to create a German state.

Twice in a generation Prussia had turned away from the liberal and constitutional path. Developments in the years after 1848 were to make plain the extent to which the liberal forces had been irrevocably weakened this time and how much the conservative elements in the bureaucracy, in the army, among the Junkers and among the middle classes had been strengthened. Prussia therefore moved deeper into the industrial age and its problems less than ever prepared politically to meet the new situation. Because the old monarchical bureaucratic framework had proved so enduring in Prussia in 1848, Germany as a whole was prevented from attaining greater unity under liberal auspices. Yet ever since 1815 those who governed Prussia had underestimated her real strength in terms of power. The old dynastic ambition of earlier Hohenzollern rulers was entirely dead. Prussia felt compelled to follow tamely in the wake of the conservative powers of Europe, Austria and Russia, and in German affairs she remained content to play second fiddle to Austria. The feeling of weakness was partly due to the conservatism which governed official policy, partly to the continued tension between conservative and liberal elements in public life and partly to the fact that the new Western provinces which Prussia acquired after 1815, were as yet imperfectly integrated with the old predominantly East Elbian Prussia. The feeling of weakness continued into the 1850s until Bismarck forcefully dispelled it. Yet the year 1848 had shown that the future of Germany depended on Prussia far more than on Austria. Both the traditional leaders of Prussia and the liberal German *bourgeoisie* learnt a lesson about the realities of political power : the former in due course became aware of the power they possessed, the latter, realizing their impotence, looked to the country where power lay.

CHAPTER VII

Prussia and the Unification of Germany
1849–1871

THE refusal of the imperial crown by Frederick William IV, the collapse of the Frankfurt Parliament, and the military suppression of the last despairing spasms of revolution did not conclusively resolve either the German question or the conflict between legitimist and parliamentary principles. Prussia had no respite from either problem. At home the imposed constitution of December 1848 continued in force, although the first lower chamber elected under it was dissolved on the day before the King gave his final refusal to the Frankfurt Parliament. In conservative circles the constitution was regarded as too liberal and many wanted it abrogated; they called it jocularly the "Charte Waldeck", after the radical leader in the Berlin Assembly of 1848. The electoral law for the lower chamber was now revised according to the three-tier system : the electorate was divided into three classes, each paying an equal amount of taxes. In practice this meant that the top division contained about 6 per cent of the electors, the second about 17 per cent and the third the remaining three-quarters or four-fifths. Each division chose an equal number of electors and they in turn elected the deputies. This strange electoral system remained in force in Prussia until 1918. After 1870 it gave the East Elbian aristocracy, gradually reinforced by the wealthy industrial and commercial classes, a political weight out of proportion to their numbers and its continuance alongside universal suffrage for the German Reichstag became one of the chief political issues of imperial Germany. Owing to the small value of the vote in the third division, the mass of voters became increasingly disinclined to use their vote.

A Chamber, thus elected in the summer of 1849, was given the task of revising the imposed Constitution. It had a conservative majority; the liberals were present in small numbers, but the radical democrats had disappeared. In the revised constitution the basic rights of the citizen were guaranteed, but the centre of gravity in the state remained undoubtedly with the King and his ministers.

The idea that ministers should also be responsible to the two Chambers was embedded in the constitution in theory but was not put into practice. The army and civil servants owed allegiance to the King only; the extent to which the Chambers could control the budget and taxation was doubtful and the government could legislate by decree in an emergency. The Second Chamber was constituted by a law of 1853 on lines similar to the House of Lords and renamed Herrenhaus. It consisted of hereditary members and members appointed by the King. Prussia, however, did not have the independent wealthy aristocracy of 18th or 19th century England and only a few of the appointed members, for example mayors of large cities, brought any knowledge of modern conditions to its deliberations. On the whole this constitution breathed a conservative air and since it received no major revision until 1918 it eventually became a glaring anachronism. In the 1850s it was, however, relatively up-to-date and it was remarkable that constitutional government survived at all in Prussia. The battles fought under this Constitution in the 1850s and '60s were realistic enough. In Austria and in a great many other German states constitutional government in any genuine sense did not survive the events of 1848.

After Frederick William's refusal of the German crown, Prussia still retained some initiative in the German question. The King wanted to further the cause of German unity if it could be done under legitimist principles and with the co-operation of Austria. Throughout 1848 his fertile brain had produced one impractical scheme after another to fulfil his dual purpose. Radowitz now proposed combining a narrower federation under the leadership of Prussia with a wider confederation including Austria. This non-Prussian Catholic who stood so close to the King had worked at Frankfurt as a member of a Catholic group of deputies and in favour of a *grossdeutsch* solution. He now returned to Berlin to advise the King and secured his approval for his proposals. On the face of it Prussia was in a strong position to carry out such a scheme, for her troops were in the process of putting down revolution all over Germany and restoring the established order.

It was the tragedy of Radowitz and Frederick William IV that just at that moment Austria was recovering her confidence and ambition as a Great Power under the able leadership of Prince Schwarzenberg. Between May 1849 and November 1850 Austria became progressively less willing to countenance any German solution other than a restoration of the Confederation of 1815 under Austrian leadership. In fact Schwarzenberg's concept went much further. He wanted to create a Middle Europe of 70 million inhabitants, including not only all German-speaking peoples but the whole of the Habsburg Empire which would become the natural leader of such a system. Austrian policy was increasingly aided by Russia and in 1850 the Tsar became the arbiter in German affairs. In the renewed conflict over Schleswig-Holstein in 1850 Prussia was inhibited from fully using her military strength against the Danes by fear of offending Russia. In the final Prussian capitulation to Austria at Olmütz in November 1850 Russia again powerfully reinforced the Austrian position. It is, however, as easy to overestimate the influence of foreign powers over these later attempts to settle the German question as it is over the course of events in 1848. Only in the Schleswig-Holstein problem, and possibly at Olmütz, was there anything like foreign intervention. Some German historians, bearing in mind the process of unification by Bismarck and giving due weight to "Realpolitik", have taken the view that any unification of Germany achieved between 1848 and 1850 would have come up against the opposition of the major powers of Europe.[1] In fact such a point was never reached and Prussian policy was in the main determined by domestic and German rather than European considerations.

Prussia's attempts at union in 1849 and 1850 met with some success. Twenty-eight of the middle and smaller German states adhered by treaty to the plan for a Union of Princes under the leadership of the King of Prussia. Bavaria and Württemberg, however, failed to do so and this, with Austrian pressure, led to the defection of the two other kingdoms, Hanover and Saxony. The erbkaiserliche liberals, who at Frankfurt had carried through the offer of the German crown to Frederick William, supported the Prussian plans wholeheartedly. A Parliament of the Union was elected and met in March and April 1850 at Erfurt. But now the tension between the Prussian plan for Germany and the Austrian intention of reviving the Confederation of 1815 became dangerous and reached flashpoint over the case of Electoral Hesse in the autumn of 1850. The Elector had tried to set aside the Constitution in his country and was faced with a popular rising. Although a member of the Prussian Union he appealed for help to the old Federal Diet, the rump of which had been reconvened by Schwarzenberg several months earlier. Radowitz, who had in the meantime become Prussian foreign minister, saw this as a case for intervention by the Prussian Union and soon Prussian and Bavarian troops, the latter acting for the Federal Diet, confronted each other in Hesse. The Prussian Government flinched from the ultimate prospect of war, partly because of the pressure of the Tsar. Radowitz resigned; Brandenburg, the Prime Minister, died at the height

of the crisis. Manteuffel, the new Premier, previously Minister of
the Interior, went to meet Schwarzenberg at Olmütz at the end
of November 1850 and signed a convention. Prussia agreed to the
restoration of the Confederation and to the end of the Union; she
withdrew from Hesse and agreed that the Confederation should
put down the rising against the Danes in Holstein.

Frederick William IV, who had always wanted to solve the
German question with and indeed under Austria, had thus nearly
gone to war against Austria. He had neither the intention nor the
nerve to pursue with resolution a policy which would again have
required an alliance with German liberalism and nationalism and
a determined use of Prussian power. Radowitz had also desired to
solve the German question with Austria, but he was prepared to
be daring and experimental. The Prussian conservatives, particularly those of the Gerlach-Stahl persuasion, were increasingly
opposed to Radowitz and his policy and tried to counteract his
influence on the King. To them their conservative principles and
attachment to a Christian, hierarchical social order were the first
priority, the interests of the Prussian state came second, and concern for Germany a long way behind. They wanted no truck with
liberalism and a Europe based on an alliance of Prussia, Russia
and Austria, the three custodians of order. Prussian official circles
continued, if anything, to underestimate the power of their country.

Olmütz was an undoubted Prussian humiliation, but it had
stopped a long way short of realizing Schwarzenberg's concept of
Middle Europe. It soon became apparent that Austrian predominance in German affairs could not be restored. Power was in fact
divided in the Confederation between Austria and Prussia. Prussian interests at Frankfurt were soon forcefully asserted by Bismarck
when he became envoy to the Diet. The lesser German states held
the balance. The Confederation could no longer be used to suppress
liberal movements in the member states, in the way it had been
in the days of Metternich. It was even more important that Austria
did not succeed in challenging the growing economic predominance of Prussia in Germany. The Austrians would have liked a
trade treaty with the Zollverein leading to their eventual admission
to the customs union. This would have degraded Prussia's position
within the Zollverein. All they got was a trade treaty, concluded
in 1853, providing for a reconsideration of their relationship with
the Zollverein six years later. When that time came their economic position relative to Prussia was even weaker and this trend
continued into the 1860s. Prussia became economically strong
enough to opt for free trade by the 1860s and on this path Austria,
with her still predominantly agrarian society and weak industries,

could not follow. The politically strongest interest in Prussia, the East Elbian Junkers, were in favour of free trade, which would help them to sell their agricultural surpluses abroad. Immediately after Olmütz the Zollverein was in fact strengthened by the adhesion of Hanover and some minor West German states; it now included a population of 35 million. All this explains much about the course of political affairs.

The 1850s were once more a period of reaction and conservatism in Prussia, but to state this too baldly would be an oversimplification. There were different shades of conservatism; the opposition of conservatives to economic liberalism produced some progressive measures—for example, limitation of child labour and hours of work. For the first time there appeared in Prussian politics a specifically Catholic Group. Frederick William's conciliatory policy toward the Catholics had not been able to erase the memory of the persecutions of the 1830s and other misunderstandings had further strengthened the feeling that the interests of the Catholic church and of Catholicism needed political assertion. Out of the small group of Catholic deputies which appeared in the Prussian Parliament in the 1850s there eventually arose the powerful Centre Party. On the liberal side the disillusionment after 1848 led to withdrawal from politics and to concentration on commerce and industry : for example, men like Hansemann and Mevissen and Camphausen became powerful figures in banking. The ideal of education, on which so much of the earlier liberalism of the German middle classes was based, faded; and even on the conservative side the Gerlach-Stahl circle was the last group to take their stand purely on ideas and principles, which in course of time became ever more remote from social and economic realities.

1848 had demonstrated crushingly the impotence of ideas without power and therefore all through the political spectrum there was a turning to "Realpolitik", a term coined by the liberal writer Rochau in 1853. Hegel's view that the essence of the state was power became popular in Germany only now. A realistic appreciation of power characterized the historical writing of the period, in the works of Droysen, Sybel and later Treitschke. From history these men drew the lesson that Germany required a strong, cohesive state. Prussia was the only existing state sufficiently strong to provide the framework for a Germany able to compete with the older European nation states. Hence Austria, a multi-national empire which could never itself obtain perfect cohesion, must be pushed out of Germany and *Kleindeutschland* must be realized round Prussia. Sybel, for example, saw the German medieval empire as an aberration and considered the Great Elector the legitimate

inheritor of Germany's national development. From this he drew
conclusions for the future : "Because the whole past has shown me
the imperial policy as the graveyard of our national well-being,
therefore I prefer 'little Germany' of 35 millions to the great
'German-Magyar-Slav-Land' of 70 million."[2] It was only now
generally accepted that Hegel's high view of the state applied *par
excellence* to Prussia and that the logical consummation of Prussia
was Germany. Such views were now widely held by the educated
liberals whose hopes had been dashed in 1848. It prepared them
psychologically to support the authoritarian Prussian state when
under Bismarck it at last took in hand again the task of German
unification.

For the moment the conduct of policy was in the hands of conservatives. There was the King, the Camarilla and the Gerlach-
Stahl circle. Among ministers Westphalen, the Minister of the
Interior, whose sister was married to Karl Marx, shared most fully
the High Tory views popular at Court. Manteuffel, the Prime
Minister, personified a more hard-headed conservatism and suffered much criticism from the King's kitchen cabinet. His attitudes
were typical of those most commonly to be found among the
higher ranks of the bureaucracy. The last traces of the liberal
humanist idealism of the reform era had by now disappeared from
the Prussian administration; it remained efficient but dedicated to
the political and social *status quo*. The views of the East Elbian
Junkers amounted to yet another variety of conservatism. Most of
them were not politically conscious; they were above all concerned
to safeguard their interests which were under attack from a number of different directions : most obviously from any recurrence
of revolution, but also from growing industrialization, from the
increasing power of the commercial classes, and from the growing
weight of the western provinces within Prussia. If men of ideas
like Stahl could help them in their stand, they were prepared to
accept them, just as the Tory squirearchy of England was prepared to accept Disraeli. This was not the only parallel between
English toryism and Prussian conservatism. The Gerlach-Stahl
circle and to some extent the Junkers, like Disraeli, toyed with the
idea of summoning up the Third Estate against the Second.
They were in favour of protective legislation for the working class,
like factory acts, they talked of social responsibility and regarded
it as much in the Prussian tradition. The Gerlach-Stahl circle were
opposed to the three-tier electoral system because it gave undue
weight to property and to the wealthy liberal *bourgeoisie*. Stahl
called it "pernicious".

Before the final failure of Prussia's German policy at Olmütz had reinforced reactionary tendencies at home, Manteuffel had succeeded, while still Minister of the Interior in Brandenburg's Ministry, in pushing through several important reforms. The most significant was the emancipation of those smaller peasants whom Hardenberg's edict of 1816 had left out. Under the law of 1850 money rents were fixed in compensation for manorial rights which were without exception abolished. A peasant had the choice of either discharging all his obligations immediately at eighteen years' purchase of the rent or paying off over forty-one or fifty-six years. Banks were set up to act as intermediaries between peasants and landlords. The number of peasants emancipated under these arrangements was far greater than those freed as a result of the reform era. There was now an entirely free market in land; more peasants became either agricultural labourers, or drifted into the towns, where they provided the labour for industry; and there was a considerable addition to the class of independent peasants. Manteuffel encountered much opposition from the Junkers in carrying through this major change and some of his other reforms foundered on this rock. In 1850 he introduced laws which ended the patrimonial police power in villages and on estates, following the abolition of patrimonial justice the year before. The predominance of the nobility in the country and provincial diets was to be lessened. But these changes were either not carried out or they were revoked.

It was opposition to the continuance of the provincial diets in their old form which first gave rise to the expression of a slightly more progressive conservatism. Its organ was the *Preussische Wochenblatt* and it became known as the "Wochenblattpartei". For the moment this group, which included Bethmann Hollweg, grandfather of the man who was to be Chancellor in 1914, and also Bunsen, represented the only kind of liberalism there was in active Prussian politics. Manteuffel continued in office no matter what happened to his policy, for he was above all concerned to serve the King. He strengthened his position against the pressures of the Camarilla by extracting from the King an order making the Prime Minister the main channel of communication between the monarch and departmental ministers. Administrative practice under Manteuffel became increasingly reactionary. Hinckeldey, the Berlin Chief of Police, a typical representative of this efficient but unimaginative officialdom, set up a comprehensive system of police surveillance of all persons he considered politically suspect. Often this included men highly placed at Court or who belonged to the wing of conservatism represented by the Kreuzzeitung and the Gerlachs. On the surface it therefore looked as if the clock had been turned back to the 1830s, but the liberal pressures were bound to revive and the German national question would not for ever remain in abeyance; all the while social and economic change was proceeding apace.

The shocks administered to the European power balance by the Crimean war were the first indication that matters would soon be in flux again. Opinion in Prussia was divided largely on ideological lines. The Camarilla, the Gerlachs and the Kreuzzeitung supported Russia as the pillar on which the established European order rested. The Wochenblattpartei and liberal public opinion beyond it supported the Western powers. The Prince of Prussia, the future King and Emperor William I, came out clearly on the Western side, although in the revolutionary days of 1848 he had been considered an extreme reactionary by the Berlin populace and had had to flee for his life. Frederick William IV felt a sense of obligation to Russia as the great conservative power, but was as usual indecisive. At times, his main concern seemed to be the recovery of the small Hohenzollern principality of Neufchâtel, which, however, in the end eluded him. Prussia remained neutral and there was no sign that she was prepared to use the opportunity presented by the war to do anything for the cause of German unity. Bismarck, from his position as Prussian envoy at Frankfurt, would have liked to assert Prussian leadership in Germany against Austria more forcefully, but he was given only a limited chance to do so. In general Bismarck supported the efforts of the Gerlachs and others to prevent Prussia from sliding into a pro-Western position. The King was forced to dismiss two prominent pro-Westerners, Bunsen and the War Minister Bonin.

As it turned out, the Prussian policy of neutrality, although the result of conflicting pressures rather than of deliberate decision, created a useful jumping-off ground for the policies which Bismarck was to pursue in the following decade. He would hardly have been free to manoeuvre as he did if Prussia had, at the time of the Crimean war, taken on a burden of Russian hostility. Austria, on the other hand, was never forgiven at St. Petersburg for her anti-Russian posture; yet she failed to earn the gratitude of France and emerged therefore much weaker diplomatically. Her traditional policy of alliances, pursued so skilfully from Kaunitz through Metternich to Schwarzenberg, had been seen to fail. The attitude of the Kreuzzeitung Conservatives was in the main ideological: they saw the enemy in nationalism, Bonapartism, constitutionalism and democracy. They wanted to preserve their Prussia—a dynastic, legitimist, non-national state, which they hoped to infuse with Christian principles. Bismarck, who probably never fully shared these ideas, was looking at the situation from the point of view of Realpolitik. The Wochenblatt Conservatives regarded themselves as the custodians of the German national idea in Prussian politics. They were determined to make good the humiliation of Olmütz, for which they put the blame chiefly on Russia. They had extravagant hopes of English support for the German national movement, combined with unrealistic and brutal plans for the carve-up of Western Russia.

In Prussian politics matters were on the move again when Frederick William IV faded from the scene. He began to show symptoms of mental illness in the summer of 1857 and his condition was aggravated by a series of strokes. His brother, the Prince of Prussia, had to take over the functions of the monarch on a temporary basis in October 1857 and a formal regency was declared a year later. This was the beginning of the so-called New Era. Prince William was in no sense a liberal : it was only his dissatisfaction with the static and indecisive policy of his brother that had brought him into apparent association with the Wochenblattpartei. In his real beliefs he was a true representative of the Old Prussia which, he felt, rested on the four pillars of monarchy, army, bureaucracy and nobility, all of them closely interlinked. He opposed liberalism, parliamentary government and nationalism based on popular sovereignty. His deepest loyalties were to Prussia and not to Germany. He had many of the Prussian virtues : he was absolutely straight and honest; he disliked all ostentation. In spite of his deep aversion to liberalism his accession to the powers of the monarchy did in fact bring about a new turn towards the liberals and roused even greater hopes. His wife, Princess Augusta, was a more genuine liberal; she was a grand-daughter of Karl August, the Grand Duke of Weimar, who had been Goethe's master.

As soon as Prince William assumed the full powers of Regent there was a ministerial reconstruction and fresh elections. Most of the new ministers were liberal conservatives of the Wochenblattpartei. The elections decimated the right-wing Conservatives and produced a moderate liberal majority. The reasons for this were that many of the voters, particularly among the peasantry, were always willing to support the line taken by the King and his Government; in the days of conservative government much direct pressure had been used to bring the voters into line. In a speech to his new ministers the Prince Regent used the phrase that Prussia would have to make "moral conquests" in Germany, by wise legislation and through steps towards unity like the Zollverein.[3] In spite of declarations that no break with the past was intended, it was widely assumed that Prussia had resumed her quest for the leadership of Germany by appealing to moderate liberal sentiment. In their chastened mood German liberals of all shades were now more likely to accept the leadership of monarchical, bureaucratic Prussia. But the conflict between "grossdeutsch" and "kleindeutsch" was still not resolved : indeed the outbreak of war between Austria and France over the future of Italy immediately raised again the old dilemmas in an acute form. Although German opinion sympathized with the Italian national movement there was an upsurge of national feeling in favour of Austria. As in the crisis of 1840 France was regarded as the hereditary enemy. German nationalism, grossdeutsch feeling, liberal aspirations and fear of France all flowed in the same direction. The choice for Prussia was either to go along with this movement and support Austria within the framework of the German Confederation; or to strengthen Prussia's position in Germany at the expense of Austria.

A few were inclined to take the second course—for example, Bismarck, who, however, at this moment had been relegated to the sidelines as Prussian envoy at St. Petersburg. He no longer saw France under Napoleon III either as a revolutionary dictatorship or a national menace. In an exchange of letters with Leopold von Gerlach in 1857, Bismarck argued against Gerlach's ideological view of Bonapartist France as a revolutionary regime and declared it to be in Prussia's interest to be on good terms with France.[4] In other memoranda of this period he continued to advocate a policy of challenging the Austrian position in Germany[5] and he was now, in 1859, appalled at the prospect of Prussia pulling Austrian chestnuts out of the fire at great risk to herself. Bismarck's view that Prussia should take advantage of Austria's weakness to unify most or all of Kleindeutschland under her own aegis was now widely shared, though some of those who did share it made strange bedfellows. Ferdinand Lassalle and Ludwig Bamberger, both of them of Jewish origin and on the extreme left of German politics, held similar opinions. Lassalle was a socialist by this time and was to become one of the founders of German socialism. Bamberger was one of the Radicals of 1848 but later came to support Bismarck's German policy through the National Liberal Party.

The Prince Regent and the Government in Berlin were in no mood to listen to Bismarck; they were on the whole inclined to support Austria, not only because of the emotional upsurge of public opinion, but also because they believed that an Austrian defeat would soon bring dangers of a French invasion across the Rhine. They wanted, however, to extract concessions from the Austrians, such as Prussian command over all German federal troop contingents in the North. Austria was still so reluctant to surrender her position in Germany that she was not prepared to make the concessions that might have brought her the positive support of Prussia. Then came, rather abruptly, the Peace of Villafranca. One of the factors which had induced Napoleon not to press his advantage unduly was undoubtedly his fear of Prussian intervention. German opinion regarded the Austrian defeat as a heavy blow and Prussian neutrality almost as treachery. The Austrian Emperor, Francis Joseph, declared publicly that he had been deserted by his natural allies. By their indecisive policy the Prince Regent and his ministers had, as in the days of Frederick William IV, gained almost nothing and made many enemies.

In spite of its disappointment with Prussia, nationalist opinion in Germany was given much encouragement by events in Italy. The "Deutsche Nationalverein" was founded, organizationally the first major attempt to resume the national and moderately liberal course which had come to a standstill ten years earlier. Again it consisted only of a group of individuals and lacked real political power. It was not even a mass movement and deliberately confined its membership, which never exceeded 25,000, to men of substance. It could not, for fear of losing support, make a clear stand on the issue of Grossdeutschland or Kleindeutschland, but many of its leaders were convinced, albeit somewhat reluctantly, that Prussia would have to take the lead. Bennigsen, one of the future leaders of the National Liberals, Schulze-Delitzsch, a former radical who had acquired a great reputation in the field of social policy and started the German co-operative movement, and Unruh, a liberal industrialist who had been a political opponent of Bismarck in the United Diet but had become his personal friend— these were the men prominent in the Nationalverein. At a moment when events seemed again to be driving Prussia and the German national movement together, developments started in Berlin which were likely to drive them apart again—the growing political and constitutional crisis over army reform.

The mobilization of the Prussian army during the Franco-Austrian war had revealed serious shortcomings. Military matters were close to the heart of the Prince Regent and he thoroughly understood the technicalities. Even before the war of 1859 his friend General Albert von Roon had been given the task of working out army reforms. He came up with a plan to lengthen the period of service in the regular army, which had stood at two years for more than a quarter of a century, to three years, and also to abolish the Landwehr of the first reserve. In a purely technical sense these proposals were not unreasonable. The number of those who could be annually called up for the regular army had for financial reasons remained stationary at 40,000 for over a generation, while the population had nearly doubled. Consequently a large number of young men were not called up while their elders might have to be summoned to serve in the Landwehr. The proposals of Roon had, however, political overtones of which their author was not at first fully aware. The lengthening of the period of service in the regular army could be represented as an attempt to inculcate recruits more thoroughly with the spirit of blind obedience and to estrange them from the attitudes and opinions of civil life. Ever since Boyen had created the Landwehr in 1814 liberal opinion had regarded it as a citizen army distinct from the regular army; while the latter could be used to protect reactionary authority the former could not. The suspicions on both sides, the liberals and the military, were fed by the memory of 1848. On the part of the liberal-conservative majority in the Landtag, now usually referred to as the Old Liberals, there was in any case growing disappointment with the results of the New Era. Some of the military advisers of the Prince Regent had never been happy with the liberal experiment, and they smelt revolution behind all opposition to the army reforms. In fact, plans were prepared for the use of military force in case of another popular uprising in Berlin. The most uncompromising military adviser of William as regent and king was Edwin von Manteuffel, the Chief of the Military Cabinet and cousin of the former Prime Minister. At times his policy seemed to be to provoke another revolution so that it, and constitutional government with it, could be thoroughly squashed. Roon, who succeeded the more liberal Bonin as War Minister in 1859, was not quite so uncompromising but he was also authoritarian in his political views and determined to give absolute priority to military requirements.

The Old Liberal majority in the Landtag was reluctant to push the Regent, who became King William I in January 1861, too much into the arms of his conservative advisers. It twice voted extra funds for military purposes on a provisional basis. In spite of these conciliatory moves the Liberals were deliberately provoked by the naming of new regular regiments and the solemn dedication of their colours. It was this deliberate flouting of constitutional procedures which led to the founding of the Progressive Party in the summer of 1861, the most important event in the development of German liberalism since 1848. Many of the great figures of Prussian liberalism appeared under the banner of this party. It included moderates who had become dissatisfied with the over-cautious leadership of Georg von Vincke, the Chief of the Old

Liberals. It contained former radicals who had, from the failures of 1848, drawn the lesson that only constitutional progress was possible: men like Waldeck, Jacoby and Schulze-Delitzsch. The Progressive Party was particularly strong in East Prussia, where many landowners and officials belonged to it. Some of the landowners had an economic interest in free trade, but for the most part these men were impelled by conviction rather than interest. There was another separate secession from the Old Liberals, known as the Bockum-Dolffs group, which had its main base in the Rhineland and Westphalia. The programme of the Progressive Party, however, was not extreme; for the time being there was no question of demanding full parliamentary government with ministerial responsibility. But the Progressives wanted to preserve parliamentary rights under the existing constitution, including control of the budget. On the military question they wanted a two-year period of service and continuation of the Landwehr, and they wanted other reforms to reduce Junker privilege—for example, changes in the county constitution, in the office of Landrat and abolition of patrimonial police power. Some of these reforms had already been mooted during the New Era but had not been carried. The Progressives became the strongest party in the Landtag in December 1861 and were even further reinforced in May 1862, after another dissolution.

In the meantime, the liberal-conservative New Era ministry had virtually disintegrated, but instead of the government moving to the left in step with the Landtag only conservative ministers like Roon remained. Yet compromise seemed to be possible on most problems other than the military question; and even on this Roon was in the end prepared to accept the two-year term of service. The King, however, remained adamant for a three-year term. Conservative German historians have tended to see a contradiction in the policy of the Progressive Party. They argue that advance towards German unity under Prussian leadership was ardently desired by these men, yet they were denying the Prussian state the military means necessary to pursue such a policy. This argument seems to overlook the fact that compromise on the technicalities of army reform was by no means impossible; but that the King and his advisers were increasingly abandoning all pretence at maintaining the constitution and were thereby throwing away the "moral conquests" which earlier they had claimed that Prussia should be making in Germany. The further Prussia moved away from liberalism, the more difficult became the position of the German national movement, and particularly of bodies like the

Nationalverein which were predominantly committed to Klein-deutschland.

It was in September 1862, when King and Parliament had reached final deadlock, that William I was at last induced to call on Bismarck to become his Prime Minister, having on several previous occasions balked at the prospect of having him in any ministerial office at all. Thus there was added to the complex parallelogram of forces impinging upon Prussia, Germany and Europe yet another factor, a dynamic personality of genius. There can be few political situations so inextricably knotted as that which faced Bismarck on his accession to power. Prussia was destined to be the leader of a united Germany, but it seemed inescapable that only a liberal Prussia could accomplish that task. But constitutional parliamentary government would mean the end of the real Prussia built on the monarchy, the army, the Junkers and the bureaucracy. Prussia's dilemma gave a chance once more to Austria to reassert her leadership in Germany. She had just entered upon a more liberal phase in her domestic policies. Schemes for reforming the German Confederation, proposed by Baden, by Saxony, by Austria, were coming thick and fast and most of them were detrimental to the Prussian interest. A bitter battle was being fought again over the Zollverein and Austria's relationship with it. Here it was Prussia that held most of the cards, for her industrial development was proceeding fast. But these great economic changes were themselves creating new problems: beyond the conflict in Prussia between the monarchical, aristocratic state and the liberal *bourgeoisie* there were the masses with their political and economic demands. Finally there were the Great Powers of Europe who were unlikely to watch passively while the map of Central Europe was being changed. How could a way be found out of this maze of contradictory pressures?

The question about Bismarck as a historical figure is whether he perverted the course of German history. The question arises because German history, from whatever system of values one judges it, took a disastrous course in the 20th century. These disasters occurred not so very long after Bismarck did his work and they were inextricably connected with what he did. Bismarck himself would have regarded them as disasters, and not only because the Reich he created did not survive. In his last days he was full of forebodings that his handiwork could not withstand the forces that were stirring—the industrial masses, the national rivalries, the dynamic ambitions of a Germany growing ever more populous and powerful. None of the tendencies of his age were created by Bismarck. He found them, and his work reinforced and speeded up some of them. It has often been said in defence of Bismarck that he was a moderate, a man who believed in a balance of power at home and abroad, a cabinet politician of the old school, a conservative Junker. Much of this is true : as Imperial Chancellor Bismarck saw social democracy, the creed to which the most active elements of the working class increasingly gave their allegiance, only as an enemy to be crushed. Here his anachronistic view of politics and society led him into grave misjudgement. On the other hand we can now appreciate that his diplomacy of balance after 1870 was a factor for peace and that the wars he undertook in the 1860s were based on a minimum use of force.

Nevertheless Bismarck did not merely cope with established forces and tendencies; he created a fresh synthesis which turned out, in the event, to have many unhealthy features. When he came to power in 1862 Prussia was, as we have seen, a monarchical Obrigkeitsstaat in which the East Elbian Junker aristocracy still occupied a privileged position and in which the army and bureaucracy played a central role; but there was a constitution and the forces of liberalism had just proved their resilience. The King felt strongly that he could not surrender control over the army to an elected Parliament, but he was very reluctant to break his oath to the constitution and there were many factors working for compromise. It is quite conceivable that Prussia might have developed gradually towards a mixed constitution, not necessarily along the lines of Western or Anglo-Saxon parliamentary democracy, but in harmony with her own traditions. It was not inevitable that liberalism in Germany as a whole should become emasculated, as it did as a result of its alliance with Bismarck. It is even conceivable that a solution might yet have been found for the Austro-Prussian dualism that would not have excluded Austria from Germany while maintaining the Danube monarchy intact. Such a solution seemed on several occasions between 1860 and 1861 within the bounds of possibility. Vienna would no doubt have fought hard before conceding equality to Berlin in German affairs, but Prussia held strong economic cards which might have made war unnecessary. The problems and tendencies of the 1860s were not of Bismarck's making, but he was not only a moderate, conservative, political craftsman, highly skilful in handling them : he was a dynamic, even demonic personality of immense will-power who forced all the trends of his age into a new mould. He cut his way through the maze and the result was a creation which transcended the Old Prussia and the Old Germany. One can think of few men in modern history who have had an equally powerful impact on their nations. Not even the first Napoleon or Lenin were quite comparable in their effect on France or Russia.

The development of Bismarck as a man and his career down to 1862 pose a number of problems. Was he a typical Junker? Or did his mother's side of the family—administrators, like his grandfather Mencken, or academics—predominate in his make-up? It was often important to him to be thought a bluff, hard-riding country Junker and he reacted against the self-conscious emphasis on *Bildung* which his mother tried to foist on him. In fact he could never be just a country squire, for his intellect and his reactions were like quicksilver : he was highly-strung and nervous, broadly educated and thoroughly literate. During the eight years he spent running his estates he got very bored, relieved the tedium by all manner of extravagant behaviour and finally escaped into politics. It was during those years that what is known as his "conversion" took place. He formed a deep emotional attachment to Marie von Thadden, the daughter of one of the foremost Pietists among the Pomeranian Junkers. She was betrothed to and eventually married a close friend of Bismarck's, who could thus never attain the object of his love. Her early death in an epidemic deeply affected him. From being a sceptic and unbeliever he found his way back to Christianity. But his faith was very much a personal matter, a means of finding peace and reassurance, and had little effect on his public actions. As far as the world at large and the sphere of politics were concerned, Bismarck's God was the stern God of the Old Testament and of Luther, who chastises His enemies. Throughout his life Bismarck was a great hater and never doubted that he was on the side of the angels. In 1847 he made his first appearance in the political arena as a member of the United Diet. He quickly became a well-known figure among the conservative Junkers and had access to all leading personalities from the King downwards. Bismarck claimed that he would have been able to bring peasants from his Pomeranian estate to rescue the King from the Berlin mobs in the spring of 1848. All the evidence about the mood of the peasantry in 1848 suggests that the peasants were themselves restive and many of them sympathetic to the revolution.[6]

After 1848 Bismarck was regarded as a conservative of the Kreuzzeitung and Gerlach-Stahl persuasion. In fact his outlook was from the beginning somewhat different from the Christian-Germanic political Romanticism of the King and the Gerlachs. He might be found expressing similar sentiments, but his priorities were different and his grasp of realities greater. In his speech supporting Olmütz, for example, delivered in the Prussian Second

Chamber, he used all the conservative anti-liberal arguments and spoke of Austria's rightful position in Germany; but he also used language about the interests of a state having absolute priority and such language would never have been used by his friends in the Camarilla. Throughout the 1850s Bismarck became ever more clearly an advocate of policies based on the strict national interest of Prussia and his views gained weight and maturity through the great store of experience of the German and European political scene which he amassed. His keen sense of the power struggle between Prussia and Austria separated him on a major issue from his political friends. In fact he was politically very isolated, for when the New Era began he became distinctly *persona non grata* in the leading circles. The reputation of the wild reactionary which still clung to him was now inconvenient. The wife of the Prince Regent harboured strong suspicions against him ever since he tried to involve her in a hare-brained scheme to set up a regency on behalf of her son in 1848. Bismarck was to rail against the intrigues of the royal ladies, Augusta and her daughter-in-law Victoria, for the next thirty years. While some considered him beyond the pale as a reactionary, others suspected him as a Bonapartist, because he advocated the maintenance of friendly relations with France and had made himself agreeable to Napoleon III personally. The constitutional struggle retrieved Bismarck's personal fortunes. He was now under consideration again as a possible minister although it was not until the conflict had almost passed beyond the point of no return that William I could bring himself to summon him.

Once installed in office Bismarck began to play the parties and the options with growing brilliance, zest and cunning. He found the taste of power overwhelmingly sweet and the pursuit of it provided the chief object for his ferocious energies for the next twenty-eight years. It is impossible not to admire his virtuosity, but it is the very brilliance with which he manipulated men and situations that raises doubts about his ultimate sense of responsibility. Every cause, every institution, every man seemed to be grist only to his mill; and it may be doubted if even the pillars of Prussia—the monarchy, army, the Junkers—ever commanded his total commitment.

The Bismarck problem is well illustrated by the two major issues which faced him immediately, the constitutional conflict at home and the Polish Revolt abroad. In the constitutional question he moved simultaneously on a number of different tracks. In front of the liberal majority in the Landtag he flashed the possibility of concessions on the military question. In conversations with individual deputies he adopted a tone of confidentiality, of apparent indiscretion, compared the King to a horse shying in front of strange objects to which it would gradually get accustomed. These tactics were designed to work upon the many divisions that existed in the liberal ranks. Thus he held out vistas of progress on the German question and it is there that he let fall the famous remark: "Germany does not look to Prussia for her liberalism, but for her power . . . The great questions of our time will not be decided by speeches and majority resolutions—that was the cardinal error of 1848 and 1849—but by blood and iron."[7] The words sounded sensational in the mouth of a minister but the sentiment was a commonplace in the great flood of speeches and writings on the German question since 1848. What none except Bismarck yet saw was that liberalism and German unification were not necessarily inseparable. Bismarck's initial dalliance with the liberals and with nationalism caused consternation in the conservative circles which had been dubious about his appointment. But he never seriously meant to come to terms with the liberals and he would espouse German nationalism in his own time and on his own terms. If the constitutional conflict had been settled by compromise Bismarck would have lost his hold over the King and he saw to it that it was not settled until great successes in foreign policy had transformed the scene. When the conflict between the Landtag and the Government was at its height in 1863, when the press was being gagged and deputies holding official positions were being disciplined, Sybel and the young Treitschke, historians who were later to sing paeans of praise to Bismarck, were highly critical of him. The shift in their position to almost uncritical adoration within a few years, is a measure of the enslavement which Bismarck imposed upon German and Prussian liberalism.

An interesting sidelight on Bismarck's toying with all options is his flirtation with democracy and universal suffrage, a flirtation which was eventually to bear fruit in the Bundestag of the North German Confederation of 1867 and in the Reichstag of the Second Empire. The idea that the authority of the state might be strengthened by an appeal to the masses and that the pretensions of the liberal *bourgeoisie* might thus be contained had been strikingly put into practice by Napoleon III. In Prussia the idea had been tried by the Conservatives who had seen their influence steadily dwindle in the Landtag since the beginning of the New Era. One of their more enterprising leaders, Hermann Wagener, had helped to found the "Preussische Volksverein" in 1861, a riposte to the foundation of the Progressive Party. It hoped to mobilize peasants and artisans against the *laissez faire* capitalism of the middle-class liberals. In spite of official support its success was limited. Bismarck, whom his experiences of 1848 had convinced of the loyalty of the masses and who had learnt much from Napoleon III, thought of universal suffrage not merely as a gambit in the context of the Prussian constitutional crisis, but as a possible aid to his German policy.

These considerations brought him into contact with Lassalle in 1863 and 1864. This remarkable man, not yet forty years of age, had carved for himself a position of significance in Prussian and German politics without the aid of any office, party or parliamentary seat. He came from a Jewish family in Breslau and he was one of the revolutionaries of 1848, a neo-Hegelian, much influenced by French socialists like Saint-Simon and Proudhon. He was convinced that the fourth estate, the workers, would have a decisive part in shaping the future and he believed in the central importance of the class struggle. He had much in common with Marx and Engels, was in friendly contact with them until 1862 or 1863 but then estrangement followed. What distinguished Lassalle from Marx was that Lassalle thought much more in terms of the German situation while Marx was concerned with a universally valid social theory. Lassalle saw that the Germans had yet to create their state and he came to think that this might be done by Prussia, but in the form of a unitary state into which Prussia would be merged. The social and the national revolution would as it were run parallel to each other. Lassalle saw the enemy in the capitalist *bourgeoisie,* in narrow Manchesterism; he was not afraid of the state and foresaw a kind of state socialism. All this was in the realm of broad, forward-looking visions; as an immediate step he founded in 1863 the "Allgemeiner Deutscher Arbeiterverein", with a programme of universal suffrage and the formation of producer associations as a first stage towards socialism. This was the first German socialist manifesto and although Marxism was later to predominate in the formation of the German Social Democratic party, the influence of Lassalle's ideas remained potent. Socialism in practice has tended to be state socialism.

The only part of Lassalle's programme that could be of immediate interest to Bismarck was the common fight against middle-class liberalism and the device of universal suffrage; but even the social programme did not strike an entirely alien note in Prussia, with its long tradition of state-promoted social welfare going back to the "peuplierung" and Pietism of Frederick William I. The meetings between the powerful Junker Prime Minister and the Jewish intellectual without a following were a strange occurrence; but both men recognized in each other political genius. Lassalle's concern was to persuade Bismarck to impose another constitution providing for universal suffrage. Bismarck toyed with the idea as a means of resolving the constitutional conflict but the outbreak of the Danish War in 1864 made this for the time being unnecessary. Bismarck kept universal suffrage up his sleeve for later use; Lassalle's career was cut short by his death in a duel in 1864.[8] The encounter between the two men illustrates the mastery, sensitivity and absence of scruple with which Bismarck played upon the political keyboard.

On the Polish question Bismarck also pursued a line entirely his own. For much of the period since 1815 Prussia had at first treated her Polish subjects, most of whom lived in the Province of Posen, with fairness and respect for their rights in matters of language and religion. Only after the rising of 1830, when Prussia seemed to be simultaneously threatened with an upsurge of French and Polish nationalism, was there a phase when Germanization became a positive policy. The national movement of 1848 was sympathetic to Polish aspirations, but began to experience the inherent clash between Polish and German nationalism.[9] Prussia put down the Polish rising in her eastern provinces for reasons of her own self-interest. Bismarck viewed the Polish question in the 1860s from two points of view: it posed a threat to the cohesion of Prussia and made her difficult frontiers even more vulnerable; secondly he feared the effects of a more liberal Russian policy towards the Poles, partly because of Prussia's own Polish problem, but even more because it might lead to a Franco-Russian *rapprochement* from which Prussia had a great deal to fear. Thus he sent Alvensleben, who as the King's General Adjutant had shared with Edwin Manteuffel the responsibility for launching William into the clash with the Landtag over army reform, to negotiate the convention by which Russia and Prussia gave each other a free hand in suppressing the Polish rising. The action outraged the majority in the Landtag and liberal opinion all over Germany. Bismarck had long passed beyond his short honeymoon with the liberal majority and was at this time not averse to sharpening the conflict. It would bind the King closer to him.

The international repercussions of the Alvensleben Convention made it appear at first that Bismarck had blundered. French and British public opinion sympathetic to Poland raged at Prussia even more than at Russia. Napoleon was sensitive to public opinion and the matter began to disturb relations between Berlin and Paris which were so precious to Bismarck. It was at this point that Napoleon offered an alliance to Austria on condition that she ceded Venetia to Italy. The Hofburg rejected this offer which would have enormously strengthened Austria in Germany and would have weakened Prussia. Even at St. Petersburg the Alvensleben Convention evoked little gratitude for Gortchakoff, the Russian foreign minister and chancellor, felt uneasy about too repressive a policy in Poland and had in fact pan-Slavist sympathies. Thus Bismarck appeared to have miscalculated and he began to lose face with the King. He adopted the tactic of playing down the Convention. French sympathy for the Poles was, however, increasingly irritating to the Russians and within a few months Bismarck was reaping dividends from his policy after all. He had demonstrated the solidarity of the conservative powers and Russian benevolence became extremely important for Prussia in the next few years. Good relations with the Tsarist Government always remained a cornerstone of Bismarck's policy.

The constitutional crisis and the Polish uprisings were problems which faced Bismarck within hours or weeks of taking office. Lurking in the background for the moment, but never far away was the German question and at its core was the relationship between Prussia and Austria. Bismarck was determined that, whatever the developments in the German problem, Prussia would block any attempt by Austria to re-establish her leadership in Germany. It was not an auspicious moment for Prussia. The constitutional crisis had alienated many Germans and Bismarck's tough attitude to the Prussian Landtag deepened the split between the mainstream of German middle class opinion and Prussia. In South Germany prejudice against the severe, militaristic state in Germany's in-hospitable North Eastern corner was never far below the surface. Austria on the other hand was winning the battle for German opinion and making the "moral conquests" which the Prince Regent had announced as the Prussian aim in 1858. The Habsburg Empire had been shaken by the defeat in Italy and by 1861 Francis Joseph was ready to try a liberal regime. Schmerling, who had been a leading moderate liberal of the grossdeutsch variety in 1848, and who was Prime Minister under the Frankfurt Parliament, was appointed Minister of State in Vienna. In step with his more liberal regime based mainly on the German-speaking population of the Austrian Empire he initiated a more forward policy in Germany. A far-reaching project for the reform of the German Confederation was tabled. The loose confederation was to become a federal state with a directory of princes and a parliament with considerable powers, composed of delegates from existing parliaments. This Austrian counter-offensive in Germany was backed up by an organization analogous to the Nationalverein, the

"Reformverein". In 1862 an observer asking himself who would create a more closely-knit German system might well have named Schmerling rather than Bismarck.

Prussia was for the moment reduced to playing a defensive game in the struggle for Germany; she held the initiative only in the economic sphere. She concluded the Franco-Prussian Trade Treaty in 1862, a natural consequence of the movement towards international free trade initiated by Cobden's treaty with France two years earlier. Prussia took this step on her own without waiting for the agreement of her Zollverein partners. For some of the South German states it created a difficult situation, but their economies were already too strongly tied to the Zollverein and to Prussia to break away. It was impossible for Austria to follow this further plunge into free trade, so the chances that she might reach an accommodation with the Zollverein receded further. But the connection between economic and political events was not so close that Austria's political initiative on the German question need necessarily have come to grief through her economic weakness. Bismarck played his economic cards for all they were worth and he was ably assisted by Delbrück, the official who had directed the Prussian free-trading policies since the 1850s and was to continue to do so until the middle 1870s. On the political side Bismarck blocked as best he could the Austrian initiatives, while at the same time holding out the possibility of an understanding to Austria. He told the Austrian envoy in Berlin, with that appalling frankness which he sometimes put on, that Austria should leave North Germany to Prussia. In return he offered that Prussia might support Austria's vital interests in Italy. He made it crystal clear that Prussia would not allow a reform of the German Confederation in Austria's favour. The Habsburg monarchy should shift its centre of gravity towards Hungary—this was Bismarck's advice. It was not heeded in Vienna.

Austrian efforts to solve the German question in accordance with Austrian and grossdeutsch ideas reached their climax in 1863. The Frankfurt meeting of German princes in August 1863 was an occasion of great splendour which aroused enthusiasm throughout Germany. Even those who had put their faith in Prussia and Kleindeutschland were all but swept off their feet. The *Wochenschrift,* the journal of the Nationalverein, could not but acknowledge the merits of the Austrian initiative and was full of bitterness towards the Bismarck regime in Berlin, which had undermined the pro-Prussian kleindeutsch position of the Nationalverein.[10] Hardly ever in his career did Bismarck swim quite so much against the tide than in his successful efforts to torpedo the Austrian reform project and the Frankfurt meeting of princes. He had to fight a nerve-racking battle with his royal master; it was after the final interview at which he obtained the King's refusal of the invitation to Frankfurt that Bismarck smashed a vase to relieve his feelings.

Bismarck's treatment of the Schleswig-Holstein question is often regarded as his masterpiece. With astonishing nimbleness he picked his way through the complexities of the problem and the diversity of purpose among the large number of interested parties. In spite of the major defeat he had only just imposed on Austria's German aims, he managed to tie Vienna to his own policy in circumstances that were to bring nothing but disadvantage to the Habsburg monarchy. The German national movement was so deeply stirred by the Schleswig-Holstein question that it was impossible for the Austrians to do nothing and at the same time retain any credibility as a German power. On the other hand, Vienna was reluctant to support the Augustenburg cause because of the dangers inherent in it to the whole legitimist position of the Danube monarchy in European affairs. The Duke of Augustenburg had liberal connections, and he owed his election as Duke in Holstein and Schleswig to a popular uprising; on paper his claims were hardly strong. Thus Bismarck managed to detach Austria from the German national movement and even from the princes of the German middle states, because all of these backed Augustenburg. He did this while using Austria to lend strength to Prussia's position in relation to the other great powers of Europe, all of whom, particularly Britain and Russia, had their own interests to pursue over Schleswig-Holstein.

From the point of view of Prussia's domestic developments the war with Denmark had a most debilitating effect on the Government's liberal opposition. Fresh elections in the autumn of 1863 had not greatly reduced the number of liberals in the Landtag, but a drop in electoral participation, particularly in the two lower sections, became very noticeable. Now Bismarck worked relentlessly on the divisions among liberals. He was proceeding from the so-called 'gap' theory of the constitution, according to which the Government was entitled to go on raising and spending revenue as long as there was a constitutional deadlock. He need therefore never have applied to the Landtag for appropriations for the Danish war, but he deliberately did so in order to stretch the opposition on the rack of their divided aims. It is from this point onwards that a growing fatigue of liberalism in Prussia can be observed. The Prussian military successes, though by no means as spectacular as they were in the later Austrian or French wars, began to swing public opinion behind the Government. It was now

being said that the military reforms had after all been necessary
and successful. Those Prussian liberals who supported the Augustenburg claims became less and less confident in their position. The
shift in opinion is most strikingly illustrated by Treitschke. He had
at first supported the Augustenburg claims as a proper solution in
the German national interest. In January 1865 he made a public
change of attitude in an article in the *Preussische Jahrbücher,* the
journal that since 1859 had addressed itself to that liberal, educated
bourgeoisie in Prussia which supported the German national movement.[11] Treitschke now came out in favour of Prussian annexation
of the two duchies. He faced squarely the conflict between what
was right in international and in German law and what was necessary to protect the German national interest in terms of power. He
now gave clear priority to the second of these considerations.

The confusion which Bismarck was sowing in the liberal ranks
was almost equalled by the illusions and doubts he produced
among conservatives. Ludwig von Gerlach was still the conscience
of the party. He wanted a solution of the Schleswig-Holstein
question in the Prussian and the German interest, but he was
contemptuous of the liberal-democratic enthusiasm aroused by the
crisis. Legitimate rights, even those of the Danish Royal House,
must be safeguarded at all costs. After the Prussian victories he
saw the chief benefit in the strengthening of the Prussian state and
in the collaboration of Austria and Prussia in the interests of
European and German order. He was disturbed by the growth of
"godless and lawless greed" in Prussia. Not many conservatives
shared to the full Gerlach's rigid legitimism; pleasure at Prussian
aggrandisement and at liberal discomfiture was widespread among
conservatives. Hotheads at Court and in military circles—for
example Alvensleben—were waiting impatiently for a *coup d'état*   •
to overthrow the Constitution of 1850. Among all shades of conservatism Bismarck, in spite of his undoubted successes, did, however, arouse uneasiness. His flirtation with the German national
movement and with universal suffrage, his refusal to squash the
liberals outright and his friendly policy towards French Bonapartism made him highly suspect. It required the War of 1866 and its
political sequel to convince a minority of conservatives that Bismarck was not their man, and to cause the majority to bend their
knee in awe before him. Thus 1866 completed the disintegration
of Prussian politics and the recasting of the system in the Bismarckian image.

Many options were open to Bismarck in 1865 and 1866. He
could have made his peace with the weakened liberal opposition
and thereby have swung public opinion throughout Germany

behind Prussia. "One doesn't shoot at the enemy with public opinion but with powder and lead", he remarked. Would Bismarck have remained in power if the Prussian constitutional conflict had been composed? As it was, the King found the minister who was so devoid of moral scruples sometimes hard to bear. William shared the conservative legitimism of Gerlach and wanted to tread the path of rectitude if at all possible. Bismarck was only able to bring him into open hostility with Austria by appealing to his pride as a Prussian officer and frightening him with the spectre of another Olmütz. Relations with Austria were the area where Bismarck had to make his most crucial choices. His conviction that Prussia and Austria would have to fight it out was of long standing, but he was not necessarily driving towards war all along. This is borne out by the Gastein Convention of August 1865, which appeared to settle the dispute over the booty from the Danish war by an amicable division of the spoils. Right up to the outbreak of war with Austria Bismarck was concerned to show that he would leave no stone unturned to reach a settlement with her on terms acceptable to him, while at the same time preparing the ground for war. His greatest success was to have secured the benevolent neutrality of Napoleon without incurring any definite commitment in return. Bismarck also obtained the alliance of Italy and he was certain of the neutrality of Russia and Britain. By the spring of 1866 the international position was so favourable to Prussia that it would have been a severe blow to Bismarck's policy if at that stage the avoidance of war had been purchased by any substantial Prussian concession. His most nerve-racking battles were again with the King who was reluctant to risk his kingdom in fratricidal strife in circumstances of doubtful morality. Bismarck was brought to the verge of nervous breakdown by these battles.

Perhaps the most striking initiative of the infinitely resourceful Prussian Prime Minister was his last-minute bid for the support of the German national movement. It came in the form of a proposal for an all-German parliament elected by direct and universal suffrage. It was the card that Bismarck had first played tentatively in opposition to the Austrian reform plans of 1863 and which he had discussed with Lassalle. The move carried little conviction with the liberals, but it certainly deepened their divisions. The right-wing liberalism represented by the *Preussische Jahrbücher* supported Bismarck's call for a German Parliament, though without enthusiasm, from a feeling that it strengthened Prussia's claim to solve the German question in her own way. Other liberals, like most of the leaders of the Progressive Party or Bennigsen and the Nationalverein, were distrustful. They refused to back the reform plan or the war unless Prussia was given a liberal regime. A liberal newspaper editor wrote : "Herr von Bismarck at the head of a feudal Government summons a German Parliament! If the devil mounts the chancel and reads the Gospel, who is likely to listen with devotion?" On the extreme left some radicals, like Rodbertus and Ruge, both veterans of 1848, and some Lasallian socialists came out in support of Prussia and Bismarck. The offer of a German Parliament brought about the final breach between Gerlach and Bismarck. Gerlach called it political bankruptcy and once more emphasized that a German settlement was possible only if the legitimist rights of both Austria and Prussia were respected. A "lacerating interview" between the two men failed to heal the breach and Gerlach described his former friend as "restless and desperate" on the eve of the war.[12] One of Bismarck's conservative ministerial colleagues, Bodelschwingh, resigned before the war started. Even the King recoiled from Bismarck's radical proposals and exclaimed "but what you are proposing to me is the Revolution". William was, however, too much in the grip of his powerful minister to resist.

The swift and sensational triumph of Prussian arms completed the disintegration of existing political groups. The beginning of the war coincided with fresh Landtag elections. The liberal groups lost over a hundred seats and the conservatives gained a similar number. If the election had come a little later, after the news of the Prussian victories in Bohemia, the result would have been even more striking. In any case, the massive hammer-blows of war produced a revolution of opinion which made the old party labels meaningless. Reassessment and self-criticism was the order of the day in all political camps. Mevissen, the liberal leader from the Rhineland who had spent his life fighting for constitutional government, wrote : "I cannot shake off the impression of this hour. I am no devotee of Mars; I feel more attached to the goddess of beauty and the mother of graces than to the powerful god of war, but the trophies of war exercise a magic charm upon the child of peace. Eye and mind are irresistibly drawn to the vast concourse of humanity doing homage to the deity of the moment, Success."[13] Baumgarten, another liberal who had become prominent in the New Era, addressed his fellow liberals : "... we must above all accept facts.... We wanted this and that, but the opposite has happened. We wanted peace and freedom; now we have a fight for power. Are we going to proclaim, amid the thunder of guns, our resolutions about freedom and peace which even amid the silence of peace convinced no one but ourselves?"[14] After the war, he argued that the middle class had shown itself incapable of leadership while the aristocracy had shown its traditional military and political qualities.

Perhaps the saddest position was that of the Prussian Catholics. They had up to this time fought with the liberals against Bismarck, for the constitution of 1850 guaranteed the rights of the Catholic Church and therefore the small Catholic parliamentary group wanted to see it strengthened. Their real sympathies were grossdeutsch. One of their leaders, August Reichensperger, wrote in his diary immediately after the battle of Sadowa: "It takes a great deal to accept such counsels of God and to avoid the conclusion that right governs only small private matters, whereas in large affairs only force, cunning and deceit rule, and that neither ends nor means are subject to moral or religious principles."[15] For the moment the small Catholic group all but disappeared; it rose again in the shape of the important Centre Party when, after 1870, the South German states entered the Reich and when the Kulturkampf stimulated Catholic resistance particularly in Prussia.

The liberal groups split when Bismarck introduced an Indemnity Bill into the newly-elected Landtag which was designed to legalize the Government's unconstitutional actions in the past. A smaller group continued to oppose the Government and to demand a genuine constitutional regime; a larger group voted for the bill for the kind of reasons which Mevissen or Baumgarten had given for their conversion. This second group formed the basis for the National Liberal Party which was soon to be reinforced from the territories that were now incorporated in Prussia, for example, Hanover and Electoral Hesse. The non-Prussian members of this new party did not have memories of years of constitutional conflict to sour their relations with the Government. The Indemnity Bill also split the conservatives. A larger group opposed this bill, as it seemed to make nonsense of years of fighting against liberalism. This group was based mainly on the older East Elbian provinces of Prussia, on the Junkers and on officialdom. The smaller group, the so-called Free Conservatives, were in favour of reconciliation with the liberals and of enthusiastic acceptance of the new order; they drew their support mainly from the Western Provinces and from Silesia. Nothing enraged Bismarck more than the breach with many of his former friends whom he accused of total lack of understanding. Both the National Liberals and the Free Conservatives were a political reflection of the fact that a new *élite*, composed of Junkers and the old official classes on the one hand and the *haute bourgeoisie* on the other. was arising. This new *élite* accepted many of the values of the Junker aristocracy.

The surrender of the liberals to Bismarck also affected the attitude of the extreme left, the Lassallians. Even Marx felt in the days of Bismarck's offer of a German Parliament that his former friend and rival Lassalle had missed his great moment. But as the collapse of the liberal resistance to Bismarck became obvious, many socialists became more attracted by Marxism and the class war. This drift was accentuated when they found that universal suffrage introduced into the parliament of the North German Federation did at least initially work in the conservative sense intended by Bismarck. In 1869 the Social Democratic Workers' Party was founded in Eisenach. It adopted Marxist principles; it was opposed to Bismarck and to Prussia and all they stood for and also to those Lassallians in North Germany who had accepted the consequences of 1866. Its leaders were August Bebel and Wilhelm Liebknecht.

The revolutionary events of 1866 changed attitudes throughout the political spectrum, but they also changed Bismarck. He always identified with the power base from which he was operating. Up to now his base had been the Prussian Government and this meant fighting Austrian pretensions in Germany, fighting the liberal opposition and sometimes even fighting the King and the conservatives. Now the Government of the North German Federation, soon to be further enlarged into the German Reich, became Bismarck's base. In the first drafts for the constitution of the Federation he had still thought in terms of making the Prussian premiership, which he would retain, the main focus of power and giving the federal chancellorship to someone else. The chief counterweight to the particularism of the non-Prussian members of the Federation was to be the Federal Parliament elected by universal suffrage. In devising this complex system of checks and balances Bismarck was undoubtedly influenced by the American Constitution and perhaps also by the experience of the Dutch Republic. He had often discussed it with Motley, the American historian of the Dutch Republic, who remained one of his few really close personal friends almost through his entire life.

As the political scene evolved in the autumn and winter of 1866 and 1867 Bismarck began to see things differently. The reformed and docile National Liberals were increasingly his natural allies. No longer was there any likelihood that an accommodation with liberalism would endanger his hold on office and power. If in the course of nature the reputedly liberal Crown Prince should come to the throne it might even help Bismarck to have made his peace with the opposition. On the other hand, the Prussian particularism of those Conservatives who had opposed the Indemnity Bill was increasingly irksome to Bismarck. It was not only a question of counterbalancing this Prussian particularism or the interests of the other governments in the federation : if the more substantial South German states, like Bavaria, should at some future date come into the federation, it would be even more important to have reasonably strong, federal institutions. These may be some of the reasons why Bismarck made considerable concessions to the National Liberals in the Constituent Reichstag which met in 1867. The office of Federal Chancellor now became the linchpin of the whole edifice and Bismarck decided to assume it himself. The Chancellor was in some sense answerable to the federal parliament, although not in the sense that he could be overthrown by it. The federal parliament had some control over the federal budget, although the budget was not to be a large one since the main powers of taxation remained with the States. Bismarck now made some concessions even on the issue of the military budget, on which he had defeated the Prussian Landtag. The military budget was agreed for a four-year term; this was later to become a seven-year term. Another important concession which Bismarck made in the Constituent Reichstag was the adoption of the secret ballot; the conservative implications of universal suffrage were thereby to a considerable extent nullified.

Thus Bismarck, who had emasculated Prussian and German liberalism, in the end adopted some liberal and even democratic features for the constitution of his new edifice. The nature of German liberalism, however, was now such that it could not and would not exploit these footholds during the half-century for which Bismarck's Reich endured. Perhaps this is hardly surprising since Prussian liberalism had been unable to exploit the footholds in the Constitution of 1850 which were in some respects much better. The Constitution of the North German Federation, and of the Reich thereafter, went further in the direction of creating a genuine federal state with considerable unitary features than was immediately realized. Bismarck had to make it look as nearly like the Confederation of 1815 as possible, otherwise the resistance in Prussia and other German states would have been too great. The National Liberals failed to obtain a Reich Ministry, they got only a Reich Chancellor. But in foreign policy and defence, and increasingly in economic affairs, it became all but a unitary state. The process of transcending even the strongest of the particularisms, namely that of Prussia, had begun and continued apace. Nevertheless the dualism between Prussia and the Reich remained a problem for a long time and Bismarck used it when it suited him.

1866 was the year of decision in the foundation of the second German empire; the completion of the edifice in 1870 was almost an afterthought. It is difficult to give a completely satisfactory answer to the question why Bismarck did not complete Klein-deutschland in 1866. Perhaps the main reason was that the risks of a French countermove were too great. In any case Bismarck had no great desire to build German unity; it was a possibility which entered into his calculations but he was not prepared to run risks to hasten it on. He was also aware of the remaining strength of South German particularism and there was in fact a recrudescence of anti-Prussian, particularist sentiment in Bavaria and elsewhere between 1866 and 1870. In 1866 Prussia had annexed outright the Kingdom of Hanover and sent her ruler packing and she had done likewise to a number of smaller states including the free city of Frankfurt. Such actions sent shudders down the spines of the remaining independent rulers and governments south of the Main. On the other hand, the South German states were tied to the North German Federation in two very important spheres, military and economic. Military alliances were concluded with the South German states to replace the military arrangements which had existed under the German Confederation. The Zollverein treaties had also to be re-negotiated and it was now impossible for any of the South German states to stand out against the industrial and commercial preponderance of Greater Prussia. A "Zollparlament" was created by which deputies from South Germany were added to the North German Reichstag for the discussion of problems relating to the whole customs union. Thus yet a third parliament came into existence, in addition to the Reichstag and the Prussian Landtag, all part of the system by which Bismarck set out to "defeat parliamentary government through parliaments". He also hoped to use it to develop the relationship between North and South Germany. In the short time of its existence little occurred to nourish these hopes; it required another outburst of German nationalist enthusiasm to unite the South German states with the North.

The clash with France was not deliberately engineered by Bismarck. As a politician he rarely created situations, but excelled in striking decisively when they had arisen. In 1866 he had certainly used the spectre of German nationalism, the *furor teutonicus,* as an additional element to prevent French interference while he settled his business with Austria. In 1867 he showed little inclination to go to war with France over Luxemburg, though he was again adept in using German nationalist emotions in the diplomatic game. Bismarck had not yet given up the notion of an understanding between France and Prussia which had for so long been a cornerstone of his policy and for which he had so often been abused by liberals and conservatives alike. He realized, however, that Napoleon's regime was an increasingly precarious one, hungry for a success to refurbish its tarnished prestige. When Napoleon's foreign minister Gramont played into his hands in the summer of 1870, Bismarck seized the opportunity with his customary ruthlessness. Perhaps his guilt lies in the fact that he made no attempt to avoid a clash which could have been avoided. The war of 1870 was, far more than those of 1864 and 1866, a modern nationalist war; it deepened the sense of hereditary hostility between two countries and saddled the new German state with another heavy mortgage upon its future.

Even after the great triumphs of 1870 it required much pressure and manoeuvre to bring the South German states into a fully-fledged Reich under the Prussian King as Emperor. Not the least of the difficulties lay with William I himself, for he was reluctant to accept the imperial title unless it was pressed upon him by his fellow rulers. He sensed the revolutionary nature of all that had happened, the affront of legitimism; above all he felt obscurely that this was the end of Prussia. Bismarck had to persuade the romantic King of Bavaria, Ludwig II, to offer his King the imperial title on behalf of all the German rulers. To make the persuasion effective he had to pay the Bavarian king a yearly secret subvention of 300,000 marks out of the "Guelphfund", the secret fund obtained through the annexation of Hanover and the confiscation of the properties of her royal house. Even then the German rulers would only accept William as German Emperor, not as Emperor of Germany; the Prussian King, who had been so reluctant to take the imperial dignity at all, wanted at least to have the title in its proper form. This was the cause of the ill-feeling between the King and Bismarck which marred the famous ceremony in the Hall of Mirrors at Versailles on 18th January 1871—trivial perhaps, but symbolic of the ambivalent nature of what had been achieved.

The events by which the second German Empire was created defy definitive interpretation. Changing perspectives have altered prevailing judgements. Up to the first World War the chorus of admiration and self-congratulation was overwhelming in Germany, expressions of doubt few and far between. After the first World War, it became fashionable to criticize aspects of the Second Reich, mainly what was considered to be its defective political system. Ziekursch, who wrote the first major history of the Bismarckian Reich after 1918, saw its tragedy in the fact that it had been created in the teeth of the prevailing liberal spirit of the age by the genius of one man. After 1945 it became even more common to question the validity of Kleindeutschland as a tightly knit state : the enormous loss of national substance which the Germans had suffered in Eastern Europe and the Balkans was plain for all to see. Not all features of Bismarck's handiwork have proved ephemeral. The German nation state survived the catastrophe of defeat in 1918 substantially intact. Even after 1945, the idea that there should be a German nation state remained alive and was, curiously enough, reaffirmed by the major world powers, on paper at any rate. The second Reich provided the framework for a tremendous economic and demographic advance which has permanently altered the face of Europe. It remains open to question whether Schwarzenberg's concept of a middle Europe of 70 million people could have been as effective. On the political side the exclusion of Austria had grave consequences. The eventual collapse of the Habsburg Monarchy destroyed one of the great historical achievements of the German people. The division of the German Catholics and their partial alienation from the state was a serious cultural and spiritual loss.

But Prussia did not win, either. Some of the admirable qualities of the old Prussian military dynastic state, for example, some of its administrative techniques, became an asset to the new state; but much of its old moderation and sobriety was lost. Perhaps most serious of all was the breach between Prussia and German liberalism caused by the constitutional conflict after 1862. In spite of many disappointments, the liberal movement and Protestant, once enlightened and progressive Prussia seemed destined for each other. Before Bismarck came to power there was a reasonable chance that Prussia would develop increasingly into a constitutional state. The Prussian *élite* was itself changing, as a result of industrialization and because of the growing importance of the Western provinces. Bismarck did not so much save the old bureaucratic aristocratic ascendancy as take over some of its characteristics into the new amalgam he created. The success of Prussian arms militarized sections of German society; the extra-constitutional position of the General Staff came to take on a sinister significance. Bismarck himself had occasion to feel the power of the military men in 1866 and even more so in 1870. Thus the new synthesis in many respects gave a new twist to the old Prussian characteristics which it took over. In any case the King and the Prussian conservatives were right in thinking that the old Prussian state had reached the end of the road. The Prussian spirit had been raised in the Hohenzollern territories east of the Elbe. Here it had experienced its finest hour after 1806. The incorporation of large, wealthy provinces on the Rhine with a long history of their own started a process of metamorphosis. In the 1860s Prussia conquered Germany but in doing so she lost her own identity.

CHAPTER VIII

Prussia in Imperial Germany 1871–1918

IN a meaningful sense Prussia ceased to exist in 1870. The great problems of the new Reich in foreign and domestic policy concerned the whole of it, rather than the two-thirds of it that in a formal sense constituted the Kingdom of Prussia. That Kingdom had itself expanded its territory by a quarter and its population by a third in 1866 and was therefore changing in character. The great social and economic transformation of Germany did even more to overwhelm the old East Elbian Prussia and its special features. What remained of the Prussian problem falls in the main under three headings. There were first of all, issues of an administrative and constitutional character affecting the relationship between the newly created Reich and the surviving state of Prussia. They never reached major proportions before 1918; but they became, curiously enough, of critical importance again under the Weimar Republic. In the imperial days there was rarely any great political divergence between the Reich Government and the Government of Prussia, but when such a divergence occurred in the Weimar period the continued existence of a Prussian Government became significant. The second major aspect of Prussia's survival lay in the continued important social and political position occupied by the Junker aristocracy. This aristocracy was in fact being replenished all the time from the ranks of the upper bourgeoisie of an increasingly industrial society, while on the other hand many Junker families grew wealthy in commerce and industry. But what were assumed to be the values of the Junkers, particularly their military virtues, set the tone until 1918, with results that were sometimes damaging and frequently ridiculous. The genuine Junkers in their turn fought a desperate rearguard action in defence of their class interest and jealously guarded the three-tier electoral system in Prussia as their major remaining bulwark. They thus became an almost entirely reactionary element in the new Reich and another of its many liabilities. In the last decade or so before the first World War many progressive Germans considered the survival of the three-tier electoral system as the only remaining significant aspect of Prussia. Thirdly, and most elusive of all, there remained the Prussian ethos and the Prussian myth. A Prussianization of Germany took place in the sense that what were assumed to be Prussian characteristics—punctiliousness, hard work, respect for law and order, but also officiousness, servility and red tape—spread throughout Germany. In some South German states, notably Bavaria, the feeling against Prussianization remained strong. The Prussian myth agitated many minds inside and outside Germany : on the one hand the great eulogy of Prussia which had been so often heard in Germany throughout the 19th century was sounded with more conviction than ever; on the other hand the picture of Prussia as the aggressive militarist core of the new Germany struck fear throughout Europe.

In the Constitution of the North German Federation and of the Reich Bismarck appeared to have solved the problem of the relationship between Prussia and Germany which had for so long prevented a solution of the German question. He had created a federation which as time went on developed increasingly the characteristics of a unitary state, but he did not dissolve Prussia as the advocates of a unitary German state had demanded in 1848. Prussia and Germany were tied together in the persons of the Emperor and King and the Chancellor and Prime Minister. As German Emperor William I and his two successors retained much of the monarchical power in the Reich which they and their predecessors had habitually exercised as Kings of Prussia. Ministers were appointed and dismissed by them and not by a parliament. The political parties in the Reichstag, unaccustomed as they were to the exercise of political power, had not by 1914 found a way of decisively changing this situation. Thus the Prussian monarchical state handed over one of its principal constitutional features to the new Reich. The misfortune was that this type of mixed constitution proved exceedingly difficult to operate in an industrialized mass society. What had been moderate and balanced in the hands of an educated *élite* became strident and erratic when under pressure from the masses to whom it had to pander but whom it would not trust.

The Chancellor-Prime Minister was the other link between Prussia and the Reich. For another two decades Bismarck shaped the evolution of this office until he fell himself victim to that dependence on the Emperor which his monarchical constitution had preserved. Bismarck created an official machine in his capacity as Chancellor and put Delbrück, the great architect of free trade, in charge of it. As the Reich developed more functions Delbrück's office, under Bismarck's ultimate control, became a central focus of power. It dealt with everything from justice to railways and before long some of these responsibilities had to be hived off and vested in separate departments. This process was facilitated by Delbrück's fall in 1876, when Bismarck was preparing the switch from free trade to protection. The officials in charge of these new separate departments were, however, not responsible ministers in the full sense, but only had the title of State Secretaries. No corporate Reich Government emerged before 1918. Various devices were adopted to regulate the relationship between the State Secretary controlling a department for the Reich and a Prussian minister dealing with the same field for Prussia. Sometimes a State Secretary also had a seat in the Prussian Government. As long as Bismarck remained in power the whole complex system of checks and balances had a sense of direction. The Iron Chancellor dominated the affairs of the Reich and the State Secretaries were clearly his servants; he was also in complete control of the Prussian ministers whom he was able to appoint and dismiss at his whim.

After Bismarck's fall there was often confusion and friction. His successors continued to combine the offices of German Chancellor and Prussian Prime Minister, except for a brief period under Caprivi; but they were far less successful in controlling either State Secretaries or Prussian ministers. Nevertheless there was even now no serious clash between Prussia and the Reich. For the man in the street both in and out of Prussia it was increasingly the Reich that mattered and engaged his attention. The Constitution of the Reich provided for a Bundesrat in which the Governments of the separate states were represented and which thus emphasized the federal nature of the union. There were fifty-eight votes in the Bundesrat; of these Prussia had seventeen and these were again controlled by the Prussian Prime Minister who was also Prussian Foreign Minister. This was a third link between Prussia and the Reich, but in practice the Bundesrat gradually declined in importance as the unitary features of the Reich became more established.

Prussia and the Reich might have diverged most seriously in the parliamentary sphere. Even an admirer of Bismarck like Treitschke believed that two parliaments so differently elected as the Reichstag and the Prussian Lower House could not for long continue side by side. In fact they did so right up to the collapse of the Hohenzollern monarchy for two main reasons : full parliamentary government was never established and the conservatives, based mainly on East Elbian Prussia and strong in both houses of the Prussian Parliament, retained their influence in the Reich Government, in spite of their weakness in the Reichstag. For a brief period after 1906, when Bülow governed with the support of a Conservative and Liberal Alliance in the Reichstag, the so-called Block, the

transformation of Germany into a genuine parliamentary state
with ministerial responsibility seemed just round the corner. It was
at this point that a change in the Prussian three-tier electoral law
became an immediate political issue. The opportunity passed :
Bülow fell, the Block broke up, the Kaiser sided with the Conservatives in resisting changes in the Prussian electoral law and
ministerial responsibility was as far away as ever.

The Prussian conservatives were the principal organized force
representing the Old Prussia in the New Empire. The course of
events since 1866 had antagonized many conservatives, especially
the legitimists of the Kreuzzeitung variety. Only the Free Conservatives who had split off from the main body of the party in
1867 whole-heartedly supported the new order. This party adopted
the name "Reichspartei" in the new Reich and obtained nearly
10 per cent of the vote in the first Reichstag of 1871. The so-called
Old Conservatives whose strength lay almost entirely in the older
provinces of Prussia soon found fresh reasons for estrangement
from Bismarck. It was now felt necessary to take in hand once
more the work of administrative reform in Prussia that had been
left unfinished in the Stein-Hardenberg era and that had withered
a second time in the 1850s. The centre of gravity in Prussia had
shifted so much to the west that local government, which was still
almost entirely in the hands of the Junkers east of the Elbe, had
to be brought up to the more democratic western conditions
throughout the land. This was the aim of new regulations concerning county (Kreis) government promulgated in 1872. Rudolf
Gneist, the distinguished Prussian constitutional historian who had
made a close study of English institutions of local self-government,
had some influence in bringing these proposals to fruition. The
office of Landrat which had usually been held by a local estate-
owner for life was now fitted into the hierarchy of professional
administrators. The overwhelming predominance of estate-owners
in the county councils was diminished and the patrimonial police
power was at last abolished. These and other modest reforms were
fiercely resisted by the Junkers, especially in the Herrenhaus. Bismarck wanted to seize the opportunity to reform the Upper House,
but in his absence the Emperor was persuaded to push the regulations through by a creation of peers. Relations between Bismarck
and the Conservatives grew more strained than ever and in exas-
peration the Chancellor resigned the Prussian Premiership in
favour of Roon. The experience of separating the two offices was,
however, short-lived and by the end of 1873 Bismarck once more
held them both.

In the meantime the Kulturkampf which might have been

thought to the taste of the Protestant Prussian Conservatives had in fact deepened the estrangement between them and Bismarck's Government. It is in the last resort difficult to find a fully rational explanation for this phase of Bismarck's policy other than the Chancellor's unquenchable thirst for battle. The Catholic group in the Prussian Lower House, known because of the position of their seats in the Chamber as the Zentrum, had been virtually shattered by the events of 1866. The incorporation of large numbers of non-Prussian Catholics in the Reich in 1870 led to the reconstitution of a party dedicated to the maintenance of the secular and ecclesiastical concerns of this religious minority. Fifteen out of the over forty million inhabitants of the new Reich were Catholics. Outside Prussia the Catholic Church had in most German states less freedom from state supervision than it had under the Prussian Constitution of 1850 and it was an obvious aim for a nation-wide Catholic party to create uniform and acceptable conditions of autonomy for the Church. At one state Bismarck regarded the reconstituted Zentrum, whose leadership was at first mainly drawn from Prussian officialdom, as a party on whose support he could hope to count, along with that of the Conservatives. The controversies arising out of the proclamation of the doctrine of papal infallibility and out of the conquest of the papal state by Italy made this increasingly impossible. When the so-called Old Catholic group began to form in opposition to papal infallibility the Catholic hierarchy in Germany demanded that the state should throw its weight against recalcitrant Catholics and Bismarck was not prepared to concede this. The lobbying of German Catholics on behalf of the Pope's temporal power infuriated him, and he feared that his foreign policy might be mortgaged by the Catholic interest in the same way as Napoleon III's had been.

Bismarck began to see the Zentrum as a real menace when other opponents of the Reich joined it. The Zentrum, hoping to broaden its base, gave hospitality to various, sometimes non-Catholic particularist interests, for example to the adherents of the dispossessed Guelph dynasty of Hanover. This brought Windthorst, himself a Catholic, but for long a minister in Hanover, into the party. He became one of Bismarck's foremost opponents, one of the few men able to measure himself against the formidable Chancellor. Even more alarming was the alliance of the Polish nationalist movement with the Zentrum. The Poles feared the new Reich. based on German nationalism, far more than they had feared the old, non-national, dynastic Prussian state. Polish support for the Zentrum spread from Posen to Upper Silesia. Perhaps the last straw in the Chancellor's eyes was the adhesion of some clerical democrats to the Zentrum. These are some of the factors which explain, though not entirely convincingly, Bismarck's bitter battle against the Zentrum and the Catholic Church.

Various aspects of the Kulturkampf became as offensive to true Prussian conservatives, and to orthodox Lutherans, as they were to Catholics. The law on school inspection of 1872 was bitterly opposed. Particularly in Prussia's eastern provinces the village pastors, closely linked with the Junkers, were the inspectors of the village schools. Now this task was put into the hands of secular officials; the Junkers disliked this as much as their English contemporaries, the squires, had disliked the penetration of school boards into their villages. The Liberals were unwilling to leave these new powers of inspection in the hand of Mühler, the Old Conservative Prussian Minister of Culture, whom they regarded as the personification of the evils of the old bureaucratic Prussian state. They forced his resignation and his place was taken by Falk, who pursued the Kulturkampf in Prussia with doctrinaire zeal. Later, long after the Kulturkampf had ended in embittered stalemate, Bismarck declared that he had never fully approved of Falk's actions. The notorious May Laws of 1873 dealt with the training of clerics and church discipline and were strongly opposed in the Prussian Upper House, which was the real stronghold of the Old Conservatives. Treitschke described the typical member of the Herrenhaus at this time : "He sits in his village, hears the pastor inveigh against the new heathens, and upsets himself about the disobedience of the servants and the tiresome assertiveness of the peasants. He measures all the events of a time of greatness against his parochial experience; as a peer of the realm he looks down contemptuously upon the virile forces of modern commerce which he hardly knows from hearsay. When he comes to the capital he puts up modestly in a bed-and-breakfast place but thinks he must keep up appearances as a pillar of the Crown. In the Upper House he then mingles with his cousins and equals; and he thus becomes confirmed in his narrow party spirit and unteachable pride."[1] In the Prussian Landtag elections of November 1873 the Conservatives were decimated. There had been 116 Conservatives, of which seventy-one were in outright opposition to Bismarck, while the remainder, under the leadership of his brother, took up a more conciliatory attitude : now they were reduced to thirty-two, of whom only a handful belonged to the irreconcilable faction. In the Reichstag elections of January 1874 the Old Conservatives retained only twenty-one seats where previously they had fifty-four. As a major organized political force the Old Conservative Party appeared to be finished. Ludwig von Gerlach had become an honorary member of the Zentrum in 1871 and later represented it in the Prussian Lower House and in the Reichstag.

In the meantime the Kulturkampf went on. Civil marriage was made obligatory and even the old Emperor found this difficult to stomach. In 1875 the paragraphs of the Prussian constitution dealing with the independence of the churches were cancelled and the salaries of priests who refused to promise obedience to the state were blocked. Hundreds of priests vacated their cures rather than risk conflict. At this time relations between Bismarck and Prussian conservatives were at their worst. Politically those who were prepared to accept the new order were entirely in the ascendant and soon a reconstituted Conservative Party was to appear which was German rather than Prussian. But socially Prussian Junkerdom was still powerful. Many still regarded Bismarck as the destroyer of their order, the man who had ruined "their" Prussia. The Kulturkampf strengthened this feeling and further fuel was added to the flames by Bismarck's remorseless persecution of Count Arnim, who was regarded in some conservative and court circles as a possible successor to Bismarck. No family had wider ramifications among the Prussian aristocracy than the Arnims. The Kreuzzeitung published articles which implied that Bismarck and some of his closest collaborators, such as Delbrück, had used their office for personal gain. In the face of Bismarck's counter-attacks against the newspaper several hundred prominent Prussians, among them many members of the nobility and many pastors, openly declared their sympathy to the editors.[2] Their attitude was symptomatic of how Old Prussia was beginning to feel overtaken by history and how this produced a posture of tenacious and negative reaction.

The majority of Prussian conservatives, however, were by now in a mood to accept the new order. The party renamed itself German-Conservative Party, a significant change. A further reform of Prussian provincial government in 1875 provided a firm base for such a party. New provincial diets were instituted, to be elected from the county councils. These diets in their turn elected officials and committees to supervise those fields of activity which were left to provincial self-government by the agencies of the central government. These changes were at first introduced in the eastern provinces of Prussia only, because these had been less affected by the Kulturkampf than the Rhineland or Westphalia. The new diets were less exclusively Junker dominated than the old ones, but still strongly conservative. The German-Conservative Party accepted the Reich and German nationalism; it wanted to preserve what it could of Prussia by emphasizing the federal nature of the Reich; and above all it looked after the economic interests of the owners

of large East Elbian estates. The party was thus well equipped to
fit into Bismarck's change of course in both its major aspects, the
move from free trade to protection and the move from liberalism
to conservatism. The East Elbian Junkers had once been in favour
of free trade, but now they wanted protection. Bismarck's alliance
with liberalism was a marriage of convenience only and reliance
on a docile conservative party suited him much better.

The threat of republicanism and socialism made Bismarck look
upon the federal structure of Germany and the survival of a multitude of governments with renewed favour. The National Liberals
had gone on hoping in vain that the Chancellor would seal his
alliance with them by forming an imperial ministry fully responsible
to the Reichstag. This was never in Bismarck's mind and the
Emperor jibbed even at the carefully hedged offer of a ministerial
post to Bennigsen who led the right wing of the Liberals. Bismarck
could scarcely restrain his satisfaction when the second of the two
attempts on the Emperor's life in 1878 presented him with the
perfect opportunity of ditching the Liberals. The Reichstag was
dissolved and new elections greatly strengthened the two conservative parties, the German-Conservatives and the Reichspartei. In
the Prussian Landtag elections of 1879 the two conservative parties
did even better and more than doubled their seats. Bismarck could
now govern with conservative support both in the Reich and in
Prussia and in consequence the last decade of Bismarck's rule was
not so stridently punctuated by domestic crises as the first sixteen
or seventeen years had been. The old Prussian conservatives had
ceased to exist as an organized political force. Writing immediately
before the first World War Count Westarp, then one of the leaders
of the German-Conservative group in the Reichstag, said that
among his colleagues there was only one left who still regretted
that Prussia had been merged in the Reich.[3]

What had happened was again not wholly beneficial for Germany. While Bismarck governed with the support of the Liberals
a great deal had been done to create common institutions for the
country, especially in the economic and legal sphere. It was increasingly the Reich that impinged on the daily life of the man in
the street and not the separate states. These developments rendered
Prussia less and less a factor of substance; in a country like Bavaria,
with a very old ethnic core, they had less effect in removing the
awareness of distinctive statehood. But the process of unification
was not completed in the constitutional sphere and Bismarck
deliberately gave up the chance of further reforming the Reich in
co-operation with the Liberals in the years 1877 and 1878. In
consequence the immensely complex federal structure of the Reich

remained to plague his successors who lacked his skill in making
the system work. The Kulturkampf had consolidated the Zentrum
which remained an astonishingly constant feature of the German
scene at least until 1933; but the existence of such a purely de-
nominational party was not wholly conducive to the political
health of the country because it often made a rational political
polarization more difficult. No sooner had Bismarck allowed the
Kulturkampf to die down than he engaged in similar bitter battles,
with no holds barred, against the Social Democrats. He used in
these domestic battles the same ruthless skill that he displayed in
foreign policy. In the case of the Social-Democratic Party the
consequences were even more disastrous for Germany than they
had been with the Zentrum. The chosen instrument of the increasingly numerous and important German working class was ostra-
cized on the political scene and never integrated into the political
process.

As for the Liberals, Bismarck's change of course in 1878 carried
further the emasculation of German middle-class liberalism. The
National Liberals became a conservative nationalist party, distin-
guishable from the German-Conservatives mainly because they
represented industrial rather than agrarian interests. They were
further weakened by secessions to the right and to the left. The
left wing of the liberal movement, the Progressives, occupied a
diminishing and uncomfortable perch between the Social Democrats and the parties on their right. The Conservatives supported
Bismarck's famous social policy of sickness and accident insurance.
This policy could be represented as a modern example of the social
welfare tradition in Prussia going back to Frederick William I. The
Prussian motto, after all, was *suum cuique*. The Conservatives as
an agrarian party were emotionally prejudiced against *laissez faire*
and the industrial entrepreneurs so that it did not come hard to
them to support policies requiring economic intervention by the
state. The German working classes did not, however, regard either
Bismarck or the Conservatives as sincere in their support of the
social policy. They realized that this policy was mainly designed
to take the wind out of the sails of the Socialists and hence it
failed to reconcile the workers to the social *status quo* or to the
ruthless suppression of the Social Democrats. The rift in the German
body politic was left unhealed.

The Prussian Conservatives were rewarded for their acceptance
of the Reich by their continuing great influence in the administration, the army and the Court. In so far as such matters can be
statistically ascertained, all the evidence shows that the Junkers,
the nobility in the old Prussian provinces, continued to maintain a

strong position right up to 1918 and in some cases beyond. Among
high officials in the central bureaucracy the Junker element dropped to 13 per cent in 1890, but was up again to 30 per cent in
1909 and 25 per cent in 1918. The Junkers were more heavily
represented still in the provincial administrations, particularly in
the East Elbian provinces. Their greatest stronghold was naturally
the officer corps of the army, particularly its senior ranks. Even
in the enormously expanded army of the first World War 20 per
cent of the general officers were drawn from the old Prussian
nobility and their position became very predominant again in the
Reichwehr; of forty-two generals in 1931 sixteen were Junkers.[4]
The reverse of the influence of the Junkers in high civil and military positions was the discrimination practised against Catholics,
Jews and those with radical political views. It was difficult for
members of these groups to gain entry into the civil service or the
officer corps and their progress on the ladder of promotion was
likely to be slow. The public service was based fairly and squarely
on those social classes which were considered "staatserhaltend",
supporters of the established order. In Prussia, Puttkamer, the
Conservative Minister of the Interior after 1881, deliberately pursued a policy of turning the bureaucracy into an appendage of his
own party.

Even more striking than the continuing great influence of the
Junkers was the homage universally paid to what were assumed to
be the values which the Junkers as a military caste held dear. The
sensational success of Prussia had made a deep impression on the
German nation. Whereas before 1866 or 1870 it was common in
South Germany to look upon the military side of the Prussian
state with both contempt and fear all this changed under the
impact of the Prussian victories fought in the cause of German
unity. What had been so long delayed seemed doubly precious;
and it appeared self-evident that Prussian military prowess had
led to achievement where other methods had failed. Thus the
Prussian army was uncritically glorified. The kleindeutsch school
of historians, Sybel, Droysen, Treitschke, who had built up the
image of the Prussian state, did the same for the Prussian army
and its officer corps. No doubt the army had played a central role
in the evolution of Prussia, but it was a new phenomenon, dating
from the wars of the 1860s, that it should have enjoyed something
like veneration among the population at large, particularly among
the educated middle class. In the past the army had been recruited
from the lowest elements in the population and the changes of the
reform era had not been able to cure this defect completely. The
Junkers were trained to service in the officer corps by rulers from

the Great Elector to Frederick the Great as a means of tying them to the state and giving them employment. The middle class on the whole held aloof from the army and by no means respected the Junker officer as a type. The use of troops in crushing the uprisings of 1848 in Berlin and elsewhere caused wide sections of the population to hate and fear the army and the officer corps.

After the wars of unification these attitudes changed radically and the historians made it seem in retrospect that the Prussian army had always been loved and adored. It was the highest aspiration of many members of the *bourgeoisie* in the new Reich to become reserve officers and the status of reserve officer was the outward and visible symbol of having arrived socially. Since Roon's army reforms the reserve officers were much more closely linked to the regular officer corps than the Landwehr officers had been. Even the holders of the highest civilian posts regarded the conferment of a military rank as an accolade. Bethmann Hollweg on his first appearance as Chancellor in the Reichstag wore the uniform of a major. Military modes of thought and expression began to permeate the patriotic bourgeoisie. Two incidents, the case of the Captain of Köpenick in 1906 and the Zabern case in 1913, each of them in a different way a *cause célèbre*, illustrate how far the militarization of sections of the German public had progressed before 1914.[5] The first incident was a comic opera affair of impersonation, showing what power a uniform possessed in Germany regardless of who wore it. The second incident was a more serious matter, affecting the position of Alsace-Lorraine in the Reich and, more fundamentally, the relationship between the civil and military authorities. The left wing parties in the Reichstag, recently strengthened in the elections of 1912, went all out to set a limit to the pretensions of the military, but even the support of the Chancellor Bethmann Hollweg, a man with a strong sense of legal rectitude, could not help them to obtain success.

The exceptional position, outside virtually all political and hardly any budgetary control, of the military authorities, headed by the General Staff, was again one of the unfortunate legacies passed on by Prussia to the Reich. In the old Prussian state it was natural for the highest military officers and offices to be directly answerable to the King. No Hohenzollern ruler after Frederick the Great had in fact the ability to exercise this control in a consistent fashion, but as long as the powers of the monarchy remained absolute there was no constitutional problem. The position of the army and the problem of parliamentary control became issues when Prussia tried to evolve into a constitutional state. Bismarck resolved the conflict

by leaving the army free of parliamentary interference and allowing only a limited degree of budgetary control by parliament. He
himself was made to feel the power of the military "demi-gods" in
1866 and 1870 when he retained his control of high policy only
with great difficulty. After 1870 he continued to fight the army's
battle against the Reichstag on the military budget, but it was a
battle which flared up again and again until 1914. On the other
hand Bismarck managed to keep the control of foreign policy
firmly in his own hands, but his successors found it much more
difficult to keep the military influence in this field at bay. The
system by which military attachés in the various capitals could
report directly to the General Staff caused even Bismarck a great
deal of trouble. Thus the Army remained a state within a state,
the General Staff and the Chief of the Emperor's Military Cabinet
important centres of power independent not only of the Reichstag but also of the political chiefs. If the Prussian Minister of
War, who controlled the entire German army except the Bavarian
contingent, showed any independence the General Staff intrigued
against him; if he played to their tune he had to stand in the
pillory for the Army in the Reichstag. One might say it had been
ever thus in Prussia; but the circumstances of the old Prussian
military monarchy were entirely different from those of the industrialized, densely populated new Reich. By some fateful application
of Gresham's law the Reich was obliterating some of the praise-
worthy characteristics of the old Prussian state, while other features
of Prussia, when metamorphosed into the new amalgam of Germany, took on very damaging characteristics. The bad was driving
out the good.

As Prussia, by being merged into Germany, became less and less
a thing of substance, the Prussian myth began to take over. To
admirers and enemies alike Prussia suggested an association of
ideas : it meant the army, militarism, the pride of the Junkers,
conservative political attitudes, the three-tier electoral system. In
German domestic affairs Prussia became, as it were, a party cry;
abroad it smacked of sabre-rattling and aggression. It escaped
notice that some of these ideas had no special connection with or
looked quite different in the Old Prussia. It was not nearly so well
known that many of the opposed ideas—anti-militarism, liberalism
and democracy and even socialism—were often more strongly represented in the areas that were at any rate nominally Prussian
than elsewhere in Germany. If Junker conservatives were strong
in the rural areas east of the Elbe, socialism was strong in some of
the great cities of Prussia, including Berlin, while the Zentrum had
wide support not only in the Rhine provinces but also in Silesia.

Nevertheless Prussia, the more elusive it became in reality, gained in potency as a myth.

One of the great makers of the Prussian myth was Treitschke. Son of a Saxon general, he venerated Prussia with the fervent attachment of an outsider. He suffered from deafness and this physical disability tinged his life with suffering and made it easier for him to ignore inconvenient realities and even the full implications of what he himself wrote and said. As a young man in the fifties he considered himself a liberal, who was looking forward to the achievement of a powerful German state through the combined efforts of Prussia and the German liberal movement. Even then he did not view freedom as an absolute value arising from natural rights, but as a condition to be achieved only within the confines of a strong state. He was absolutely opposed to democracy and did not consider the masses fit to be entrusted with power. Initially he was highly suspicious of Bismarck and the line he took in the Prussian constitutional conflict. Within a few days of Bismarck's assumption of power in 1862, Treitschke wrote to his brother-in-law : "You know how passionately I love Prussia but when I hear a shallow Junker like this Bismarck boast of the iron and blood by which he intends to dominate Germany, I can only say it is hard to tell whether he is more vulgar or ridiculous."[6] But by 1865 his opinion of the Prussian Prime Minister had changed, though he was then still reluctant to become an official propagandist for Bismarck. Treitschke's longing for a unitary German state was passionate and he could not but regard Bismarck's achievement of it as a miracle. Under the impact of events Treitschke's German-Prussian nationalism became ever more strident and exclusive. He was at first gloomy about the constitution of the North German Federation and the Reich because they left too much scope for the particularism of the smaller German states. In his view of German history this particularism was the root of all evil. It was this one-sidedness amounting often to distortion, combined with a great literary gift in the writing of history, which gave Treitschke his impact. Looking outside of Germany he saw nothing but enemies who could be held at arm's length only by the exercise of power and force. His national egotism prevented him from seeing that other nations might feel themselves threatened by this constant harping on the power of the new German Reich. Thus he nurtured a whole generation of Germans in a self-righteous chauvinism which could be highly dangerous. The occasional qualifications about the ethical basis of state power, or the need to retain a European sense, with which he interspersed his lectures, were all too easily overlooked. Even the policies of Bismarck, which were in fact so subtle, were made to look like crude exercises in power politics.

The impact of Treitschke's rhetoric was like a drug : in a breathless torrent, made doubly difficult to follow owing to the faulty articulation caused by deafness, his views poured out, yet in sentences perfecly formed and highly polished. All the emotions and prejudices associated with imperial Germany were to be found there : glorification of war as a purifying and spiritualizing experience, the innate aristocracy of the German nation, the venality of the French, the rapaciousness of the British, the materialism of America, the subversive influence of the Jews and many other such stereotypes. Treitschke's lectures were one of the rituals of Berlin; among the students close to him were Heinrich Class, the future head of the Pan-German League, and Alfred von Tirpitz, the future head of the German Navy. Treitschke was in full sympathy with German colonial aspirations and looked forward to the time when Germany would be challenging Britain on a wider world scene. He supported the annexation of Alsace-Lorraine and felt that countries like Switzerland and the Netherlands which had become separated from the German body politic might be reunited with it. Treitschke was probably most influential as a lecturer, but he was also an active pamphleteer and writer of articles and for many years edited the *Preussische Jahrbücher*. His major work was his large German history, a book written entirely from the Prussian point of view.[7] The Prussian state is seen as charged with the destinies of Germany from an early date; the Habsburg is the destroyer of German unity and 1870 the culmination of divine purpose and rationality in German history. As history Treitschke's work is not original and it is hardly objective; it is effective as literature and supplied a kind of bible for Prussia-Germany.

Treitschke sat in the Reichstag for thirteen years from 1871, for the first eight of them as a National Liberal. He belonged to the extreme right of the party. In 1874 the perennial question of the military budget was before the Reichstag and the compromise of a seven-year period for military appropriations was finally reached. Treitschke was almost the only National Liberal member who was prepared to go all the way with the Government. He accurately judged that his colleagues' concern for constitutional niceties carried far less weight with the public at large than Bismarck's threat of resignation. In 1878 Treitschke was the only National Liberal who voted for Bismarck's Socialist Law when it was introduced for the first time. He still had no sympathy whatsoever for working-class aspirations. For several years he had engaged in controversy with Gustav Schmoller, one of the leading

"Pulpit Socialists" who had founded the *Verein für Socialpolitik* in 1872. This association did much to prepare the ground for Bismarck's social policy. Schmoller, an economist, foresaw that the workers would demand a greater share of the social product and felt that they were morally entitled to it. He argued from a deep knowledge of current social problems, of socialist theory and of the Social Democratic Party. Treitschke's counter-arguments came from an academic ivory tower. He knew nothing about the workers and preferred to quote Aristotle : "Who is engaged day after day in menial work can only rarely raise his thoughts above his own narrow interests."[8] He claimed that men like Schmoller were abetting a revolutionary egalitarian conspiracy and were no better than demagogues. Thus Treitschke's vote for Bismarck's repressive measures against the Socialists could have surprised no one. What was more surprising was that most of the National Liberals followed Treitschke's example when, amid the hysteria produced by the second assassination attempt on the Emperor in 1878, the Socialist Law was introduced a second time. It was the party's final capitulation to Bismarck and presaged its disintegration. Treitschke left the party in the following year. He was now profoundly conservative, if he had ever been anything else, and an uncritical follower of Bismarck.

Treitschke was one of the makers of the Prussian myth because his vision of the new Germany was nationalist, expansionist and militarist and at the same time he represented her as the continuation and culmination of the old Prussia. It was not necessarily the truth and some of Treitschke's friends saw clearly the change that had taken place in him. Theodor Mommsen, another great German historian of the 19th century, had shared the same enthusiasms in his youth. He wanted a centralized, powerful Germany led by Prussia and he thought that Bismarck had produced it. Mommsen wrote to his brother in 1866 : "It is a wonderful feeling to be present when world history turns a corner. It is no longer a hope but a fact that Germany has a future and this future will be determined by Prussia. This is a prodigious fact for all time to come."[9] Later Mommsen became deeply disillusioned by the new Germany and turned his back on it. As early as 1871 he wrote about Treitschke : "When I see that our good Treitschke, minister, lyric poet, and lieutenant in one person, is the true evangelist of our time, holding forth in all sincerity, you can understand why I don't wish for anything but a quiet corner, a refuge for my old age; that I think I still deserve."[10] This was addressed to Gustav Freytag, great literary figure and distinguished Prussian liberal, who agreed about Treitschke : "His liberalism arose indignantly out of the

courtly loyalty of a newly ennobled Saxon family, his contacts with
old Prussians strengthened his faith in Prussia, but the old family
tradition did not release him completely, his awe of old blood
became strong, and out of his estrangement from his family grew
an emotional need to acknowledge only the good side of the Prussian Government".[11]

Treitschke has the dubious distinction of having made anti-
semitism respectable in Germany. He is the link between the instinctive anti-semitism and administrative discrimination against
Jews common in Prussia and the demagogic, racialist anti-semitism
which began to arise in Germany in the 1880s. Between 1815 and
1870 Prussia continued to be relatively progressive in her attitude
to the Jews compared with other German states. The list of Jews
influential in Prussian public life is long and this state of affairs
went on after 1870. Eduard Simson, later ennobled, presided
over the Frankfurt Parliament in 1848 and headed the delegation
which offered the Crown to Frederick William IV. He was President of the Lower House of the Erfurt Parliament in 1850, of the
Prussian Lower House in 1860 and 1861 and of the North German
and later of the German Reichstag from 1867 to 1874. In 1871
he again headed the parliamentary delegation which asked King
William I to accept the imperial crown offered him by the German
princes. He was not a figure of major political significance, but a
man who could fill a representational role with dignity. Eduard
Lasker, on the other hand, occupied a vital position in Prussian
and German politics. He came from the extreme eastern frontier of
the Hohenzollern monarchy and entered the Prussian Lower House
as a Progressive in 1865. He was one of the founders of the
National Liberal Party and the leader of its left wing. In the 1870s,
when the National Liberals did much to accomplish the legislative
unification of Germany, Lasker did more than anybody to carry the
burden of the parliamentary work involved. His moment of truth
came in 1878 when he found it extremely hard to vote for the
Socialist Law. He had increasing doubts whether the National
Liberals were still his party and he finally left them in 1880. Lasker
was one of those liberals who hoped that it would be possible to
keep Bismarck to a liberal policy; his world vanished when Bismarck deprived him and his like of their political base. When
Lasker died in 1884 the Emperor prevented any official representation at the funeral; when Bismarck was attacked for this in
the Reichstag he replied in phrases full of hatred for the dead
man.[12] Nothing could illustrate better how thin the veneer of
parliamentary and constitutional government was in the new
Germany.

Ludwig Bamberger was another leading National Liberal of Jewish extraction. He came from Mainz, where the Jews were much more assimilated than in Lasker's birthplace. He took part in the Revolution of 1848, had to emigrate and worked in the family banking business in London and Paris. He thus became an expert on financial and monetary matters and it was in this capacity that he made his chief contribution to German unification. Bismarck and Delbrück relied much on his advice. Bamberger was, like Lasker, deeply troubled by the decline of German liberalism, but he must himself bear some of the blame for it. Like so many liberal Germans from the commercial and industrial classes, he was blind to the social and economic demands of the workers and wholly addicted to *laissez faire*. This left the liberal movement very vulnerable to attacks from the right and from the left. Bamberger left the National Liberal Party, like Lasker, and joined the *Deutsch-Freisinnige* (Left-Liberals). He became thoroughly disillusioned with the new Germany, not least because of the anti-semitism that disfigured it. He replied to Treitschke's pamphlet "A Word about our Jews" with an essay entitled "Germans and Jews".[13] Bamberger had a brief moment of triumph during Frederick III's short reign, when he helped to force the ultra-conservative Prussian Minister of the Interior, Puttkamer, out of office. Mommsen, the historian, published Bamberger's speeches and writings and hailed him as one of the genuine liberals in the Bismarckian Reich.

The anti-semitism to which Bamberger was sensitive was stimulated by the economic depression of the 1870s, by the fears aroused among the lower middle class and the peasants through the speed of industrialization, by the increasing stridency of German nationaalism, perhaps even by the presence of prominent Jews such as Lasker and Bamberger in the liberal movement. Even Bismarck, during the phase of his collaboration with the Liberals, was not immune from anti-semitic attacks in the Kreuzzeitung and elsewhere and much was made of his connection with Jewish bankers like Bleichröder.[14] Treitschke was not a racialist, but the unbridled language he used about the Jews was grist to the mill of demagogues. All the stereotypes about Jews, their prominence in left-wing movements, their subversive characteristics, their critical and unconstructive spirit, all this can be found in Treitschke. He therefore forms a link to the politically organized anti-semitism that was to be found on the conservative side of German politics from the 1880s onwards and of which the Court Chaplain Stöcker was the first well-known exponent.

The fall of Bismarck in 1890 marks the end of an epoch. It has often been pointed out that the Emperor William II embodied to a remarkable extent in his person the qualities of the new age which now dawned for Germany. He was no villain and he desired nothing more ardently than to be enveloped in an atmosphere of admiration and approval, preferably expressed through a continuous procession of parades, festivities and ceremonies. The outward bombast and bellicosity which, unfortunately for his country, he so often exhibited in his public pronouncements masked an inner insecurity and lack of confidence. He was intelligent, had a quick grasp and a good memory, but was totally lacking in application and concentration. He interfered in the running of the governmental machine in short, sharp, inconsistent bursts which often did great damage. He was impetuous and never lost the type of immaturity common among well-to-do undergraduates. Nothing could be more remote from the austere qualities of traditional Prussia than the Byzantine personality of the last German emperor.

The Germany which William II ruled, the most dynamic country in Europe, was transforming itself at great speed away from the kind of society that Prussia had once been. Thus Prussia continued to survive only in the shape of a series of specific problems, and on the other hand, more significantly, as an idea or myth. The specific problems were similar to what they had been ever since 1870 or 1867. There was the constitutional problem of the relationship between Prussia and the Reich, now made more difficult to cope with by the absence of Bismarck who alone had been able to impart direction to the complex system he had created. Especially in the years immediately before 1914 the Reichstag moved to the left and strong pressures built up to transform Germany into a genuine parliamentary monarchy. The Prussian Lower House remained a conservative stronghold, buttressed by the three-tier electoral system. Conservative forces throughout Germany clung to this stronghold with great tenacity. The problem thus often presented itself in the guise of a conflict between Prussia and the Reich. In this conflict Prussia represented all that was traditional or reactionary. Hence the idea or the myth of Prussia remained very much alive. The German-Conservatives in the Reichstag and their counterpart in the Prussian Landtag had become mainly a party representing the agrarian interest, but they used the high-flown language of loyalty to traditional Prussian values to cover their essentially negative position. Their opponents saw themselves fighting a Prussian amalgam of Junker privilege, militarism and anti-liberalism. Thus Prussia seemed still to be alive when it was in fact fast fading away.

None of Bismarck's successors managed to keep the complex constitutional machinery of the Reich and Prussia working in

harmony. The position of Prussian Prime Minister was not constitutionally strong. Even Bismarck, when he was fighting for survival
in 1890, had had to unearth a long-forgotten royal order granted
to Manteuffel in 1852, under which ministers were to communicate
with the sovereign only with the consent of the Prime Minister.
Bismarck's successors often found it impossible to impose any
unity on the Prussian Government and ministers pursued mutually
inconsistent policies. As for the Reich, it occupied an ever more
substantial position in domestic policy. The State Secretaries of the
Reich became important figures in their own right. Posadowsky, for
example, State Secretary for the Interior from 1899 to 1907,
brought the no-holds-barred battle against the Social Democrats to
an end and tried to alleviate the class conflict by constructive and
reasonably progressive social policies. In the Reichstag he worked
with the support of the Zentrum. The Conservatives who were
dominant in the Prussian Landtag and in the Prussian Ministry,
were not happy with the course followed by Posadowsky, but no
attempt was made to bring them into line. In fact on matters of
particular concern to them Bülow, the Chancellor and Prussian
Prime Minister, went as far as he could to humour them. An
important economic project of the early years of this century, the
Mittellandcanal linking Rhine, Weser and Elbe, was opposed by
the Prussian Conservatives because they feared that it would
cheapen imported grain. Bülow allowed them to delay the project
for years and in the end left out the section of the canal linking
Hanover with the Elbe, thus depriving it in large part of its value.
Even the Kaiser, who took a great interest in economic development, was infuriated by the selfishness of his Junker subjects.

The three-tier electoral law defied all attempts to abolish it
before 1918. An important change was made in 1893, arising out
of the Prussian taxation reform which was being carried out by the
Minister of Finance Miquel, once a prominent National Liberal.
The taxation reform was itself a technically very accomplished
piece of work, showing that the famous efficiency of the Prussian
bureaucracy was not yet dead. It took the form of a progressive
income tax based on returns by the taxpayer himself. It put Prussian finances on a very sound basis, as opposed to the considerable
financial difficulties in which the Reich continued to find itself,
owing to the restricted sources of revenue over which it had direct
control. The reform had, however, the effect of making the Prussian electoral system even more plutocratic than it was already. In
many electoral districts there was only one elector in the highest
of the three classes. This was now counteracted by creating smaller
electoral districts in towns. This had the effect that in the poorer

quarters of cities anybody who paid tax at all might well find himself in the highest electoral class. On the whole this helped the Prussian Conservatives with their strong agrarian bias and the Zentrum. The question of the Prussian electoral law never came to rest again from this moment. The whole balance of the German constitution was based on it; without the conservative bulwark of Prussia the introduction of a genuine parliamentary regime would have been inevitable.

Increasingly the German political scene was dominated by a confrontation of conservative and left wing forces : the monarchy, the court, the Junkers, the higher bureaucracy, the officer corps, the industrialists and the *haute bourgeoisie* on the one hand; the Social Democrats, the trade unions, left wing liberalism, even the Zentrum, a party with deep popular roots, on the other. The conservative forces were not without popular support, for they had the powerful drives of nationalism and imperialism on their side. Organizations like the Pan-German League and the Navy League organized this support. But conservatism could not have remained so firmly entrenched if it had not had the help of the Prussian electoral law. There was a minor modification of it in 1906, when the distribution of seats, which favoured rural over urban areas, was slightly altered by the creation of ten additional urban seats. For the first time a handful of Social Democratic deputies were able to enter the Prussian Lower House. In the meantime electoral reform in other German states, for example Baden, Bavaria and Württemberg, made the Prussian electoral system look more of an anomaly than ever. Bülow announced electoral reform for Prussia in 1908, but it was on this issue that the Conservative-Liberal coalition with which he worked in the Reichstag showed the first signs of breaking down. His successor Bethmann Hollweg introduced a modest reform in 1910. The highest taxation payments were in future to be disregarded in the division of electoral classes; and persons of "cultural merit" were to be included in the highest electoral class, whatever their taxation position. Curiously enough such persons were to include both men with an academic education and retired non-commissioned officers. The Socialists were outraged by these proposals and Rosa Luxemburg organized some highly effective demonstrations against them. Yet the Conservatives refused to swallow even those modest reforms and they came to nothing.

There the matter rested until 1917. Bethmann Hollweg then tried to revive the question of franchise reform in Prussia, as well as consitutional reform of the Reich, as a means of buttressing the declining morale of the nation. In his Easter message of 1917 the

Kaiser promised the introduction of a secret and direct franchise into Prussia and in July 1917 he promised the abolition of the three-tier electoral system. The reforms were to be introduced after the end of the war. In fact these promises were the immediate cause of the down-fall of Bethmann Hollweg. This Chancellor personified in himself the division between West German liberalism and old Prussian conservatism. He came of a patrician family from Frankfurt who had entered the Prussian service in the 19th century and had became East Elbian landowners. It was again significant that the forces determined to prevent democratic reform in Germany even at this late stage were identical with those still pressing for an annexationist peace in 1917 and 1918. The Prussian Landtag was still refusing to pass the promised reforms in May 1918. An equal franchise was not proclaimed in Prussia until two weeks before the final collapse and then it was much too late to be noticed.

Thus the Prussian electoral law was in fact a German problem and the failure to modernize it a German failure which contributed to the German defeat in the first World War. It was the same with the Conservatives. The party which had been reorganized in 1878 as the German-Conservatives was still Junker-led and still made much of its Prussian patriotism. But Prussian patriotism was now part and parcel of German nationalism and indistinguishable from it. The Conservatives, for example, were now firm supporters of the policy of Germanizing those provinces of Prussia which had considerable numbers of Polish inhabitants. This policy was not in accordance with the traditional attitude of Prussia to her Polish inhabitants, although, admittedly, there had been phases much earlier in the 19th century when German schools and the German language were imposed on the Poles in Prussia. But after 1870 the pressure on the Poles became much more severe and ruthless. Bismarck started it during the Kulturkampf : he carried the anti-Polish policy a step further in the 1880s when he expelled a considerable number of Poles who did not possess German nationality. His motives then may have been partly foreign political : he wanted to gain Russian goodwill with his anti-Polish policy; failing better relations with Russia he did not want Germany to be burdened with a hostile Polish population on her sensitive eastern frontier. There was a short respite in the anti-Polish policy under the Chancellorship of Caprivi; partly again because relations between Russia and Germany were strained following the German failure to renew the Reinsurance Treaty in 1890. After Caprivi an aggressive policy to boost the German element on the eastern frontier and weaken the Poles was again pursued until the outbreak of war in 1914. The Conservative party always supported the anti-Polish policy and, here as in other matters, it was now far more German than Prussian.

Apart from forming an element in the German Right Wing the Conservatives specialized in representing the agrarian interest, but this was also increasingly a German rather than a Prussian concern. In 1893 the Agrarian League was founded to mobilize opposition to Caprivi's trade policies. This organization supplied the Conservatives with a broader popular base throughout Germany. It indulged in a demagogic, often anti-semitic style of campaigning which would have been anathema to an older generation of Prussian conservatives. Henceforward the Conservatives, as opposed to the Free Conservatives or Reichspartei which now drew its support mainly from industry and commerce and from academics, were often called the Agrarians. Occasionally the Conservatives still took up what might be called a pure Junker position. Thus in 1891 the Prussian Minister of the Interior at last took in hand the reform of government in rural districts in the seven eastern provinces of Prussia, in order to complete the structure of Prussian local self-government. The aim was to merge the administration in estates, which was always in the hands of the landowner, with the village administration, so as to create a modest measure of self-government at this lowest level. But the Conservatives prevented this process from being made mandatory and a decision by the Prussian Government as a whole was required in each individual case. Thus only a few hundred estates were in this way amalgamated with their local communities, when it had been estimated that the number might be as high as 16,000. The narrowness of the Conservatives as a party of interest frequently caused embarrassment to the Emperor and the Government. There were occasions when officials had to be warned against campaigning for the Agrarian League. The embarrassment was mutual, for William II did not always measure up to what the Conservatives considered fitting in a Prussian king. In December 1898 the Chancellor, the South German Prince Hohenlohe-Schillingsfürst, wrote in his diary: "I must strive to keep Prussia within the Reich, for all these gentlemen don't care a fig for the Reich and would rather give it up today than tomorrow." The narrowness and rigidity of the Junkers must often have given this impression, but Hohenlohe was being unduly pessimistic. The glory of Prussia and the glory of Germany were now completely intermixed in the minds of the Junkers.

The great problem of Germany's position in the world, the central issue of the decades preceding 1914, had little connection with the problem of Prussia. Nationalism and Imperialism were universal forces which held sway in many nations. The new Germany had arrived late and enjoyed an exceptionally dynamic rise to wealth and power. It was perhaps inevitable that such a nation should join the international scramble for influence and territory with undiscriminating zeal. Even so intelligent a man as Friedrich Naumann, who tried before 1914 to give a new direction to German politics by creating a compound of monarchical, parliamentary and socialist ideas, believed in a world role for Germany. The conduct of German foreign policy before 1914 was often unwise. It may be that the strains and stresses of German domestic politics, aggravated by the artificially strong anti-liberal position based on Prussia, added to the bellicosity and nervousness of the makers of German foreign policy. It is by no means certain, however, that if public and parliamentary opinion had had a greater and more direct influence on the German Government, the result would have been much better. Opinion everywhere in Europe before the first World War was susceptible to the appeal of chauvinism. It was one of the legacies of the German and the Prussian past that German public opinion was more than averagely immature. The Reichstag had little experience in handling foreign affairs : on the right it tended to regard criticism of official foreign policy as almost treasonable; on the left suspicion of the military and a tendency to attack the military budget, regardless of realities, was endemic. It seems therefore at least doubtful if a fully parliamentary regime would have made a better job of German foreign policy than the Kaiser's semi-authoritarian system.

Once the war had broken out the German system seems again to compare unfavourably with the parliamentary democracies of the West. Certainly the absence of a political focus of power allowed decisions such as the adoption of unrestricted submarine warfare to be taken on almost exclusively military grounds. But was it any easier to adopt realistic and limited war aims in Lloyd George's Britain than it was in the Germany of the *Vaterlandspartei*? The Prussian Conservatives were no doubt usually to be found on the side of the annexationists and those who were fighting for an all-out victory. Their motives were, at any rate partly domestic, for they felt that only a complete victory for Germany could keep intact the system of aristocratic government to which they were so closely attached. The drive to make Germany into a world power was supported in many sectors of German life, from industrialists and bankers like Emil Kirdorf and Arthur von Gwinner to academics like Max Scheler and Hans Delbrück, and there was nothing specifically Prussian about it. It need not concern us here whether this drive was, or amid the passions unleashed by war turned into, a quest for hegemony or whether it was a more modest demand for equality with other world powers. If German bellicosity contributed to the outbreak of the war and if German ambitions helped to prolong it, this was a German, not a Prussian affair. The picture which some of the world had of the bad Prussians dragging the good Germans into war was remote from reality. Much more relevant is the fact that the collapse and the revolution of 1918 did not form a drastic break with the past. The German amalgam, to which Prussia had contributed many elements and within which these Prussian elements sometimes had a retarding effect, was not radically different after 1918 from what it had been before. This explains many of the problems which beset the Weimar Republic.

CHAPTER IX

EPILOGUE: *The Weimar Republic and the Nazi Regime 1918–1945*

THE Revolution of 1918 might have marked the end of Prussia. Its most characteristic elements seemed to disappear. The House of Hohenzollern which had created the Prussian state and had celebrated the quincentenary of its acquisition of Brandenburg in 1915 was exiled. It was never thereafter to play an important role in German affairs. The question of a Hohenzollern restoration moved into the realm of discussion on one or two occasions but never became practical politics. Some of the Kaiser's sons made rather discreditable incursions into German politics, in some cases under Nazi auspices, but such matters were only of minor significance. The House of Hohenzollern disappeared into the limbo of history with a suddenness and a finality which even in retrospect appears astonishing.

The second Prussian element which disappeared in 1918, though with a good deal less finality, was the important political position of the Junkers and the Prussian political classes. The defeat of 1918 was to a large extent their failure, and their privileged position was necessarily at an end. Many of them, however, remained in high positions, for the leaders of the Republic had neither the desire nor the will to dispense with their services. The democratic politicians were anxious to ensure continuity and expertise in administration; they also had something of an inferiority complex in the face of their former masters. The old ruling classes on their side did not fully accept the Republic: indeed, it was one of its greatest liabilities that so many of its public servants bore it so little loyalty. This was naturally not a specifically Prussian problem, for the *élite* of pre-1914 Germany was a mixture of aristocratic elements from all over Germany, of men who had risen in the public service and of others who had grown wealthy in industry and commerce. The third major element which disappeared in 1918 was the three-tier electoral system.

It is therefore surprising that anything survived of Prussia at all and it would of course be a distortion of history to overestimate the surviving aspects and look at them independently from German developments. Ever since 1870 Prussia had increasingly become merely a facet of the general German situation and this was even more so after 1918. Nevertheless Prussia survived as a constitutional entity and because the Reich as well as the separate Länder had fully parliamentary regimes a divergence between them could assume a more critical significance than under the Empire. The Prussian myth or idea also survived, but because the reality had become comparatively insubstantial, it could be handled with greater abandon. Men as diverse as Oswald Spengler and Adolf Hitler used it their own way and for their own ends.

There seemed many good reasons why the constitution of the German Republic should be unitary. It was after all the over-complex mixture of federal and unitary elements in Bismarck's constitution which was widely thought to be one of the reasons for Germany's failure in the first World War. A number of different solutions to the problem were possible. Prussia could be kept intact and could retain its leading position as in Bismarck's Reich, or Prussia could be divided into its component provinces and these, along with the former South German states, would all become roughly equal members of one unitary state; or Prussia could become immediate Reich territory, as proposed in 1848, and one might hope that the remaining German states would eventually merge into it. Variants on these three major possibilities were also feasible. Hugo Preuss, who more than any other single person was responsible for the constitution of the Weimar Republic, produced a first draft in which the traditional German tribes and regions would have only limited self-government and the creations of dynastic accident would entirely disappear. Prussia would thus be dissolved into its various components. The opposition to this scheme did not come from Prussia. The Prussian Government of the November Revolution had declared that "the old Prussia, reactionary to its very foundations, should be transformed as rapidly as possible into a fully democratic part of a unitary people's republic."[1] The parties which now ruled Prussia and which had been for so long excluded from any share in political power could see no further reason for continuing the defunct dynastic state. As late as December 1919 the Prussian Constituent Assembly was still prepared to give up a separate Prussian constitution in favour of a unitary German state. The medium-sized German states, however, regarded the dissolution of Prussia as too high a price to pay for being themselves degraded to mere provinces of a unitary German state. Thus a compromise was finally reached and the constitution of the Weimar Republic became more unitary than that of Bismarck, but the German states were not abolished but merely reduced in number. Prussia continued to exist.

The Weimar Republic was more unitary than the Second Empire because the Reich had much greater financial and economic powers; sovereignty rested with the people, and the Reichsrat, the principal federal organ analogous to the old Bundesrat, had advisory functions only. Yet the survival of separate states, even with limited powers, did in fact put a more severe strain on the Weimar Republic than the old dynastic states did on the federal structure of the Empire. This was because the states were now fully-fledged political organisms and the complexion of their parliaments might diverge from that of the Reichstag. This happened above all in the case of Bavaria. Its right wing monarchist government after 1920 found itself out of step with Berlin and refused to support fully the attempt of the Reich Government to protect itself against its domestic enemies. The assassinations of Erzberger and Rathenau were only the most sensational of a long series of political murders and the Bavarian Government would do little to help in tracking down the perpetrators. The separatist policies of the Bavarians were seen at their most striking in the murky story of the Hitler-Putsch of 1923. The Bavarian Government all but connived in this affair and only crushed it at the last moment; even the unity of the Reichswehr was in danger of breaking down.

Prussia, on the other hand, became the chief pillar of the Republic. In a reversal of roles, it was now the most staunchly republican of the Länder where previously it had been regarded as the bulwark of reaction. The parties of the so-called Weimar Coalition, the Social Democrats, the Zentrum and the Democrats, successors of the left-liberal Freisinnige, had in fact always been strong in Prussia and only the three-tier electoral system had produced the illusion that the country was a conservative stronghold. In November 1918 Paul Hirsch, a Social Democrat and a Jew, became Prussian Prime Minister. He was only the third commoner to hold the office; the two previous non-noble Prussian premiers were Ludolf Camphausen in 1848 and Georg Michaelis, scion of an old family of Prussian officials, who was Reich Chancellor and Prussian Prime Minister for a few months in 1917. This indicates better than anything the magnitude of the political change which occurred in 1918. Hirsch had been one of the small group of Social Democrats who entered the Prussian Lower House in 1908 and fought the unequal struggle against the three-tier electoral law. His seniority propelled him, an unassuming man, into the highest office and he remained there during the period of provisional constitutional arrangements.

In 1920, following the Kapp-Putsch, Otto Braun, another Social Democrat, became Prussian Prime Minister. He had come into the Socialist movement as an organizer of East Prussian agricultural workers. Except for two brief periods in 1921 and 1925 he retained his office until Papen ended the existence of an independent Prussian government on 20th July 1932. For most of these years, he had at his side another of the strong men of German Social Democracy, Carl Severing, the Minister of the Interior. This minister controlled the police in Prussia, and therefore in three-fifths of Germany including the capital and this was a power bastion of great significance for the Weimar Republic, especially in its final agony. The Braun-Severing regime, known to their opponents as the "red tsars of Prussia", presented a point of stability on the German political scene where chancellors and cabinets were constantly changing. The Social Democrats, who in principle were in favour of an unitary German state, could now on occasion and for tactical reasons, be found idealizing the virtues of the Prussian state, clean administration and social responsibility. For most of the twelve years of the Braun-Severing regime the Prussian government consisted of the three parties of the Weimar Coalition, but between 1921 and 1925 the German People's Party, the right-wing liberal party to which Stresemann belonged, was also represented in the Cabinet in a so-called Grand Coalition. Within the fairly narrow limits set by the Weimar Constitution to the sphere of action of the separate Länder, the Prussian administration had considerable achievements to its credit, particularly in the cities, and traces of this, for example, progressive housing developments, can still be seen in Germany today. The Prussian administration had considerable influence on legislation in the Reich. Prussia had a Staatsrat analogous to the Reichsrat. It was elected by the provincial assemblies and could initiate legislation, though it had only a suspensory veto. For most of the Weimar period Konrad Adenauer, the Burgomaster of Cologne, was its chairman.

The continued existence of the Weimar Coalition Government in Prussia became a matter of major political significance when, with the appointment of Brüning in the spring of 1930, the Reich Government ceased to rest on a parliamentary majority. After the disastrous Reichstag elections of September 1930, which catapulted the Nazis from the position of a fringe splinter group to that of the second largest party, Germany became even more ungovernable and Prussia was the last bastion of Republican legitimacy. Severing, who had been Reich Minister of the Interior in the last fully parliamentary Reich Cabinet, now reverted to the position of Prussian Minister of the Interior; his predecessor Grzesinski became Berlin Chief of Police; Grzesinski's deputy was Dr. Bernhard Weiss, a Jew. This trio bore the full brunt of the Nazi fury, whipped up in Berlin by Goebbels. The traditional right wing had always regarded it as a particular affront that "their" Prussia was under the sway of the red-black coalition. They had not given up hope that a reform of the German political system in accordance with conservative anti-parliamentary ideas might be achieved through Prussia. The machinery was put in motion for a referendum to require the dissolution of the Prussian Landtag. It was one of those occasions, which had become numerous since 1929, when the parties of the respectable "national opposition" made common cause with the Nazis. The Communists, in their blind hatred of the Socialists, threw in their support for good measure. The vote in favour of a dissolution was not large enough to be fully binding, but it still augured badly for the future of the Weimar Coalition in Prussia. This was in August 1931. In April 1932 the Prussian Landtag elections, the third of the five major elections to be held in Germany in 1932, ended the majority of the Braun Government. There was no majority for the right wing parties either and the Communists, with whom nobody would treat, held the balance. The Braun Government stayed in office as caretaker but Otto Braun himself seemed to give up the game as lost when he went on sick leave early in June.

In the meantime Papen had been installed as Reich Chancellor. His Cabinet, which did not enjoy a vestige of parliamentary support, was as pure a reincarnation of the old monarchist aristocratic Junker Governments of the imperial era as could be imagined. Papen himself was a Westphalian Catholic who had served in a Potsdam guard regiment. Schleicher, the man who made him Chancellor and who was his Minister of Defence, had served in the same regiment as the two Hindenburgs, father and son. Gayl, the Minister of the Interior, was another Prussian Junker and reserve officer; Schwerin-Krosigk, bearer of a famous Prussian name, became Minister of Finance, a post which he continued to hold till 1945. Papen and his friends, as part of their plan to give Germany a new, more authoritarian and possibly monarchical constitution, conceived a scheme to remove what remained of the Republican government of Prussia and take it over themselves : severe street fighting in Altona, during the electoral campaign for a new Reichstag, gave them their excuse to act. On 20th July 1932, Braun, Severing and the other Prussian ministers were barred from their offices and Papen made himself Reich Commissar for Prussia.

Grzesinski, Weiss and countless other officials of known republican convictions were swiftly removed. It will always remain a debatable point whether resistance to this illegal act might have been possible. Twelve years earlier a general strike had brought about the collapse of the Kapp-Putsch, but now the ability of the unions to use this weapon, even if they had been willing, was sapped by mass unemployment. It is certain that the absence of resistance was another nail in the coffin of the Weimar Republic. Legal proceedings brought by the displaced Prussian and other German governments reached no definite conclusion before the advent of Hitler to power made them academic. The control of the Prussian Government, particularly of the Ministry of the Interior through Göring, was a major factor in the swift establishment of the Nazi dictatorship when Hitler took office six months later. If any single date can be named for the final disappearance of Prussia it is 20th July 1932.

The Braun-Severing Government was unfortunately not the only aspect of Prussia which survived in the Weimar Republic. The fault line which ran through German politics before 1918 separating the nationalist, imperialist, conservative right from the anti-military, socialist, liberal left continued to divide the Germans, perhaps even more bitterly, in the Republic. The constitutional advantage to be derived from the existence of Prussia had lain with the Right in Imperialist Germany and was, as it were, transferred to the Left in the days of the Republic. The Right, however, continued to cherish the Prussian idea and hoped that it might even recapture the constitutional advantage; eventually, in Papen's coup of July 1932, it did so. The successor of the German-Conservative Party of the Empire, and to a lesser extent of the Free Conservatives, was the German-National People's Party, usually known as the "Deutsch-Nationale" (DNVP). The name itself reveals something of the dilemma in which this party found itself. It was an amalgam of interests and tendencies, ranging from East Elbian Junkers, monarchists and various agrarian associations to the Christian-Socialists, racists and anti-semites who had existed on the fringe of the right wing even in imperial days. In the early twenties it had a considerable popular following as a "collecting basin" of the right and reached its peak in 1924. The need to become a mass movement was difficult to swallow for those conservatives who clung to older ideas of monarchical and aristocratic government and caused tension in the party. A further dilemma was added when the consolidation of the Republic in the middle twenties posed the question whether the party should continue in opposition or participate constructively in government. Opposition was not an attitude for which German conservatives were emotionally well equipped. The election of a genuine Prussian field marshal, Hindenburg, as President of the Republic in 1925 made it easier for the DNVP to join the government. They now had an "Ersatzkaiser".

The period in government proved unrewarding for the party and they lost heavily in the Reichstag elections of 1928, which signalled a general swing to the left. This was the main reason why Count Westarp, a Prussian Junker who had been a Conservative leader since before 1914, was removed from the party leadership and replaced by Hugenberg. The party now switched to a much more radical course of opposition to the Republic; there was less emphasis on monarchy, aristocracy and Prussianism and more on demagogy and exploitation of nationalist and economic resentments. The link with the extreme racist right, which had virtually been cut in the mid-twenties, was re-established and above all common cause was made with the Nazis, in the first instance over the Young Plan. The concept of the "National Opposition" was born. The disastrous consequences of Hugenberg's course for his party and for Germany are only too well-known.

It is naturally more difficult to establish a direct link between the Deutsch-Nationale and Prussia than it was to link the pre-1918 German-Conservatives with Prussia. The link lies in the fact that in organizations like the DNVP or the *Stahlhelm*, its paramilitary counterpart, there were many men who considered themselves conscious Prussians and the Prussian ideology was made much of. When Treviranus, Westarp and others left the Hugenberg dominated DNVP in 1930 to form the Conservative People's Party, one may see in their move a stirring of the old Prussian conservative conscience against Hugenberg's unprincipled opportunism. Treviranus and his group liked to think of themselves as the German Tory Democrats, but it was one of Germany's many political tragedies that it had never produced a popular conservative party and a moment of profound crisis was hardly likely to provide the occasion for filling the gap. The Conservative People's Party received only negligible electoral support; these men were officers without an army. In any case the claim to Prussianism of the conservative variety was not the monopoly of the organized conservative parties and was shared by many who did not come from the old provinces of Prussia. For example, Papen was as a Westphalian Catholic aristocrat by no means a typical Prussian. He sat on the extreme right of the Zentrum in the Prussian Lower House until his party disowned him when he accepted the Chancellorship in 1932. Nothing was more precious to him, however, than his former status as an officer in a Prussian Guard Regiment and he was therefore, like many others, an elective Prussian.

The survival of the Prussian Junker and his values can be seen at its purest in the Reichswehr. This force was very much the personal creation of its first Chief, General von Seeckt, who until dismissal in 1926 was a major figure in the development of the Weimar Republic. Seeckt epitomized even in his appearance the typical Prussian officer; he had proved himself a brilliant staff officer in the first World War. His loyalty to the Republic was conditional rather than absolute and his frequently quoted remark, made at the time of the Kapp-Putsch, "Reichswehr does not shoot at Reichswehr" well illustrates his attitude. Seeckt was very conscious of the Prussian heritage and he wrote in his biography of Moltke about the Prussian state: "It differs as much from the Anglo-Saxon liberal concept of the state, which sees it as an insurance agent for commerce and industry, as it differs from the Marxist concept, which regards its ultimate purpose to be like a mechanical beehive. The Prussian state rests on mutual service. In the Prussian concept of the state there lives the voluntary subordination into a structure of which each individual is a necessary part. *L'état c'est moi* is the motto of every Prussian. This the world cannot understand because it cannot feel it. Hence it regards the Prussian state with suspicion."[2] When in September 1918 Count Hertling, the Reich Chancellor, who was a Bavarian, made a speech advocating an equal franchise in Prussia, Seeckt wrote to his wife: "And what does a Bavarian know about the Prussian dynasty? and is there no Prussian who will answer him? This is worse than Bethmann and worse than anything that is happening or can happen at the front. . . ."[3]

It fell to Seeckt to choose and train the officers of the Reichwehr. Because the force was so small he could be highly selective. He preferred candidates of aristocratic birth and from old military families, but he could also demand high educational qualifications. He thus got an officer corps with a high proportion of Junkers, a politically reliable instrument in the hands of its leaders but not necessarily reliable for the Republic, and high technical competence. When parliamentary government broke down after 1930 the Reichwehr became again a major political factor in Germany and its influence was exercised mainly through its "political cardinal" Schleicher. Thus by a roundabout route the Prussian Junker influence was almost back to where it had been under the Kaiser. Another route lay through Hindenburg, the Ersatzkaiser, who was himself a Prussian Junker officer. It is generally supposed that the opposition of East Elbian landowners to the agrarian

policy of the Brüning Government played a part in the downfall
of the last effective Chancellor of the Republic. The estate owners
of East Prussia grew indignant about what they called agrarian
bolshevism and communicated their sentiments to their fellow
squire, the Reich President. This was one of the ways in which
Hindenburg's confidence in Brüning was undermined.

Thus Prussia was neither the property of the Left nor of the
Right. In any case it was nothing but an illusion that Prussia had
any existence independent of Germany. During the Weimar period
it was conceivable that Bavarian separatism could have come into
the realm of practical politics; but Prussia and Germany had been
virtually synonymous for at least a generation. The more nebulous
Prussia became as an independent entity the more active were the
makers of the Prussian myth. The Left tried it in a small way on
the strength of the Braun-Severing regime and its achievements,
but in the main the Prussian myth was again to be found on the
Right. It was part and parcel of the anti-democratic, anti-western,
anti-liberal, militarist, Fascist and sometimes nihilist philosophy
which did much to undermine the Weimar Republic. It is difficult
now to sympathize with men like Oswald Spengler, Moeller van
den Bruck, Carl Schmitt and even Ernst Jünger who from an
attitude of huge intellectual pride and extreme presumption chip-
ped away at the foundations of European civilization. They were
acutely sensitive to the deep malaise and disillusionment in defeated
Germany and they argued from this to Western society in general.
In fact they greatly underestimated the staying power of Western
civilization and their cultural pessimism is not without Schaden-
freude. Rejection of civilization as it was with its existing systems,
capitalism, socialism, democracy, and liberalism, led to the demand
for a brave new world, governed by strong *élites,* unafraid of
struggle, ultra-modern and technical. All this was known as the
"Conservative Revolution" a paradoxical term which covered up
a great deal of pseudo-profundity and uncertainty. There was, to
be fair, also much idealism in this movement and the young who
were thirsty for ideals listened most avidly to these prophets. But
besides idealism there was also the urge to destroy, a nihilism
which entered deeply into the Nazi movement. The prophets themselves felt the urge, from their superior knowledge, to proclaim
the coming doom.

In so confused a movement of ideas the exact emphasis varied
widely from one writer to another. Carl Schmitt, for example, was
an academic political scientist and constitutional lawyer of great
intellect. His writings on constitutional law did much to make the
presidential government of the Brüning era respectable and he

finally came to justify the bloodbath of 30th June 1934 in an article entitled: "The Führer protects the Law".[4] Schmitt contended that the legitimacy of justice lay in the legislator's ability to enforce it; the essence of the political was that it was based on a friend-enemy relationship. Ernst Jünger was a pure artist, remote from political reality, yet often given to visions of the future dominated by a hard generation of soldiers and workers. He had been through the first World War and much of his writing is on war as a spiritual experience. The opening passage of his war diary *In Storms of Steel,* which during the second World War reached an edition of several hundred thousand, conveys well the flavour of his writing. "We had left lecture and schoolrooms and work-tables and had been welded together, in the brief weeks of training, into a great, enthusiastic body. Grown up in an age of security, we all yearned for the exceptional, the great danger. Then the war had made us drunk. We went out in a shower of flowers, in a drunken mood of roses and blood. The war must make it real to us, the Great, the Strong, the Solemn."[5] In another of his widely read books, *War as a Spiritual Experience,* he wrote: "The essential is not what we are fighting for, but how we are fighting."[6] What Jünger really wanted is difficult to tell and he hid his doubts behind the stoical mask of the warrior. He was honest enough to repudiate the stab-in-the-back myth on the grounds that Germany's defeat must have been due to her spiritual inferiority. He was a proud and aloof man who to his credit never compromised with the Nazis.

It is not difficult to see why the image of Prussianism held great appeal to the men of the Conservative Revolution. Oswald Spengler and Moeller van den Bruck both devoted books to it. Spengler was probably the doyen of the neo-Conservative movement and one of the most influential intellectual figures of the Weimar period. In 1919 he published a small book called *Prussianism and Socialism.*[7] It developed the thesis that German socialists and Prussian conservatives had really much in common and that the alien element that was being imported was the liberal parliamentary democracy of Weimar. The Prussians were the only true socialists and Frederick William I was "the first conscious socialist". Spengler contrasts the Marxist idea of the public ownership of the means of production with the old Prussian idea of controlling by legislation the national productive forces while leaving scope for individual talent and enterprise. In the Prussian economic system freedom is enjoyed through the rules of the game which are imposed. *Prussianism and Socialism* also contains much of the stock Spenglerian ideas, struggle as the fundamental fact of life and politics, war as a higher form of human existence, reform and improvement as an enterprise doomed to failure and insignificance. The book ends with a characteristic passage: "The most valuable among the German workers must unite with the best representatives of the old Prussian political spirit, both determined to create a strictly socialist state, a democracy in the Prussian sense, both tied together by a common sense of duty, by the consciousness of a great task, by the will to obey in order to rule, to die in order to win, by the strength to make tremendous sacrifices in order to fulfil our destiny, to be what we are and what without us would not exist. We are socialists. We do not intend to have been socialists in vain."

Moeller van den Bruck is chiefly known for his book *Das Dritte Reich* in which he extols the concept of a new Reich, in the medieval sense of the word, as the means of rescuing European civilization from the slough of liberalism and materialism. He believed that Prussianism was perhaps the most distinctive gift which the Germans could bestow upon the world. In a book called *The Prussian Style* he wrote: "Strength of organization is the essence of Prussianism. Strong organizers gave to what is Prussian at an early stage the shape and the colour which distinguishes it from what is German."[8] Moeller van den Bruck thus thought, like Jünger, primarily in esthetic, apolitical terms. He once met Hitler in the early twenties and is supposed to have remarked "This fellow will never grasp what it is all about". Self-conscious elitism was very characteristic of the ideologues of the Conservative Revolution. Their doctrines are a kind of *jeu d'esprit* which became a *trahison des clercs* when the Weimar Republic began to disintegrate. They had provided images and myths through which even liberally-minded Germans could come to accept what was happening and lose the will to resist it.

The Prussian myth was in the air during the Weimar period. It is not surprising therefore that so accomplished a propagandist as Hitler also used it. There is an enormous literature both from supporters and opponents of National Socialism showing links from Frederick the Great through Bismarck to Hitler. The most striking instance of the direct political use of the Prussian idea by Hitler was the famous Day of Potsdam, 21st March 1933. Hitler owed his rise to power to some extent to the support of the Conservatives, principally the DNVP. This was so from the moment when Hugenberg first joined with the Nazis in opposition to the Young Plan in 1929. The Cabinet which Hitler formed on 30th January 1933 ostensibly contained a majority of Deutsch-Nationale and even after the elections of 5th March 1933, the Nazis had a majority in the Reichstag only in combination with the DNVP. It was one of the secrets of Hitler's success that he could be all things to all men. In the weeks after his assumption of office and before he had concentrated dictatorial power in his hands it was particularly important to give the impression of continuity in order to allay the fears of the German middle classes. The slogan "Nationale Erhebung" or "Nationale Revolution" dominated the mass media. The Germans were being persuaded that what was taking place was not a take-over by a revolutionary party but the resumption of Germany's great national destiny which had been so treacherously interrupted in November 1918. Hitler still needed the Reichstag to pass the Enabling Law in order to wield dictatorial power securely and the Day of Potsdam was arranged to prepare the mood two days before the meeting of the Reichstag.

It was the first big occasion for which the scene was set by Goebbels as Minister for Propaganda and Enlightenment. The central figures were Hindenburg and Hitler and there is a well-known photograph of the latter, unusually dressed in morning coat, bowing low in front of the former, in full Field Marshal's uniform. Other features to emphasize the continuity between the old Prussia and the new Nazi Germany were the use of the Garrison Church at Potsdam, the massive display of the old imperial colours as well as of the swastika, the descent of Hindenburg into the crypt of Frederick the Great, the empty chair left for the Kaiser and the presence of the Crown Prince as well as numerous generals of the imperial army in their uniforms. Even Brüning and the Zentrum deputies in the Reichstag had somehow got themselves to the Garrison Church, but significantly had had to enter by a side door;[9] two days later they were to vote for the Enabling Law. The day of Potsdam made a great impression inside and outside Germany. Many a nationally-minded German felt he could now safely throw in his lot with the new rulers of his country. It was a great time for illusions and what was made to look like a conservative restoration was in fact the seizure of unlimited power by a gang of extremists.

When he took office as Chancellor in January 1933 Hitler was for the moment prevented from also occupying the position of Reich Commisar for Prussia which had been held by Chancellors since Papen's coup of the previous July. This post now reverted to Papen, who was also Vice-Chancellor, one of the many safeguards against Nazi extremism which were demolished or circumvented by Hitler with such fatal ease. In spite of all this the really crucial prize, the Prussian Police, fell to Göring, as commissarial Prussian Minister of the Interior. Within days Nazi officials had been introduced into the Prussian Police; the regular force was diluted by turning large numbers of the SA into auxiliary police. It was a striking example of poacher turned gamekeeper and one of the principal means of applying terror in preparation for the Reichstag elections of March 1933. As soon as the elections were out of the way the complete "Gleichschaltung" of the Länder began. Commissars representing the Chancellor were installed, with full powers, in a number of German states; within a month these were renamed Reichsstatthalter and became, on paper at any rate, the supreme authority in all German states. The Länder parliaments were dissolved and reconstituted with the same party composition as the Reichstag which was by now completely Nazi-controlled.

In Prussia a slightly different procedure was followed. The Chancellor himself assumed the powers of Statthalter and Papen resigned his office of Reich Commissar; Göring became Prussian Prime Minister and exercised the powers of Statthalter on Hitler's behalf. The Prussian Landtag did not have to be reconstituted as it had been elected at the same time as the Reichstag in March 1933. In January 1934 a further step was taken towards reducing the separate German states to mere adminstrative organs: the Länder Parliaments, mere charades though they were, ceased to exist altogether. Constitutional tidiness, even constitutions as such, were, however, of little consequence to Hitler, who never bothered formally to abolish the Weimar Republic. In the same way the purely administrative vestiges of the Länder did not entirely disappear. In the case of Prussia nearly all its ministries were merged with the corresponding Reich ministries; but the Prussian Finance Ministry survived and Göring continued to include the position of Prussian Prime Minister among his many titles and offices. The Nazi regime was a totalitarian dictatorship with an almost unparalleled concentration of power at the top; underneath this umbrella, a proliferation of empires and of national and local bosses jockeyed for position. What remained of the administrative authority of the Länder competed in this free-for-all.

Thus Prussia ended, not with a bang but a whimper. But there was one final spasm of a nobler kind, the part which Prussians and the Prussian idea played in the resistance to the Nazis. Again the situation was not clear-cut and it would be absurd to emphasize the Prussian element as an independent factor in the resistance. This is illustrated by the rise of the Confessing Church, the first dramatic instance of resistance to the penetration of National Socialism into all facets of German life. The Lutheran churches were particularly vulnerable to the appeal of Nazism; they had a long tradition of submission to the state and had shared to the full the nationalist intoxication of Prussia and Germany. Lutheran

pastors always mixed "Potsdam and Bethlehem" and had to a
large extent lost contact with the democratic and socialist elements
of the population. The so-called German Christians, who believed
in a Germanized, de-judaized Christianity, had much support,
particularly in the Church of the Old Prussian Union, even before
1933. When, however, the Nazis tried in 1933 to take the Lutheran
churches by storm for the German-Christians, strong resistance
developed and the Confessing Church was born, in which many
conscious Prussians like Bodelschwingh and Niemöller were prominent.

Similarly the Reichswehr had played its part in allowing Hitler
to come to power and many of its senior officers were Prussian
Junkers. An officer of this kind, Field Marshal von Blomberg,
played a crucial role in the collaboration of the army and the
Nazi regime. It did not, however, take long for a group of important officers in the Army High Command to become fully aware
of the criminal nature of the regime they were serving. Some of
the military conspirators against Hitler were not Prussian Junkers :
Ludwig Beck for example, very much a central figure, came of a
middle class family from the Rhineland, but his education and
training was that of a Prussian officer. The military conspirators
were so important in the resistance because they were the only
group which held the means for action. In the wider resistance
movement many famous Prussian names appear—Moltke, whose
Silesian estate gave its name to the Kreisau circle, Kleist-Schmen-
zin, York von Wartenburg, Schwerin von Schwanenfeld, von der
Schulenburg and many more. There were also representatives of
Prussian socialism, for example, Julius Leber. It is possible to show
that some of the old Prussian conservatives within the DNVP who
opposed Hugenberg's collaboration with the Nazis later moved on
to resistance against the Nazis. It is possible to show that certain
recurring Prussian ideas—a peculiar blend of liberal conservatism,
the combination of authoritarianism and socialism, the bridging of
Western and Eastern values—crop up again in the resistance. All
this should not be pushed too far. It is perhaps sufficient to say
that some of these brave men, in deliberately embracing a lost
cause and donning the shirt of Nessus as an act of atonement, felt
themselves to be acting from a Prussian sense of duty.

The outcome of the second World War made any reconstitution
of Prussia impossible. A large part of the old Prussia, all the provinces that lay east of the Oder-Neisse line, were denuded of their
German populations. Most of Pomerania and Silesia and all of
East and West Prussia are now no longer inhabited by Germans
but by Poles; the exception is the northern part of East Prussia,

including Königsberg, now renamed Kaliningrad, which is part of the Soviet Union. Breslau is now Wroclaw, Stettin is Sczecin and Chemnitz, formerly in Saxony, now in East Germany, is Karl-Marxstadt. The formal abolition of the Prussian state by a law of the Allied Control Council in 1947 was therefore hardly necessary and is a tribute to the potency and persistence of the Prussian myth.

Prussia was far too prolonged and varied as a historical phenomenon to be summed up in a stereotype. It started as a military-dynastic state, in common with a good many others. Its poor resources, exposed strategic position and lack of natural cohesion forced it to be more efficient than other dynastic states; accident endowed it with three rulers in rapid succession who had the will and the ability to overcome the natural handicaps of their state. The Great Elector started the process of giving administrative cohesion to his territories and creating an army to give his state European standing. Administrative and economic progress, the Lutheran religion and the Pietist movement enabled Frederick William I to create a state which was beginning to have a formative influence on its citizens. The army was, however, the most important product of this state and with the instrument created by his father Frederick the Great was able to make his country into a major European power and a German power second only to the Habsburgs. The glitter of the Prussian King's personality gave his country the reputation of being the most advanced of enlightened despotisms. Eighteenth-century Prussia was entirely a dynastic, non-national state, but at the end of the century the great flowering of contemporary German culture was beginning to make its impact. This created the inner resources through which Prussia, in spite of her massive military defeats, was able to survive the Napoleonic storm. The years after 1806 were her finest hour, when men from all over Germany, nurtured in the school of German humanist idealism, laboured to reform Prussian civil and military institutions. They succeeded only partially.

Prussia emerged with a brand of liberal conservatism peculiar to herself. She was still an absolute monarchy, an Obrigkeitsstaat which left no political initiative to its citizens. But this was tempered by the rule of law, some liberal administrative practice and an established tradition of religious toleration. Prussian liberal conservatism was embodied in its ruling class, a combination of a service and a territorial aristocracy. The territorial aristocracy had since the beginning of the 18th century been accustomed to serve the King and the state through the army. The Prussian state after 1815 was still not based on the principle of nationality and was on the defensive against this principle, even though the country was now, with its reluctantly accepted western provinces, overwhelmingly a German state. A nation so constituted had to undergo great changes to meet the challenges of nationalism, industrialism and democracy. It was the tragedy of Prussia that she failed to adapt herself in time and instead handed on her pre-modern characteristics to hang like an albatross round the neck of the new Germany. A chance of coming to terms with the new age was missed in 1848, but some elements of constitutional government were saved from the wreckage. A second chance was missed between 1858 and 1862, if it ever genuinely existed. Instead Bismarck imposed his own highly individual solution to the dilemmas which faced his country. Bismarck did not create a Greater Prussia; he created a new country and many Prussian characteristics entered into it, but Prussia as an independent entity ceased to exist. Many of the qualities which Prussia handed on to Germany made the new Reich formidable and successful and some have survived to the present day. But others turned out to be liabilities; for example, the excessive prestige of the army and its freedom from parliamentary or even political controls. The veneration of things military had been enhanced by Bismarck's policy in Prussia and by the victorious wars of unification.

Those who wanted to see the Prussian state survive as a living organism after 1870 were quickly disappointed. It survived as a constitutional quirk of the new Germany; it lived on in the consciousness of many of its citizens and it received a new incarnation as a potent myth. Because the history of the Prussian state culminating in the new Germany seemed an unparalleled success story, the image of Prussian power politics was projected backwards. In South Germany Prussia had always conjured up visions of the drill square, the barrack room and of Junker backwoodsmen, but not of a Machiavellian super-power. Now all this changed and abroad, too, the Germany of the poets and thinkers became the Prussia-Germany of efficient and aggressive power. This picture was reinforced because as a constitutional factor in the new Germany Prussia did strengthen the nationalistic, militaristic, expansionist forces in politics. It was less easily noticed that many millions of Socialist voters also lived in Prussia. Perhaps when Prussia was being talked about it was the agrarian areas east of the Elbe and the Junkers that were really meant. But the dynamic sector of the German nation that wanted to make Weltpolitik was industry and commerce, the middle classes for whom new and undreamt of horizons were opening. The Junkers still set the tone socially, in common with other German aristocrats, but the German ruling *élites* were now recruited from a number of population groups; from the economic point of view the Junkers often lagged in the race. As Prussia was no longer a definite independent country, myth became often more important than reality. And so it continued even after the debâcle of 1918.

Now that Prussia has disappeared beyond a shadow of doubt it is possible to view these developments and these misunderstandings more dispassionately. Even the Prussian myth is now a matter of history. Can there be any future for Prussia? It seems unlikely. It was after all a state that made a nation of its citizens and there was never any ethnic basis to it. Now that this state has disappeared there is nothing left to build on. On the other hand the Prussian state has left a legacy that has become absorbed into the modern German nation. That nation for the moment lives divided among three states, West and East Germany and Austria. At least two of these owe a good deal to the legacy of Prussia.

Notes

Introduction

1. Sybel in a letter to Herman Baumgarten.
2. F. Meinecke, "Kultur, Machtpolitik und Militarismus", reprinted in *Preussen und Deutschland im 19. und 20. Jahrhundert* (1918), pp. 475–509.

Chapter I: Origins

1. A. Moeller van den Bruck, *Der Preussische Stil* (1931), pp. 13 f.
2. W. Hubatsch, "Kreuzritterstaat und Hohenzollernmonarchie. Zur Frage der Fortdauer des Deutschen Ordens in Preussen", *Festschrift Hans Rothfels* (1951).
3. E. Caspar, *Hermann von Salza und die Gründung des Deutschordenstaates in Preussen* (1924).
4. L. von Ranke, *Zwölf Bücher Preussischer Geschichte*, Second Book, Fourth Chapter, p. 213 (1931 edition).

Chapter II: Prussia Becomes a State 1688–1740

1. Quoted by J. A. R. Marriott and C. G. Robertson, *The Evolution of Prussia* (1937), p. 101.
2. Gottfried Arnold, *Unparteyische Kirchen- und Ketzer-Historie* (1699).
3. Frederick the Great used this expression of his grandfather. For his opinion of Frederick I, see Political Testament of 1752 in Friedrich der Grosse, *Die Politischen Testamente*, translated by F. von Oppeln-Bronikowski (1922), p. 50.
4. Carl Hinrichs wrote the only full biography of Frederick William I. The work was not completed beyond the first volume, published in 1941, which ends with the King's accession.
5. I. Macalpine, R. Hunter, C. Rimington, "Porphyria in the Royal Houses of Stuart, Hanover and Prussia. A Follow-up Study of George III's Illness", *British Medical Journal*, 1968, vol. 1, pp. 7–18.
6. H. Rosenberg, *Bureaucracy, Aristocracy and Autocracy. The Prussian Experience, 1660–1815* (1958), p. 89.
7. Hajo Holborn, *A History of Modern Germany 1648–1840*, p. 197.
8. G. Ritter, *Staatskunst und Kriegshandwerk. Das Problem des "Militarismus" in Deutschland* (1965), vol. i, pp. 28 f.

Chapter III: Prussia becomes a Great Power 1740–1786

1. R. Koser, *Geschichte Friedrichs des Grossen* (1963 edition), vol. i, pp. 141–157.
2. *Histoire de mon Temps,* chapitre 2.
3. Quoted by O. Hintze, *Die Hohenzollern und ihr Werk* (1915), pp. 345 f.
4. To Finckenstein, Koser, op. cit., iii. 35.
5. Koser, op. cit., iii. 121.
6. *Politische Testamente,* p. 232.
7. *Politische Testamente,* p. 239.
8. Goethe, *Dichtung und Wahrheit,* Erster Teil, Zweites Buch.
9. H. Ritter von Srbik, *Deutsche Einheit. Idee und Wirklichtkeit vom Heiligen Reich bis Königgrätz* (1935–42), i. 106.
10. Comte de Mirabeau, *De la Monarchie Prussienne sous Frédéric le Grand,* 4 vols. (1788).

Chapter IV: The Decline of Old Prussia 1786–1806

1. Quoted by P. Binswanger, *Wilhelm von Humboldt* (1937), p. 95.
2. *Beiträge zur Berichtigung der Urteile des Publikums über die Französische Revolution,* published anonymously.
3. Prose sketch for an unfinished poem *Deutsche Grösse* (1801).
4. Quoted by F. Meinecke, *Weltbürgertum und Nationalstaat* (third edition, 1915), p. 67.
5. Quoted by O. Hintze, *Die Hohenzollern und ihr Werk,* p. 406.
6. R. Kayser, *Kant* (1934), p. 257.
7. O. von Bismarck, *Gedanken und Erinnerungen* (1898), vol. i, chapter 12.
8. Gordon A. Craig, *The Politics of the Prussian Army 1640–1945* (1955), p. 26.
9. O. Tschirch, *Geschichte der öffentlichen Meinung in Preussen vom Baseler Frieden bis zum Zusammenbruch des Staates (1795–1806)* (1934), ii. 76–89.
10. P. Paret, *Yorck and the Era of Prussian Reform 1807–1815* (1966), p. 111.
11. In a letter to her father in April 1808.

Chapter V: The Reform Era 1806–1813

1. Remark by Brinckmann, quoted by J. Droz, *Le romantisme allemand et l'état: résistance et collaboration dans l'Allemagne napoléonienne* (1966), p. 114.
2. F. Meinecke, *Weltbürgertum und Nationalstaat,* chapter 8.
3. For a careful reassessment of Humboldt's personality, see S. A. Kaehler, *Wilhelm von Humboldt und der Staat* (1927).
4. Freiherr vom Stein, *Briefe und Amtliche Schriften,* edited by E. Botzenhart (1957–65), vol. ii, part I, pp. 380 ff.
5. For the Riga Memorandum, see L. von Ranke, ed., *Denkwürdigkeiten des Staatskanzlers Fürsten von Hardenberg* (1877–81), vol. iv, Appendix.

6. *Einghabe der Lebus-Beeskow-Storkowschen Stände,* handed to Frederick William III's secretary on 10th June 1811.
7. G. H. Pertz, *Das Leben des Feldmarschalls Grafen Neithardt von Gneisenau,* ii. 112–142.

Chapter VI: Liberation, Reaction and Revolution 1813–1849

1. J. G. Droysen, *Das Leben des Generalfeldmarschalls Graf Yorck von Wartenburg* (1913), i. 190–1.
2. Dated Breslau, 17 March 1813, and written by State Councillor Theodor von Hippel.
3. B. G. Niebuhr, *Preussens Recht gegen den sächsischen Hof* (1814).
4. "Über die englische Reformbill", partially published in 1831 in the *Allgemeine preussische Staatszeitung.* The censor prevented complete publication.
5. *Leben Jesu* was translated into English by George Eliot.
6. Held at Hambach in the Bavarian Palatinate on 27th May 1832.
7. Theodor von Schön, *Woher und wohin? Oder der preussische Landtag im Jahre 1840* (1841).
8. Johann Jacoby, *Vier Fragen, beantwortet von einem Ostpreussen,* in *Gesammelte Schriften und Reden* (1877), i. 116 ff.

Chapter VII: Prussia and the Unification of Germany 1849–1871

1. For an interpretation of this kind, see P. Wentzke, *1848: Die unvollendete Revolution* (1938).
2. H. von Sybel, *Die deutsche Nation und das Kaiserreich* (1862).
3. Speech to the newly appointed ministers, 8 November 1858.
4. Bismarck, *Gedanken und Erinnerungen,* vol. i, chapter 8.
5. For example in the so-called "Prachtbericht", a report to the Prime Minister, Manteuffel, of 26 April 1856. Bismarck, *Werke in Auswahl,* edited by G. A. Rein and others (1966), ii. 100–109.
6. See E. Jordan, *Die Entstehung der konservativen Partei und die preussischen Agrarverhältnisse von 1848* (1914).
7. Declaration in the ninety-fourth meeting of the Budget Commission on 30 September 1862. Bismarck, *Werke in Auswahl,* iii. 3.
8. The plot of George Meredith's novel *The Tragic Comedians* is based on Lassalle's career.
9. Wilhelm Jordan, a liberal deputy, was the first to assert German national rights against the Poles in a speech in the Frankfurt Parliament. See J. Droz, *Les révolutions allemandes de 1848* (1957), pp. 293 f.
10. H. Rosenberg, *Die nationalpolitische Publizistik Deutschlands. Vom Eintritt der neuen Ära in Preussen zis zum Ausbruch des deutschen Kriegs* (1935), ii. 698 f.
11. H. von Treitschke, "Die Lösung der schleswig-holsteinischen Frage. Eine Erwiderung", *Preussische Jahrbücher, vol. XV* (1865).
12. Quoted by O. Pflanze, *Bismarck and the Development of Germany. The Period of Unification, 1815–1871* (1963), p. 297.

242   PRUSSIA : MYTH AND REALITY

13. Quoted by J. Ziekursch, *Politische Geschichte des neuen deutschen Kaiserreichs*, i. 189.
14. H. Baumgarten, *Partei oder Vaterland? Ein Wort an die norddeutschen Liberalen* (1866).
15. J. Ziekursch, op. cit., vol. i.

Chapter VIII: Prussia in Imperial Germany 1817–1918

1. J. Ziekursch, *Politische Geschichte des neuen deutschen Kaiserreichs*, ii. 260.
2. The five articles in the Kreuzzeitung, entitled "Ära Camphausen-Delbrück-Bleichröder", were written by Perrot, an agrarian journalist. Those who declared their solidarity with the paper were known as the "Deklaranten".
3. Count K. Westarp, *Konservative Politik im letzten Jahrzent des Kaiserreichs*, 2 vols. (1935).
4. N. von Preradovich, *Die Führungsschichten in Osterreich und Preussen 1804–1918* (1955).
5. The story of *Der Hauptmann von Köpenick* was dramatized by Carl Zuckmayer.
6. Quoted by H. Kohn, *The Mind of Germany* (1961), p. 150.
7. Heinrich von Treitschke, *Deutsche Geschichte im neunzehnten Jahrhundert*, 5 vols., (1879–94).
8. A. Dorpalen, *Heinrich von Treitschke* (1957), p. 199.
9. Quoted by Kohn, op. cit., p. 184.
10. Quoted by Dorpalen, op. cit., p. 187.
11. Quoted ibid., p. 188.
12. E. Hamburger, *Juden im öffentlichen Leben Deutschlands. Regierungsmitglieder, Beamte und Parlamentarier der monarchischen Zeit 1848–1918* (1968), pp. 283 f.
13. H. von Treitschke, *Ein Wort über unser Judentum* (1880); Ludwig Bamberger, *Deutschtum und Judentum* (1880).
14. For example in Perrot's Kreuzzeitung articles of 1875.

Chapter IX: Epilogue: The Weimar Republic and the Nazi Regime 1918–45.

1. F. Hartung, *Deutsche Verfassungsgeschichte vom 15. Jahrhundert bis zur Gegenwart* (8th edition, 1964), p. 317.
2. H. von Seeckt, *Moltke. Ein Vorbild* (1931).
3. F. L. Carsten, *Reichswehr und Politik 1918–1933* (1964), p. 118.
4. Carl Schmitt, "Der Führer schützt das Recht", *Positionen und Begriffe im Kampf mit Weimar—Genf—Versailles, 1923–1939* (1940).
5. Ernst Jünger, *"In Stahlgewittern"*, *Werke* (1960–64), vol. I, p. 11.
6. E. Jünger, *"Der Kampf als inneres Erlebnis"*, *Werke*, vol. 5.
7. *Preussentum und Sozialismus,* in O. Spengler, *Politische Schriften* (1932), pp. 1–105.
8. A. Moeller van den Bruck, *Der Preussische Stil* (1931).
9. K. D. Bracher, W. Sauer, G. Schulz, *Die nationalsozialistische Machtergreifung. Studien zur Errichtung des totalitären Herrschaftssystems in Deutschland 1933/34.* (1962), pp. 144–152.

Chronology

1134: Albrecht the Bear becomes Margrave of Brandenburg
1226: Golden Bull of Rimini empowers the Teutonic Order of Knights to rule the territory of the Pruzzi
1320: End of the Ascanian dynasty
1356: Golden Bull of Emperor Charles IV confirms status of Brandenburg as Electorate
1415: Burgrave Frederick VI of Nuremberg, of the House of Hohenzollern, becomes Elector of Brandenburg
1466: Teutonic Order has to accept Polish suzerainty at the second Peace of Thorn
1473: Dispositio Achillea
1511: Albrecht of Brandenburg-Ansbach becomes High Master of the Teutonic Order
1525: State of the Teutonic Order secularized as Duchy of Prussia
1539: Reformation in Brandenburg
1598: Family Treaty of Gera
1609: Brandenburg claims the Cleves-Jülich succession
1613: Elector Johann Sigismund converts to the Reformed Church
1618: Johann Sigismund acknowledged as Duke of Prussia; Thirty Years War begins
1640: Reign of the Great Elector begins
1648: Brandenburg acquires Eastern Pomerania in the Peace of Westphalia
1660: Duchy of Prussia becomes sovereign in the Peace of Oliva
1675: Great Elector defeats Swedes at Fehrbellin
1688: Reign of Frederick III begins
1697: Peace of Ryswick
1701: Coronation at Königsberg of the Elector of Brandenburg as Frederick I, King in Prussia; War of Spanish Succession begins
1713: Reign of Frederick William I begins; Peace of Utrecht
1720: Acquisition of Stettin
1723: Foundation of General Directory
1730: Imprisonment of Crown Prince
1740: Reign of Frederick the Great begins; First Silesian War
1744: Second Silesian War
1745: Prussian possession of Silesia acknowledged in Peace of Dresden
1756: Seven Years War begins
1757: Prussian victory at Leuthen
1759: Prussian defeat at Kunersdorf

1760: Russians enter Berlin
1763: Peace of Hubertusburg
1772: First Partition of Poland
1778: War of the Bavarian Succession (Potato War)
1786: Reign of Frederick William II begins
1792: War of the First Coalition against France
1793: Second Partition of Poland
1795: Peace of Basle; Third Partition of Poland
1797: Reign of Frederick William III begins
1801: Peace of Lunéville
1803: Prussia acquires mediatized territories of Münster, Paderborn and Hildesheim
1805: War of the Third Coalition
1806: End of the Holy Roman Empire; Prussia declares war on France and is defeated at Jena and Auerstädt
1807: Peace of Tilsit; Ministry of Stein
1808: Stein dismissed
1810: Hardenberg becomes State Chancellor
1812: Convention of Tauroggen
1813: War of Liberation begins; Battle of Leipzig
1815: German Confederation founded; Frederick William III promises a constitution
1817: Union of Lutheran and Reformed Churches
1819: Resignation of Humboldt and Boyen
1830: July Revolution in France
1834: German Zollverein comes into effect
1840: Reign of Frederick William IV begins
1847: Prussian United Diet summoned
1848: Year of revolution
1849: Frederick William IV refuses German imperial crown
1850: Convention of Olmütz
1854: Crimean War
1858: Prince William becomes Prince Regent—New Era begins
1859: War between Austria and France in Italy
1861: Reign of William I begins
1862: Bismarck becomes Prime Minister of Prussia
1864: War with Denmark over Schleswig-Holstein
1866: War between Prussia and Austria—Battle of Sadowa
1867: North German Federation founded
1870: Franco-Prussian War
1871: William I proclaimed German Emperor; Kulturkampf begins
1878: Law against the Socialists passed
1879: Germany abandons free trade
1883: Sickness insurance introduced
1888: Reign of Frederick III; Reign of William II begins
1890: Bismarck dismissed
1897: First Naval Law
1900: Bülow becomes Chancellor

1908: *Daily Telegraph* interview
1909: Bethmann Hollweg becomes Chancellor
1912: Social Democrats become largest party in Reichstag
1917: Easter Message of Emperor promises reform of Prussian electoral law
1918: End of Hohenzollern monarchy
1920: Otto Braun becomes Prime Minister of Prussia; Kapp Putsch fails
1923: Hitler Putsch in Munich fails
1925: Hindenburg elected President of the Republic
1929: Death of Stresemann
1930: Brüning becomes Chancellor
1932: Papen takes over the Government of Prussia as Reich Commissar
1933: Hitler comes to power—Göring becomes Prussian Minister of the Interior
1934: Law for the Reconstruction of the Reich abolishes parliaments in all German Länder
1944: Failure of July plot against Hitler
1947: Allied Control Council dissolves the State of Prussia

Select Bibliography

General Works:
Braubach, Max, Der Aufstieg Brandenburg-Preussens, 1640–1815, Freiburg 1933.
Carr, William, A History of Germany 1815–1945, London 1969.
Craig, Gordon A., The Politics of the Prussian Army 1640–1945, Oxford 1955.
Gebhardt, Bruno, Handbuch der deutschen Geschichte, 4 vols., 8th edition, Stuttgart 1958–60.
Hartung, Fritz, Deutsche Verfassungsgeschichte. Vom 15. Jahrhundert bis zur Gegenwart, 8th edition, Stuttgart 1964.
Hintze, Otto, Die Hohenzollern und ihr Werk, Berlin 1915.
Hintze, O., Geist und Epochen der preussischen Geschichte, Leipzig 1943.
Holborn, Hajo, A History of Modern Germany, 2 vols., London 1965.
Jany, Curt, Geschichte der königlich-preussischen Armee bis zum Jahre 1807, 5 vols., Berlin 1928–37.
Kohn, Hans, The Mind of Germany. The Education of a Nation, London 1961.
Mann, Golo, The History of Germany since 1798, translated from the German, London 1967.
Marriott, J. A. R., and Robertson, C. G., The Evolution of Prussia. The Making of an Empire, new edition, Oxford 1937.
Meinecke, Friedrich, Weltbürgertum und Nationalstaat, 3rd edition, Munich 1915.
Meinecke, F., Preussen und Deutschland im 19. und 20. Jahrhundert, Munich 1918.
Ramm, Agatha, Germany 1789–1919. A Political History, London 1967.
Ranke, Leopold von, Zwölf Bücher Preussischer Geschichte, edited by Georg Küntzel, 3 vols., Munich 1930.
Ritter, Gerhard, Staatskunst und Kriegshandwerk. Das Problem des "Militarismus" in Deutschland, 4 vols., Munich 1964–68.
Rothfels, Hans, Ostraum, Preussentum und Reichsgedanke, Leipzig 1935.
Scherer, Wilhelm, Geschichte der deutschen Literatur, bis zur Gegenwart, ergänzt von Th. Schultz, Vienna 1948.
Schnabel, Franz, Deutsche Geschichte im 19. Jahrhundert, 4 vols., Freiburg 1929–37.
Schoeps, H. J., Preussen. Geschichte eines Staats, Berlin 1966.
Srbik, Heinrich von, Deutsche Einheit. Idee und Wirklichkeit vom Heiligen Reich bis Königgraetz, 4 vols., Munich 1935–42.
Treitschke, Heinrich von, Deutsche Geschichte im 19. Jahrhundert, 5 vols., Leipzig 1879–94.

SPECIAL PERIODS

Origins to 1740:

Barraclough, Geoffrey, *The Origins of Modern Germany,* 2nd edition, Oxford 1947.

Carsten, F. L., *The Origins of Prussia,* Oxford 1954.

Caspar, Erich, *Hermann von Salza und die Gründung des Deutschordensstaates in Preussen,* Tübingen 1924.

Hinrichs, Carl, *Friedrich Wilhelm I., König in Preussen. Jugend und Aufstieg,* Hamburg 1941.

Hinrichs, C., *Preussen als historisches Problem,* Berlin 1964.

Hubatsch, Walter, *Kreuzritterstaat und Hohenzollernmonarchie. Zur Frage der Fortdauer des Deutschen Ordens in Preussen,* in *Festschrift für Hans Rothfels,* edited by W. Conze, Düsseldorf 1951.

Oestreich, Gerhard, *Politischer Neustoizismus und niederländische Bewegung in Europa und besonders in Brandenburg-Preussen,* Groningen 1956.

Tümpel, Ludwig, *Die Entstehung des brandenburg-preussischen Einheitsstaates im Zeitalter des Absolutismus, 1609–1806,* Breslau 1915.

Waddington, Albert, *Le Grand Électeur Frédéric Guillaume de Brandebourg. Sa Politique extérieure, 1640–1688,* Paris 1905–8.

1740–1815: (see also previous period)

Arendt, H., *Rahel Varnhagen. The Life of a Jewess,* London 1958.

Barnard, F. M., *Herder's Social and Political Thought,* Oxford 1965.

Binswanger, Paul, *Wilhelm von Humboldt,* Frauenfeld 1937.

Bruford, W. H., *Culture and Society in Classical Weimar, 1775–1806,* Cambridge 1962.

Brunschwig, Henri, *La Crise de l'État Prussien a la Fin du XVIIIe Siècle et la Genèse de la Mentalité Romantique,* Paris 1947.

Cassirer, Ernst, *Die Philosophie der Aufklärung,* Tübingen 1932.

Dorn, W. L., *Competition for Empire, 1740–1763,* New York 1940.

Droysen, J. G., *Das Leben des Generalfeldmarschalls Graf Yorck von Wartenburg,* 2 vols., Berlin 1913.

Droz, J., *L'Allemagne et la Révolution française,* Paris 1949.

Droz, J., *Le Romantisme allemand et l'Etat: Résistance et Collaboration dans l'Allemagne napoléonienne,* Paris 1966.

Fichte, J. G., *Reden an die deutsche Nation,* with introduction by Hermann Schneider, Leipzig 1924.

Fischer, Horst, *Judentum, Staat und Heer in Preussen im frühen 19. Jahrhundert. Zur Geschichte der staatlichen Judenpolitik,* Tübingen 1968.

Ford, G. S., *Stein and the Era of Reform in Prussia, 1807–1815,* Princeton 1922.

Frédéric le Grand, *Oeuvres,* edited by J. D. E. Preuss, 30 vols., Berlin 1846–57.

Friedrich der Grosse, *Die Politischen Testamente,* translated by F. von Oppeln-Bronikowski, Berlin 1922.

Geiger, Ludwig, *Geschichte der Juden in Berlin,* Guttentag 1871.

Gooch, G. P., *Frederick the Great,* London 1947.

Haussherr, Hans, *Hardenberg. Eine politische Biographie,* 3 vols., Cologne 1963.

Horn, D. B., *Frederick the Great and the Rise of Prussia,* London 1964.

Kaehler, S. A., *Wilhelm von Humboldt und der Staat,* Munich 1927.

Kayser, Rudolf, *Kant,* Vienna 1935.

Koser, Reinhold, *Geschichte Friedrichs des Grossen,* new edition, 4 vols., Darmstadt 1963.

Meinecke, F., *Das Zeitalter der deutschen Erhebung 1795–1815,* third edition, Berlin 1924.

Paret, Peter, *Yorck and the Era of Prussian Reform,* Princeton 1966.

Pascal, Roy, *The German Sturm und Drang,* London 1951.

Pertz, G. H., and Delbrück, Hans, *Das Leben des Feldmarschalls Grafen Neithardt von Gneisenau,* 5 vols., Berlin 1864–80.

Pinson, Koppel S., *Pietism as a Factor in the Rise of German Nationalism,* New York 1934.

Ritter, Gerhard, *Stein. Eine politische Biographie,* Stuttgart 1958.

Rosenberg, Hans, *Bureaucracy, Aristocracy and Autocracy. The Prussian Experience, 1660–1815,* Cambridge, Mass., 1958.

Schmitt, Carl, *Politische Romantik,* Munich 1925.

Schneider, Reinhold, *Fichte. Der Weg zur Nation,* Munich 1932.

Shanahan, William O., *Prussian Military Reforms. 1768–1813,* New York 1945.

Simon, Edith, *The Making of Frederick the Great,* London 1963.

Simon, W. M., *The Failure of the Prussian Reform Movement, 1807–1819,* Ithaca 1955.

Smith, R. G., *J. G. Hamann, 1730–1788. A Study in Christian Existence,* London 1960.

Stadelmann, Rudolf, *Scharnhorst. Schicksal und geistige Welt,* Wiesbaden 1952.

Stein, Freiherr vom, *Briefe und Amtliche Schriften,* edited by E. Botzenhart, 6 vols., Stuttgart 1957–65.

Tschirch, Otto, *Geschichte der öffentlichen Meinung in Preussen vom Baseler Frieden bis zum Zusammenbruch des Staates,* 2 vols., Weimar 1934.

Vleeschauwer, H. J. de, *The Development of Kantian Thought. The History of a Doctrine,* translated by A. R. C. Duncan, London 1962.

Wolff, H. M., *Heinrich von Kleist als Politischer Dichter,* Berkeley 1947.

1815–1870: (see also previous period)

Anderson, E. N., *The Social and Political Conflict in Prussia 1858–64,* Nebraska 1954.

Becker, Otto, *Bismarcks Ringen um Deutschlands Gestaltung,* Heidelberg 1958.

Bismarck, Otto von, *Gedanken und Erinnerungen,* 1898, various editions.

Bismarck, O. von, *Werke in Auswahl,* edited by G. A. Rein and others, 3 vols., Stuttgart 1966.

Böhme, Helmut, *Deutschlands Weg zur Grossmacht. Studien zum Verhältnis von Wirtschaft und Staat während der Reichsgründungszeit 1848–1881,* Cologne 1966.

Brandenburg, Erich, *Die Reichsgründung,* 2 vols., Leipzig 1922.

Bussmann, Walter, *Das Zeitalter Bismarcks,* Konstanz 1958.

Busmann, W., *Treitschke: Sein Welt-und Geschichtsbild,* Göttingen 1952.

Dorpalen, A., *Heinrich von Treitschke,* New Haven 1957.

Droz, J., *Le Liberalisme Rhénan, 1815–1848,* Paris 1940.

Droz, J., *Les Révolutions Allemandes de 1848,* Paris 1957.

Eyck, Erich, *Bismarck. Leben und Werk,* 3 vols., Zürich 1941-44.

Friedjung, H., *Der Kampf um die Vorherrschaft in Deutschland, 1859 bis 1866,* tenth edition, Stuttgart 1916.

Hamburger, Ernest, *Juden im öffentlichen Leben Deutschlands. Regierungsmitglieder, Beamte und Parlamentarier in der monarchischen Zeit 1848–1918,* Tübingen 1968.

Hamerow, Theodore S., *Restoration, Revolution, Reaction. Economics and Politics in Germany 1815–1871,* Princeton 1958.

Howard, Michael, *The Franco-Prussian War,* London 1961.

Jordan, Erich, *Die Entstehung der konservativen Partei und die preussischen Agrarverhältnisse von 1848,* Munich 1914.

Klein, Ernst, *Von der Reform zur Restauration. Finanzpolitik und Reformgesetzgebung des preussischen Staatskanzlers K.A. von Hardenberg,* Berlin 1965.

Marcks, Erich, *Der Aufstieg des Reiches. Deutsche Geschichte 1807–1871/78,* 2 vols., Stuttgart 1936.

Meinecke, F., *Radowitz und die deutsche Revolution,* Berlin 1913.

Meyer, A. O., *Bismarck: Der Mensch und der Staatsmann,* Stuttgart 1949.

Mommsen, Wilhelm, *Bismarck. Ein politisches Lebensbild,* Munich 1959.

Mosse, W. E., *The European Powers and the German Question, 1848–71, with special reference to England and Russia,* Cambridge 1958.

Muralt, Leonhard von, *Bismarcks Verantwortlichkeit,* Göttingen 1955.

Neumann, S., *Die Stufen des preussischen Konservatismus. Ein Beitrag zum Staats-und Gesellschaftsbild Deutschlands im 19. Jahrhundert,* Berlin 1930.

Oncken, Hermann, *Lassalle. Eine politische Biographie,* 4th edition, Stuttgart 1923.

Oncken, H., *Preussen und Polen im 19. Jahrhundert,* in *Deutschland und Polen,* edited by A. Brackmann, Munich 1933.

Pflanze, Otto, *Bismarck and the Development of Germany. The Period of Unification, 1815–1871,* Princeton 1963.

Preradovich, N. von, *Die Führungsschichten in Oesterreich und Preussen 1804–1918,* Wiesbaden 1955.

Richter, W., *Bismarck.* Translated from the German by B. Battershaw, London 1964.

Ritter, Gerhard, *Die preussischen Konservativen und Bismarcks deutsche Politik 1858–1876,* Heidelberg 1913.

Rosenberg, Hans, *Die nationalpolitische Publizistik Deutschlands. Vom Eintritt der Neuen Ära in Preussen bis zum Ausbruch des deutschen Kriegs*, 2 vols., Munich 1935.

Rosenzweig, Franz, *Hegel und der Staat*, 2 vols., Munich 1920.

Schoeps, H. J., *Das andere Preussen*, Berlin 1955.

Stahl, Friedrich Julius, *Die Philosophie des Rechts 1830–1837. Eine Auswahl nach der 5. Auflage (1870)*. Introduced and edited by Henning von Arnim, Tübingen 1926.

Sybel, Heinrich von, *Die Begründung des Deutschen Reiches durch Wilhelm I*, 7 vols., Munich 1889–94.

Taylor, A. J. P., *Bismarck. The Man and the Statesman*, London 1955.

Valentin, Veit, *Geschichte der deutschen Revolution von 1848–49*, Berlin 1930–1.

Wentzke, Paul, *1848: Die unvollendete Revolution*, Munich 1938.

Windell, George C., *The Catholics and German Unity 1866–1871*, Minneapolis 1954.

1870–1945: (see also previous period)

Balfour, Michael, *The Kaiser and his Times*, London 1964.

Bergsträsser, L., *Geschichte der politischen Parteien in Deutschland*, 6th edition, Mannheim 1932.

Born, K. E., *Staat und Sozialpolitik seit Bismarcks Sturz*, 2 vols., Wiesbaden 1957–9.

Bracher, K. D., *Die Auflösung der Weimarer Republik. Eine Studie zum Problem des Machtverfalls in der Demokratie*, 2nd edition, Stuttgart 1957.

Bracher, K. D., W. Sauer, G. Schulz, *Die nationalsozialistische Machtergreifung. Studien zur Errichtung des totalitären Herrschaftssystems in Deutschland 1933/4*, 2nd edition, Cologne 1962.

Braun, Otto, *Von Weimar zu Hitler*, New York 1940.

Carsten, F. L., *The Reichswehr and Politics 1918 to 1933*, Oxford 1966.

Conze, Werner, *Die Zeit Wilhelms II. und die Weimarer Republik. Deutsche Geschichte 1890–1933*, Stuttgart 1964.

Dorpalen, A., *Hindenburg and the Weimar Republic*, Princeton 1964.

Eyck, Erich, *Das persönliche Regiment Wilhelms II. Politische Geschichte des deutschen Kaiserreiches von 1890–1914*, Zürich 1948.

Eyck, Erich, *Geschichte der Weimarer Republik*, 2 vols., Zürich 1954.

Fischer, Fritz, *Germany's Aims in the first World War*, London 1967.

Goldschmidt, Hans, *Das Reich und Preussen im Kampf um die Führung*, Berlin 1931.

Hartung, Fritz, *Deutsche Geschichte 1871–1919*, Stuttgart 1952.

Hughes, H. Stuart, *Oswald Spengler. A Critical Estimate*, New York 1952.

Jünger, Ernst, *Werke*, 10 vols., Stuttgart 1960–4.

Kitchen, Martin, *The German Officer Corps 1890–1914*, Oxford 1968.

Klemperer, K. von, *Germany's New Conservatism. Its History and Dilemma in the Twentieth Century*, Princeton 1968.

Meinecke, F., *The German Catastrophe: Reflections and Recollection,* translated by Sidney B. Fay, Cambridge, Mass., 1950.

Moeller van den Bruck, Arthur, *Der Preussische Stil,* Munich 1931.

Morsey, Rudolf, *Die oberste Reichsverwaltung unter Bismarck 1871 bis 1890,* Munich 1957.

Mosse, George L., *The Crisis of German Ideology. Intellectual Origins of the Third Reich,* London 1964.

Neumann, S., *Die Deutschen Parteien. Wesen und Wandel nach dem Krieg,* Berlin 1932.

Oncken, H., *Das Deutsche Reich und die Vorgeschichte des Weltkrieges,* 2 vols., Leipzig 1933.

Pulzer, P. G., *The Rise of Political Anti-Semitism in Germany and Austria,* New York 1964.

Röhl, J. C. G., *Germany without Bismarck: The Crisis of Government in the second Reich, 1890–1900,* London 1967.

Rothfels, Hans, *The German Opposition to Hitler. An Assessment,* London 1962.

Scheler, Max, *Der Genius des Krieges und der deutsche Krieg,* Leipzig 1915.

Schieder, Theodor, *Das deutsche Kaiserreich von 1871 als Nationalstaat,* Cologne 1961.

Schmitt, Carl, *Positionen und Begriffe im Kampf mit Weimar – Genf – Versailles,* Hamburg 1940.

Severing, Carl, *Mein Lebensweg,* 2 vols., Bielefeld 1950.

Spengler, Oswald, *Preussentum und Sozialismus,* in *Politische Schriften,* Munich 1932.

Stern, F., *Kulturpessimismus als politische Gefahr,* Stuttgart 1963.

Westarp, Count Kuno, *Konservative Politik im letzten Jahrzehnt des Kaiserreichs,* 2 vols., Berlin 1935.

Ziekursch, Johannes, *Politische Geschichte des neuen deutschen Kaiserreiches,* 3 vols., Frankfurt 1925–30. .

Index